DIRECTORS IN PERSPECTIVE

General editor: Christopher Innes

Vsevolod Meyerhold

What characterizes modern theatre above all is continual stylistic innovation, in which theory and presentation have combined to create a wealth of new forms – naturalism, expressionism, epic theatre, etc. – in a way that has made directors the leading figures rather than dramatists. To a greater extent than is perhaps generally realized, it has been directors who have provided dramatic models for playwrights, though of course there are many different variations in this relationship. In some cases a dramatist's themes challenge a director to create new performance conditions (Stanislavski and Chekhov), or a dramatist turns director to formulate an appropriate style for his work (Brecht); alternatively a director writes plays to correspond with his theory (Artaud), or creates communal scripts out of exploratory work with actors (Chaikin, Grotowski). Some directors are identified with a single theory (Craig), others gave definitive shape to a range of styles (Reinhardt); the work of some has an ideological basis (Stein), while others work more pragmatically (Bergman).

Generally speaking, those directors who have contributed to what is distinctly 'modern' in today's theatre stand in much the same relationship to the dramatic texts they work with, as composers do to librettists in opera. However, since theatrical performance is the most ephemeral of the arts and the only easily reproducible element is the text, critical attention has tended to focus on the playwright. This series is designed to redress the balance by providing an overview of selected directors' stage work: those who helped to formulate modern theories of drama. Their key productions have been reconstructed from promptbooks, reviews, scene-designs, photographs, diaries, correspondence and – where these productions are contemporary – documented by first-hand description, interviews with the director, etc. Apart from its intrinsic interest, this record allows a critical perspective, testing ideas against practical problems and achievements. In each case, too, the director's work is set in context by indicating the source of his ideas and their influence, the organization of his acting company and his relationship to the theatrical or political establishment, so as to bring out wider issues: the way theatre both reflects and influences assumptions about the nature of man and his social role.

Christopher Innes

Vsevolod Meyerhold

ROBERT LEACH

CAMBRIDGE
UNIVERSITY PRESS

Published by the Press Syndicate of the University of Cambridge
The Pitt Building, Trumpington Street, Cambridge CB2 1RP
40 West 20th Street, New York, NY 10011-4211, USA
10 Stamford Road, Oakleigh, Victoria 3166, Australia

First published 1989
First paperback edition 1993

Printed in Great Britain at the University Press, Cambridge

British Library cataloguing in publication data
Leach, Robert, 1942–
Vsevolod Meyerhold. – (Directors in
perspective).
1. Soviet Union. Theatre. Directing.
Meierkhold, V.E. (Vsevolod Emilevich),
1874–1940. Critical studies
I. Title. II, Series
792'.0233'0924

Library of Congress cataloguing in publication data
Leach, Robert.
Vsevolod Meyerhold/Robert Leach.
    p.   cm. – (Directors in perspective)
Bibliography.
Includes index.
ISBN 0 521 26739 0
1. Meïerkhol'd, V. Ė. (Vsevolod Ėmil'evich 1874–1940 – Criticism
and interpretation. I. Title. II. Series.
PN2728.M4L43 1989
792'.0233'0924 – dc 19   88–23430

ISBN 0 521 26739 0 (hardback)
ISBN 0 521 31843 2 (paperback)

Contents

Illustrations

ix

Preface

This book attempts to explain what has long been obscured – Meyerhold's 'system'. He never wrote a book which spelt this out in so many words, and most of his subsequent interpreters have approached his career chronologically. Though such an approach has its strengths, it does tend to underestimate the continuity in the work itself, its oneness. Having worked practically and intensively on 'biomechanics' and allied styles for more than a decade, I am convinced there is such a 'system' in Meyerhold's work, and though during his life the emphases often changed, and changed drastically, this fundamental oneness should be reasserted. At all times, he sought for the unique features of theatre, and found them in popular styles of acting, in constructional and architectural settings, in plays organized in non-naturalistic patterns, in the artistic 'grotesque'. By adopting a non-chronological method of examining his work, I hope I have highlighted the often-obscured consistency in Meyerhold's complete career.

Moreover, this method reveals that the essence of what Meyerhold did was genuinely original, and it suggests we should view him less as a theatre director and more as a pedagogue. The word is chosen carefully, for a pedagogue is a teacher, a researcher and a practitioner in one, and that is what Meyerhold was. The structure of his work required a school, a 'workshop' and a theatre, a difficult combination, but the only one which truly allowed him to develop. The book attempts to show why and how these three strands were interdependent, and what are the implications for theatre – now as much as then.

In undertaking the work which allowed me to complete this book, I incurred two major debts. The first of these is to the British Council, to Moscow University and to the Central State Archive of Literature and Art (TsGALI) in Moscow who together enabled me to take advantage of the British–Soviet Cultural Exchange Visits scheme to spend a term in Moscow researching the Meyerhold Archive in the autumn of 1985. I would like particularly to record my thanks for their help and kindness to Elena Yakovlevna Lukianova and Marina Iskoldovna in the Foreign Department of Moscow University, and to Professor Boris Semyonovich Bugrov in the Philology Department of the University; to Valentina Jacque and Valeria Issakovich of *Soviet Literature*; and to Svetlana Treskova who was an utterly invaluable guide, interpreter and mentor in Moscow. Among other things, they helped to obtain for me the elusive tickets for certain Moscow theatres which deepened my understanding almost as much as anything found in the archives, especially Pluchek and Yutkevich's production of *The Bedbug* and Lyubimov's production of *Ten Days that Shook the World*.

My second debt is to the Dean and Faculty of Arts at the University of Birmingham for allowing me study leave to go to the USSR; and to my colleagues in the Department of Drama and Theatre Arts not only for covering my absence, but also for putting up with the disruptions of biomechanical practical work over many years. In particular, I wish to record my thanks to my former head of department, the late Jocelyn Powell, who not only allowed me to continue my work in this field, but positively encouraged it, and who, before his devastatingly early death, discussed much of what is written here, especially chapter 3, with me, constructively and mercilessly. It was a privilege to work with him, and the existence of this book is in no small measure due to his inspiration. To the students who have been involved in my courses and who have taken part in my productions, I am incalculably grateful – they truly have taught me just about all I know about how Meyerhold's system actually works. I would like to thank especially Matt Beer, Marcus Fernando, Rick Harwood and Mandy Stevens who worked with me on biomechanics solidly for two years.

Finally, my thanks must go to my wife, Anita, for living with biomechanics for so long, for helping me with choreography, for discussing major and minor points in this book, for letting me get on with it, and last but not least for making so many cups of coffee. Ya tebya lyublyu.

R.L.

1   A life

Meyerhold was born on 28 January (old style) 1874 in Penza, a city about 550 kilometres south east of Moscow. He was the eighth child of a wealthy German businessman, and was christened Karl Theodore Kasimir. His elder brothers were all his father seems to have felt were necessary, so the young Karl was largely ignored, or rather left to the cultural pretensions of his mother. She was known in the local artistic and musical circles as a generous patron and perhaps the earliest surviving photograph of Meyerhold shows him at the age of five with the actor Dalmatov who was staying at the Meyerhold house while appearing as a guest artist in Penza.

As German citizens in the Russian empire, the family's position was somewhat vulnerable. Article 1 of the *Collected Laws of the Russian Empire, 1832* said: 'The Tsar of all the Russias is an autocratic and unlimited monarch; God himself ordains that all must bow to his supreme power, not only from fear, but also from duty.' Meyerhold was born in Alexander II's reign which had begun with high hopes of reform, engendered by the abolition of serfdom, but which was now simmering down to a sullen unease and which would end in 1881 with Alexander's assassination. His successor Alexander III was a contemptuous and perhaps contemptible martinet who died in 1894 and was in turn succeeded by Nicholas II, a not unintelligent man who however was absurdly weak-willed for an 'autocratic and unlimited monarch'.

Such unpredictable instability in the emperors did not make for a tranquil empire, and the misery of many serfs, for example, was as great after emancipation as it had been before. Reforms were called for, but resisted. Some peasants emigrated abroad, others to the cities which were beginning to industrialize. For those who stayed put, famine was a constant shadow and the anarchistic 'Narodniks' party carried some of their aspirations. For those in the towns, strikes or attempts to strike were met frequently with loaded guns and a merciless massacre. Yet Russia was expanding, emerging from a near-medieval stagnation, and this process quickened after the appointment of Count Witte as Minister of Finance in 1892. Witte made the country attractive to foreign capital investment and encouraged projects like the trans-Siberian railway.

Though the Meyerholds were very far from being peasants, by partially neglecting their eighth child they left him a good deal to the company of people of whom they, as energetic German capitalists, might not have wholly approved – gardeners, peasants, disaffected radicals exiled to Penza and others. One of these was Alexei Remizov, a minor poet and journalist, who arrived there in 1890 and a dozen years later became literary manager of Meyerhold's first theatre company. Certainly Meyerhold knew of 'socialism' in his youth and certainly he felt himself to be at least a 'radical'. In the mid 1890s, when he led the Penza Popular Theatre, an amateur group whose aim was to bring culture to the masses, he was able to unite his artistic and social interests in a manner not always possible later.

Though he had been a somewhat slow learner at school, he had developed a quick appreciation of the theatre, both the popular travelling fairground shows which included mountebanks, popular farces often with radical, as well as rude, overtones, pantomimes, puppet shows and the like, and the more conventional fare of Penza's civic theatre, where he saw many of the world's classics performed by leading actors on tour.

It was a time of theatrical change and expansion throughout Europe. Following Wagner, whose work first captured Meyerhold's imagination in the early 1890s, Ibsen and Strindberg were giving a new and topical seriousness to the theatre, soon to be capitalized on by Hauptmann and Shaw, while writers like Wedekind and Maeterlinck considerably developed the possibilities of the medium in the 1890s. Following the Duke of Saxe-Meiningen's troupe, theatre companies throughout Europe were approaching the drama with more care and sensitivity. In Germany, the Deutsches Theatre and the Freie Bühne made notable contributions, and in France the Théâtre Libre and in England the Independent Theatre Society were part of the same movement. In Russia, the playwright Ostrovsky, chafing against the Imperial monopoly of the theatre, and arguing for 'a national theatre . . . for democratic spectators: workers, handicraftsmen, needy intellectuals',[1] was instrumental in breaking the monopoly in 1882. Shortly afterwards F.A. Korsch opened a private theatre in Moscow which set new standards and was only overtaken by the Art Theatre itself sixteen years later.

In 1892, Meyerhold's father died. He seems to have been something of a weight round his son's neck. Certainly now the young Karl found himself. In 1895, he changed his forenames to Vsevolod Emilevich and his surname from Meyergold to Meyerhold, and took Russian citizenship. He went to Moscow University to study law and the following year, 1896, married Olga Munt. After a serious attempt to become a musician, thwarted when the orchestra he auditioned for refused him,[2] he left the Law Faculty to study drama at the

1. Chekhov's *The Seagull* at the Moscow Art Theatre, 1898. (*left to right*) Konstantin Stanislavsky as Trigorin, Vsevolod Meyerhold as Treplev, Olga Knipper (later Mrs Chekhov) as Arkadina

Moscow Philharmonic Society under Vladimir Nemirovich-Danchenko. This change of course marks the start of a new phase in Meyerhold's life.

ORIENTATION

At the Philharmonic School he won First Prize for acting when he graduated in 1898, and was immediately invited to become a founder member of the new Moscow Art Theatre. He played Vassily Shiusky in the inaugural production, Alexei Tolstoy's *Tsar Fyodor Ivanovich* which opened on 14 October 1898, and later Treplev in the famous production of *The Seagull* that same year. But gradually he fell out of favour, particularly with Nemirovich-Danchenko, and in January 1902 quarrelled fiercely with Stanislavsky. For pressing financial reasons Stanislavsky was at this time changing the theatre into a joint stock company, and Meyerhold was not invited to become a partner, prompting Chekhov to write on 17 February 1902, 'The Art Theatre did not do right in not making Meyerhold and Savina shareholders.'[3] He left the company and travelled abroad, returning in the autumn. Then, with Alexander Kosheverov, he founded the Company of Russian Dramatic Artists which made its debut at Kherson on 22 September 1902 with Meyerhold's first professional production – *The Three Sisters* by Anton Chekhov.

This bald summary glosses over much, inevitably. By 1902 Meyerhold was clearly looking to enter a larger theatrical world than he felt Stanislavsky's company could offer. Ever since a memorable terror had gripped him, on 24 August 1895, Meyerhold had mistrusted the method of acting by emotional saturation. On that day he had performed A.N. Apukhtin's monologue, *The Madman*, at a student gathering and had become so absorbed, 'I felt myself becoming mad.'[4] From then, he had regarded this method as 'a narcotic'[5] and by 1902 was becoming aware of other kinds of theatre. He probably saw Otodziro Kawakami's Japanese company on tour in Moscow that year, and may have been aware of Reinhardt's experiments in theatricality which were overshadowing Brahm's naturalism in Germany. Beyond that – though Meyerhold probably knew little or nothing of it – Appia, Fuchs and Craig were writing revolutionary tracts on potential developments in theatre practice as part of the general burgeoning of science and technology exemplified by, for instance, Freud's work, or the new quantum theory of physics, or the beginnings of air travel.

But Meyerhold's mind was moving in the same direction without them. It was a question of how and where and when to strike out in the new directions he sensed, as a note he wrote in his diary in Italy that summer shows: 'The water trembles, the sky is mysteriously silent, and the stars shake down dreams. In everything is a caress, a caress without end. The water, the sky, the mountains, the wind caress . . . but in the sound of the waves is a caress and a call to arms! To arms!'[6] In European drama the new stirrings seemed to find their most articulate expression in the symbolism of Maeterlinck and Przybyszewski, which found echoes in Russia in the work of Vyacheslav Ivanov, Alexander Blok, Andrei Bely and others. No one had yet found the way to stage their new plays because nobody had yet found the way to effect what many spoke of – the 'fusion' of spectator and performer. To search for this became Meyerhold's self-imposed task, first with the Comrades of the New Drama (as his provincial company became in 1903) and then in 1905, back in Moscow working again with Stanislavsky, at the new Studio Theatre.
- This last was a relief from the intense pressures of keeping a provincial company viable – in three seasons, he had staged 164 new productions – though it is not without significance that in 1904 he referred to the actors in the Comrades of the New Drama as 'performers who have trained at my school',[7] and for crowd scenes he had gathered a group of fifty or more young people who were invited not only to appear on stage but also to attend classes in 'declamation' and 'scenic art' given by Meyerhold.

The Theatre Studio was set up when Nemirovich-Danchenko and Stanislavsky began to fear that the Art Theatre was losing touch with modern developments in drama. Having heard of Meyerhold's experiments in the provinces, they decided to ask him to head this new enterprise, and Meyerhold leapt at the chance – not least because it enabled him to return to the mainstream of Russian cultural life. At the Theatre Studio, he said afterwards, he had striven for 'the renovation of dramatic art by means of new forms and new methods of scenic presentation'.[8] The emphasis was pedagogical and the idea of such a studio wholly original. 'There was,' wrote Stanislavsky, 'no place for . . . daily performances, complicated obligations and a strictly calculated budget . . . This was not a finished theatre and not a school for beginners, but a laboratory for the experiments of more or less experienced actors.'[9] For Meyerhold it was an almost ideal situation from which he learned much, both practically as far as stagecraft was concerned and organizationally with regard to running such an institution. But his work, for whatever reason, horrified Stanislavsky when he attended a dress re-hearsal, and not one of the plays worked on so assiduously – Maeterlinck's *Death of Tintagiles*, Ibsen's *Love's Comedy*, Przybyszweski's *Snow* and Hauptmann's *Schluck und Jau* – was ever presented to the public. Only Stanislavsky's dramatic intervention itself at the dress rehearsal, shouting 'Lights! Lights!' like Claudius during Hamlet's play, perhaps showed Meyerhold what spectator–performer 'fusion' might mean.

One contributory reason for the Studio's failure to present its work was the first Russian revolution which through 1905 increasingly disrupted life. Stanislavsky, essentially a non-political man, understood little of what was going on, whereas Meyerhold wanted to 'burn with the spirit of the times', [10] and put the theatre at the service of the people. Certainly Meyerhold was considered of the 'left'[11] at this period of massive upheaval, though closest to which of the opposition groupings – liberal 'westernizers', peasant Social Revolutionaries or worker Social Democrats (Mensheviks or Bolsheviks) – is by no means clear. Perhaps none of these particularly, though he almost certainly thought of himself as a socialist.

The expansion of Russia since about 1890 had been at a rate of something like eight per cent per annum. Coal production had doubled between 1890 and 1900, iron and steel production had increased five or sixfold. In 1894 Russia had eight technical schools; ten years later she had over a hundred. In 1900, forty per cent of all industrial enterprises had been in existence less than ten years, and, ominously enough, over thirty per cent of all invested capital came from abroad. The immediate social consequences were a largely disaffected countryside, where the peasants were still legally obliged to carry passports, and massively growing industrial cities, where the new proletariat lacked housing, transport, sanitation, and much else besides. In the 1890s, while the economy was expanding, the situation was just containable, despite famines, unrest, strikes and assassinations. After 1900, when a depression set in, it was not.

The disastrous Russo-Japanese war of 1904–5 largely failed to rally the poor and the exploited or the westernized intellectual democrats to the tsar's support, and the birth of his haemophiliac heir, Alexei, did not raise his popularity either. 'Bloody Sunday', the mutiny on board *Battleship Potemkin*, the flood of scurrilous and satirical magazines and finally the setting up of Soviets of Workers' Deputies – the first, in Petersburg, chaired by Leon Trotsky – all these indicated more tellingly which way the wind was blowing. In December virtually the whole country went on strike.

But by then Meyerhold was on his way back to the Comrades of the New Drama in Tiflis. Despite the failure of the Studio, his path had become clear: he wanted a pedagogical base for his work, which would research the problems inherent in creating a stylized theatre, perhaps allied to the Symbolist movement, but one which could also embrace both a radical content and a popular form. The theatre, as a tool to assist in radical change, was a concept he never dropped.

EXPERIMENT AND ACHIEVEMENT

In the years immediately following the abortive 1905 rising, it was as if Russia was in a state of shock, and the contending forces were pausing for breath. The tsar gave some ground – the 1832 article proclaiming him an unlimited autocrat was repealed and the requirement for peasants to carry passports was annulled. But Nicholas II played cat and mouse with any elected assembly, or Duma, while an unannounced reign of terror against liberals, Jews, socialists and other dissidents was allowed to continue unchecked. The pendulum swung the tsar's way till about 1910, then it began to swing back.

1910 was the year Leo Tolstoy, prophet, writer and inspiration for many religious progressives, died. His death seemed a sort of watershed culturally as well as politically. Symbolism, for instance, the dominant artistic move-ment in Russia, began to recede then. It had centred on the enigmatic Vyacheslav Ivanov, who believed that the mysticism of the poetic symbol put man in touch with the supernatural. After the Moscow Theatre Studio collapsed, Ivanov and the Petersburg Symbolists appealed to Meyerhold to help them found a theatre in which actor and audience would fuse in mysterious communion, an idea which for a short time excited Meyerhold. But the Torches Theatre, as it was to be called, never materialized beyond the dreams enunciated at Ivanov's Wednesday gatherings. These centred round

2. Meyerhold's relationship with Vera Komissarzhevskaya, as seen by a contemporary cartoonist

set-piece discussions on philosophy, religion, poetry, the occult and so on, and it is quite likely that Meyerhold was present when the flat was raided by the police on 29 December 1906. But nothing came of that either. Nevertheless, in 1910, Meyerhold did present a production of Calderón's *The Adoration of the Cross* in a room in Ivanov's flat, by then called the Tower Theatre because it was in an old tower, and it proved to be an extremely successful experiment, though it was not repeated.

Meyerhold's work with Symbolist drama, however, with the Comrades of the New Drama and at the Theatre Studio induced a brilliant 'progressive' actress who had left the Alexandrinsky Theatre to set up her own company, Vera Komissarzhevskaya, to offer Meyerhold the post of artistic director of her venture in 1906. Her father had been an associate of Stanislavsky, but she was interested in the 'new' artistic movements, especially the 'new' drama, and even held 'Saturdays' in imitation of Ivanov's 'Wednesdays'. Meyerhold accepted her offer, and scored a number of remarkable successes at her theatre, notably with *Hedda Gabler*, Maeterlinck's *Sister Beatrice*, and Blok's *The Fairground Booth*, all in 1906. However, Komissarzhevskaya felt she was losing the helm of her theatre and, supported by her brother, Fyodor, who had ambitions of his own to direct, she ousted him. Meyerhold sued her, but lost his case.

His last production for Komissarzhevskaya was of Sologub's *Death's Victory* (1907) in which Meyerhold played the part of the poet. At the end of the first performance Sologub was crowned with a laurel wreath, and later he

3. Meyerhold as Pierrot in Blok's *The Fairground Booth*. Photo taken in 1907

appeared as a witness for Meyerhold against Komissarzhevskaya. The following year he published the most significant Symbolist theatrical manifesto, *The Theatre of One Will*,[12] in which he argued as Meyerhold did for the removal of the footlights, though for Sologub this was to ease the mystical fusion of performer and spectator. Meyerhold had already rejected these 'squeezed lemons and picked chicken bones of the little world of the liberal-mystic intelligentsia',[13] as Trotsky later put it, by staging Blok's *The Fairground Booth* in which the mystics were presented as cardboard cutouts and Pierrot, played by Meyerhold, had his illusions shattered when 'suddenly all the scenery rolls up and flies away'.[14] As Meyerhold was to write in 1915, 'The way of the Mystery and the way of the Theatre do not merge.'[15]

Soon after Meyerhold and Komissarzhevskaya parted company, V.A. Telyakovsky, Director of the Imperial Theatres in Petersburg, sent for the young director, and, much to his surprise, asked him to join his staff. Much to everyone else's surprise, this iconoclastic democrat accepted, and for nearly ten years held his post, becoming secretary to the group of directors attached to the Imperial Theatres and producing some brilliant work. He was at first resisted by some of the actors – Roman Apollonsky, for instance, doing his best to sabotage Meyerhold's first production at the Alexandrinsky, Knut Hamsun's *At the Gates of the Kingdom*. But in the end, such irritations proved insignificant. Much more important, *At the Gates of the Kingdom* was the production when Meyerhold first worked with Alexander Golovin. The two were to become fast friends and collaborated closely till 1917. For another leading actor, Yuri Yurev, Meyerhold's arrival was 'a liberation',[16] and his performance as Don Juan in Meyerhold's production of Molière's play in 1910 proved to be one of his greatest triumphs. And Meyerhold was able in the Imperial Theatres to demonstrate his mastery of opera, too. A recent critic wrote of his 1909 production of *Tristan and Isolde*: 'In its time it was amazing and never since has there been seen such a blending of movement and mise-en-scène woven from a musical score.'[17] The comment indicates that Meyerhold had already developed his 'system': the performers based their work on movement which was blended with the *mise-en-scène* by musical – or rhythmic – techniques.

Productions such as *Tristan and Isolde* and *Don Juan* put Meyerhold on a par with Diaghilev's Russian artists working in western Europe, and in 1913 he did in fact go to Paris to direct Ida Rubinstein in Gabriele D'Annunzio's *Pisanelle*, with settings by Leon Bakst and music by Ildebrando Pizzatti, at the Châtelet Theatre. Though this was the city where Maeterlinck, Verhaeren Appollinaire and others were living, where cubism was causing scandals and where an 'advanced' labour movement was creating unrest, Meyerhold was not apparently particularly excited by the project, and had no further associations with such productions.

Instead, he developed his own work under the pseudonym 'Dr Dapertutto', forced on him by the terms of his contract with the Imperial Theatres. Dr Dapertutto had no theatre so his presentations – twenty-four in all – took place in little theatres, assembly rooms, cabarets, even private flats.

The most important venues were the Cove little theatre in Petersburg, where he presented a triple bill in 1908; the House of Interludes, where the audience sat at tables to eat and drink while watching and where he presented a pantomime version of Schnitzler's *Columbine's Scarf* and Znosko-Borovsky's *The Transfigured Prince* in late 1910; the Casino Theatre in the holiday resort of Terioki in Finland, where he produced Andreev's *To the Stars* in 1907, and five more plays with a large group of friends in 1912; the Tenishevsky Street Hall, where he staged two of Blok's plays in 1914, and the hall on Borodinskaya where he presented an evening of short *études* and 'antics appropriate to the theatre' with his own students in 1915; and the Comedians' Rest, a cabaret theatre where he was a partner and where he revived *Columbine's Scarf* in 1916.[18] In a letter written in 1911, Meyerhold noted that Italian *commedia dell' arte* players had performed in Russia in the eighteenth century. 'Resonant echoes' of their style, he asserted, 'can still be heard in the fairground booths of central Russia' and 'the *commedia dell' arte* tradition . . . is firmly implanted' there.[19] This was the tradition he was seeking to return to the mainstream of Russian theatre, not only with his productions of *Columbine's Scarf* and *Harlequin the Marriage Broker*, but also with *Don Juan* at the Alexandrinsky and, later, *The Magnanimous Cuckold* and other productions mounted after the revolution. *Commedia dell' arte* seemed the ideal antidote to the theatre of emotion and the naturalistic play, and it also spurred the actor towards physical, movement-based performance.

Other work of this period was geared to the same end. He adapted a story of circus life into a melodrama, *The Lady from the Box*, presented (not by Meyerhold) at the Foundry Theatre in February 1909, and a Japanese Kabuki play, *Terakoya*, also presented in 1909 at the same theatre. The previous year he had published a long essay 'On the History and Technique of the Theatre' in a book by various hands, *Theatre, a Book About the New Theatre*. Here he had discussed first the need for the theatre audience to act as 'a fourth creator, in addition to the author, the director and the actor',[20] and then the problems this posed for the actor – the problems of the mask, of movement, and so on. In 1912 this essay was reprinted in his book, *On Theatre*, which tacitly focussed Meyerhold's thought on the forestage, that is, the meeting-point between creative spectator and *commedia*-style performer. His contributions to his journal, *The Love of Three Oranges*, which ran irregularly from 1914 to 1916, continued the discussion, though it appears his concerns were still sometimes misunderstood, to judge from the entry in the diary of Alexander Blok, poetry editor of *The Love of Three Oranges*, for 6 March 1914, where he speaks bitterly of how with Meyerhold 'the sideshow [is] transferred to the stage of the Mariinsky' and how he displays 'a return to savagery (and not art)'. Then he writes: 'After I had written this, Meyerhold came to see me and, after a tedious argument, suddenly he was able to tell me about himself and his world in such a way that, for the first time in my life, I felt in him a living, feeling, loving man.'[21]

The journal was really the publication of Dr Dapertutto's Studio, where Meyerhold attempted to train actors to achieve what he regarded as the only genuinely theatrical style. He had been teaching regularly since 1909, and in 1913 opened his own Studio where the curriculum included not only voice work and movement, but also theatre history, as well as a special course in *commedia dell' arte* taught by V.N. Soloviev. Other theatre practitioners were following somewhat similar lines, though usually without the pedagogical input. Nikolai Evreinov, for instance, who succeeded Meyerhold at Vera Komissarzhevskaya's theatre, had mounted productions of old plays like *Robin and Marion* to try to recapture some of the primal fun of theatre. He was a musician (taught by Rimsky-Korsakov), historian, poet, and theoretician of corporal punishment as well as theatre, and a brilliant talker. He, too, tried to reintroduce *commedia dell' arte* techniques and was deeply involved in the kind of fringe theatre and cabaret world where Dr Dapertutto operated. Typical of this was the Stray Dog which 'by 1911–12 . . . had become the centre of literary life in the city – rather than Vyacheslav Ivanov's "Tower" . . . The Dog opened late, and the talk and the wine often flowed on till dawn.'[22] It typified Petersburg's 'silver age', brittle and brilliant, the pre-revolutionary intelligentsia's last flare-up, which became increasingly frenetic as time passed. In 1916, the last full year of tsarism, 'the farce theatres, the operetta, the *café-chantant* and the once-worried cinema thrived'. In the cinemas, 'in the intervals between the pictures [there were] music-hall turns – the two dwarfs, the gentleman who sings society songs, the fat lady and her thin husband . . .'[23]

Meyerhold worked in this milieu but his work, pedagogical and exemplary, took more cognizance of what major artists like Isadora Duncan, Max Reinhardt and Edward Gordon Craig were doing abroad than this self-indulgence at home. In Russia he was probably more interested in the Futurist movement, whose first theatre productions, Mayakovsky's *Vladimir Mayakovsky, a Tragedy* and Kruchenykh's *Victory Over the Sun* at the Luna Park Theatre in December 1913, he attended. Their work was explained by a group of young critics, headed by the aggressive Viktor Shklovsky, and known as 'Formalists', who introduced a quite new and challenging way of approaching art. The function of art, they proclaimed, was to 'make strange' the subject matter, thereby forcing us to 'see it anew', and a frequent method by which art achieved this was by drawing attention to its own artistic devices – the painting did not attempt to conceal its paint, the poem its conscious use of words, and the theatrical presentation its theatricality. It was an approach which was extraordinarily close to Meyerhold's own and one which yielded remarkably rich rewards in the newly arising worlds of post-cubist art and modern music – the paintings of Tatlin, Malevich, Chagall, Kandinsky and others, for example, 'made strange' their worlds and often drew attention to the 'artificiality' of their art, taking inspiration, for instance, from old ikons rather as Meyerhold took inspiration from the fairground booth.

And just as these avant-garde seeds were growing in the midst of suffocating 'silver' decadence, so the seeds of revolution were growing in the corruption and incompetence of the last years of tsarist government. And this, too, affected Meyerhold closely. In 1905 he had welcomed the revolution, and in 1906 argued that 'theatres must be democratic',[24] emphasizing the hunger and poverty of the beggars in his production of *Sister Beatrice*. By 1911, the reactionary forces felt themselves strong enough to persecute Nijinsky so as to drive him off the Petersburg stage altogether and to speak of 'the handful of aliens who control the Imperial Theatres', making clear that they were referring especially to 'that Jew' Meyerhold.[25] But as the Government and the Union of Russian People (the notorious 'Black Hundreds') conspired, the oppressed and the exploited began to fight back. In 1911, only 166 strikes by workers were recorded in Russia; in 1912, there were 2032, in 1913 2404, and in the seven months to July 1914 4098. One trigger for the increase was the incident at Lena in Siberia on 4 April 1912 when unarmed workers, demonstrating for the release of their arrested leaders, were shot down by soldiers. By 1914 the situation was so bad that barricades were being erected in the streets of Petersburg.

At first the war changed all this. There were some initial military successes, though also some catastrophic losses, notably at Tannenburg and Masurian Lakes. By the end of 1914, Russia was just holding her own, but 1915 gradually turned into a year of horror. Poland, Lithuania and Latvia were lost with 150,000 men killed and 700,000 wounded. The year 1916 saw a temporary respite when General Brusilov launched an offensive, but it did not last long and it became obvious that Russia could bear no more. The tsar took control at the front, incompetently. Rasputin was shot at home, but it made no difference. For the common people, the facts were that a bag of potatoes which had cost one rouble in 1914 cost seven roubles at the beginning of 1917, and a pound of meat which had been about twelve kopeks had risen to about seventy. The workers started striking again. In 1915 there were 928 strikes. In 1916 1284. And in the first two months of 1917 there were 1330 strikes. Then the tsar abdicated.

It was the end of Dr Dapertutto, too. He was perhaps no longer needed, for much of Meyerhold's extra-curricular energy had begun to be devoted to film making. In 1915 he completed *The Picture of Dorian Gray*, which Leyda has called 'undoubtedly the most important Russian film made previous to the February revolution',[26] and in 1917 *The Strong Man* which was perhaps less impressive but still contained an important element of the Meyerhold method, presenting 'not whole scenes, but only sharp fragments of the whole'.[27] Moreover, the war years contained some of Meyerhold's most exciting stage productions at the Imperial Theatres – Lermontov's *The Two Brothers* (1915), Calderón's *The Constant Prince* (1915), Ostrovsky's *The Storm* (1916) and finally Lermontov's *Masquerade* which received its premiere the day before the February revolution broke out. It was the richest, most lavish show ever presented in Russia, and Kugel recorded how as the brilliant crowd left the theatre, having paid fabulously inflated prices for their seats, 'somewhere in the distance there was shooting and cries for bread'.

A new world was lurching into being.

TRIUMPH 1917–1930

Between the February and October revolutions of 1917, Russia trembled between two worlds. Even in cultural matters there was much manoeuvring for positions as blocks were formed and re-formed, the red flag was flown over the Mariinsky Theatre and cabarets and *cafés chantant* opened and closed. Meyerhold allied himself with the Freedom of Art group, a 'left' alliance, and continued to work for the Imperial Theatres, but on a hitherto banned trilogy by the nineteenth-century author, Alexander Sukhovo-Kobylin. The Provisional Government's inability to end Russian involvement in the world war probably more than anything else robbed them of support and by September there were Bolshevik majorities on both the Petrograd and Moscow Soviets. The second revolution of the year at the end of October (old style) was hardly a surprise.

A week after seizing power, the Bolsheviks appealed to all artists to meet their representatives to discuss the organization of the cultural life of the country. Only a few responded – the poets Blok and Mayakovsky, Larissa Raisner, a young politically active writer who was later to fight in the Red Army, perhaps a couple of painters. And from the world of theatre, Meyerhold alone came forward. It was a bold decision for a man of his eminence and respectability as probably the leading director in the former Imperial Theatres. But he shared passionately the desire expressed by Blok

to redo everything. To arrange things so that everything comes new; so that the false, dirty, dull, ugly life which is ours becomes a just life, pure, gay, beautiful . . . 'Peace and the brotherhood of nations' – that is the banner beneath which the Russian revolution is taking place. For this its torrent thunders on. This is the music which they who have ears to hear must hear.[28]

Probably at the instigation of Boris Malkin, the party official who had met the few artists to respond to its appeal, Meyerhold was appointed deputy head of the Theatre Department of Narkompros (People's Commissariat of Education) when it was established in January 1918. He organized a series of classes for them and in August of that year joined the Bolshevik Party. Ehrenburg has commented on this: 'The fact that he became a Communist was not accidental: he was firm in the knowledge that the world must be changed. This knowledge was not based on other men's arguments but on his own experience.'[29] He continued to work at the former Imperial Theatres with diminishing enthusiasm, the one interesting work he did there in 1918 being Stravinsky's *The Nightingale*, presented in May at the Mariinsky after the composer had specifically requested that he produce it. It might be added that the Stravinsky scholar, Victor Borovsky, has noted that the questions raised by the 'inherent theatricality' of Stravinsky's thought were answered by 'various people in the theatre; the one who should be mentioned first and foremost is Vsevolod Meyerhold'.[30] The times, however, were wrong for this development. In the early autumn, Meyerhold brought Mayakovsky to the Alexandrinsky to read his play *Mystery Bouffe* to the company: their outraged reaction probably decided him finally to sever his links with these theatres. This first version of Mayakovsky's 'heroic, epic and satiric representation of our era', despite enormous problems encountered in preparing it, was a memorable celebration of the first anniversary of the Bolshevik revolution.

It was, however, Meyerhold's last production for exactly two years, as he was caught up in the whirling fortunes of the Civil War and the invasions of Russia by Germany, Britain, the USA and other western countries. At first, the opponents of Bolshevism – managers, bureaucrats, and so on – went on strike. When this brought meagre results and the peace of Brest-Litovsk was signed, they began to fight in earnest under a series of tsarist generals – Kolchak, Deniken, Vrangel and others. The Bolsheviks struck back. The Red Army had been formed in 1918 and in little over two years its enthusiasm, coupled with its efficiency, had defeated the Whites. Meyerhold had been forced in 1919 to travel to Yalta for health reasons. The Whites had arrested him as a Red, he had escaped and joined the Red Army, where, by the way, he organized theatricals. In summer 1920, he was summoned to Moscow, where he was appointed director of the Theatre Section of Narkompros.

No doubt he was pleased to return. He discovered that the old cultural world he had known had fragmented, but art had not stood still. Especially on

4. A 'mass spectacle', Petrograd, 1920

important days like May Day or the 7 November revolutionary anniversary the cities changed their appearance under huge canvasses, float-like decorations and other revolutionary banners and flags, and were likely to be subsumed in a 'mass spectacle' – a vast open-air theatrical performance with hundreds – sometimes thousands – of performers, usually celebrating some aspect of peasant or working-class revolt. It was reminiscent of a gigantic fairground booth. Thus in 1920 Kandinsky proposed a theatrical dimension to the called-for 'monumental' art which would rely largely on movement and gesture,[31] as the fairground performance and the mass spectacle also did.

But in spite of the enthusiasm there were dire problems, not least in getting enough food for the actors to eat. In November 1917, all theatres had been nationalized, but by 26 August 1919 they had to be nationalized again. A company like that of the Nezlobin Theatre, re-formed as a collective in 1917, hung together till 1921, when the theatre was taken from them and they were 'assigned finally to the cold, damp and ill-equipped Zon Theatre',[32] whither Meyerhold himself had also moved. The Moscow Art Theatre was floundering, Komissarzhevsky had deserted his company and emigrated. Meyerhold therefore faced much work in his new post at Narkompros.

And much was what he did. Huntly Carter remembered him at this period 'looking . . . like a typical workman in blouse, top boots and cap, dining on black bread and hard boiled eggs, living in a bare, cold and cheerless flat, and yet doing work that might reasonably cause English theatre managers to give up their jobs and take to road-sweeping.'[33] Mikhail Zharov recalled a talk to

5. Meyerhold the Bolshevik, 1921

young theatre workers: 'Meyerhold with his dishevelled hair – still "Doctor Dapertutto" – sat on the little school stage with "folded" legs (he was very adept at "folding" one over the other) and spoke intoxicatingly, enthusing himself with his own inspiration.' 'So Meyerhold came into our youth,' Zharov continues, 'and we gave the heat of our ardour to him.'[34] He called for nothing less than 'October [i.e. a revolution] in the theatre'. Organizing the Theatre Department along military lines, he conducted a frontal assault on the bastions of the old, privileged academic theatres through the columns of the Department's journal, *Theatre Herald*.

Meyerhold took his stand with Pushkin, who more and more in the last twenty years of his life seemed to offer Meyerhold inspiration or wisdom. According to Pushkin, 'drama originated in a public square and constituted a popular entertainment. The common people, like children, require amusement, action. The drama confronts them with a strange and unusual incident . . . Laughter, pity and terror are the three chords of our imagination, vibrated by dramatic enchantment.'[35] With this as his basic premise, Meyerhold suggested that in the absence of a genuinely Soviet repertoire, the contemporary theatre should learn from the Italian theatre of the seventeenth and eighteenth centuries and make its own, improvised from scenarii. The keys to such a development lay in, first, theatricality (even Ostrovsky 'bore in mind the power of laughter in the theatre', he noted[36]), improvisation and 'physical culture', and, second, in 'tendentiousness', and he quoted Aristophanes, Molière, Shakespeare's *Henry V* and other plays as examples of what he meant here.

To demonstrate his theses in action, he set up the 'First Theatre of the RSFSR' as 'a model . . . of the new proletarian theatrical collective',[37] a 'Theatre of the Red Flag', which also had pedagogical aims. There were to be four sections, for (1) artistic agitation, to be headed by A.S. Serafimovich, (2) a neoclassical section under Valery Bryussov, (3) a section for socialist plays, headed by Larissa Raisner, and (4) a section for new forms to be led by Mayakovsky. While the work of these sections was to proceed in 'the mirror hall with its small stage . . . and all the rooms adjacent to it', 'the large stage . . . will be given over to the production of plays from the heroic-monumental repertoire.'[38] This large scheme was never actually set in motion, but a start was made on the repertoire with Meyerhold's production of *The Dawns* by Emile Verhaeren on 7 November 1920. A particular feature of this show was that Meyerhold soon discovered how to build into it an opportunity for despatches from the Civil War front to be read out, which caused a sensation on at least one occasion. However, despite some popular success, Lenin's wife Krupskaya, Lunacharsky, the Commissar for Education, and other party dignitaries, disliked it. Neither did many of them care much for his next production, an updated version of Mayakovsky's *Mystery Bouffe*, which was received with much enthusiasm, however, by the soldiers and workers whom Meyerhold had come to regard as *his* spectators.

Throughout this period, he had general support from many 'left' organizations and individual practitioners, even though there was a good deal of quibbling and petty backbiting. The Proletkult (Organization for Proletarian Culture) and TEREVSAT (Theatres of Revolutionary Satire) pursued what were in fact Meyerholdian lines, theatre tickets continued to be available free of charge, former students like Sergei Radlov in Petrograd and Andrei Zonov in Moscow were active and influential, and Platon Kerzhentsev's widely-read book, *The Creative Theatre*, the first version of which was published in 1918, was plainly written in Meyerhold's shadow. As for the Party he had joined, Boris Malkin worked hard to raise Meyerhold's star in it. He and Meyerhold, as well as Mayakovsky, Brik and others, were members of the 'Kom–Fut' (Communist–Futurist) group and in the spring of 1921 Malkin tried to gain Lenin's interest in and commitment to *Mystery Bouffe*, though with little success. Meyerhold's real influence, however, was summed up by Yuri Olesha in 1934, when he wrote:

If there is indeed a new art that came into existence after the October Revolution, an art that now amazes the world, a Soviet art, then one can safely say that the first years of that art had a name. Meyerhold. He invented everything that others now claim as their own. The whole system of contemporary Soviet theatre derives from him.[39]

At the time, matters can hardly have seemed so simple. By 1921, the period of 'war communism' was over, but the country was still largely broken down and chaotic, with tsarism, anti-semitism and the like by no means dead, strikes and assassinations too frequent, hunger ubiquitous and a gradual but inexorable depopulation of the cities occurring. Lenin's New Economic Policy (NEP), which reintroduced some limited capitalist organization to the dismay of many of his supporters, was adopted by the Party in March 1921, and a new era began. As for Meyerhold, the Party's refusal to give him more than the flimsiest support led him to resign from the Theatre Department in April; a few months later, the First Theatre of the RSFSR's subsidy was withdrawn and the theatre closed; and finally his marriage to Olga Munt came to an end. He, too, needed a new start.

The NEP period was to provide an intense climate to work in, exhilarating, bitter, confused and demanding. Basically, after 1921, both the trade unions and the Soviets lost power to the Party. The left were not necessarily opposed to this: after all, the function of a trade union, which was needed in a capitalist state to defend workers, was not at all obvious in a workers' state; and the Soviet was the vehicle the Kronstadt mutineers upheld as opposing the Party. But there was nevertheless something worrying in the fact that power (and power struggles) were concentrated so exclusively in the Party. If Trotsky was correct when he said in 1924, 'one can be right only with the party and through the party',[40] then effective opposition to policy trends was virtually impossible. The left, who had fought and won the revolution – and Meyerhold certainly considered himself one of them – found themselves opposed to many developments of the NEP period, but powerless to do much about it. They had lost touch with the proletariat when, after the revolution, they had had to organize and manage the new institutions of the

Soviet Union. Now, as these jobs were taken over by bureaucrats, they found themselves swamped by new party members (the very bureaucrats who were taking over) and reduced to an even smaller minority. Meyerhold's own career – organizer at the Theatre Department till 1921, followed by a return to his first job of theatre practitioner 'organized' by others (as described below) through the 1920s and 1930s – is entirely typical, even down to the way he fell out of favour in Stalin's heyday in the 1930s.

During the NEP period, Meyerhold and the 'left' group supported the nationalized concerns against the entrepreneurial 'NEPmen', with the ironic result of course that they thereby strengthened the state bureaucracy. Trotsky's calls for centralized planning, industrialization and 'machinization' had this effect, too, though his demands for certain kinds of democratic procedures which made him popular with some in the Party did not. Trotsky symbolized the 'left' until his fall in 1927 and though he was a lonely and somewhat cranky figure, victim, too, of a mysteriously persistent illness, he still inspired enormous admiration and respect. In the intra-party battles of 1923 and 1924, Trotsky's followers were able to demonstrate on the streets against Stalin and his agents in impressive numbers, and the Komsomol and student organizations had to be thoroughly purged and closely watched to eradicate Trotsky's influence.

It was perhaps Meyerhold's misfortune that he and his theatre were at least partly identified with Trotskyism, especially at the end of the 1920s when Stalin was speaking of Trotsky as a traitor ('the united front from Chamberlain to Trotsky'[41]). Boris Malkin, the member of Kom–Fut who had been secretary to the All Russian Congress of Peasants' Deputies and a member of the All Russian Central Executive Committee and head of its Central Press Agency, and who tried to help Meyerhold in the early years of Soviet power, was of Trotsky's faction, and as such was arrested in the 1930s. Meyerhold's production of *Earth Rampant* in 1923 was dedicated 'to the Red Army and the first soldier of the RSFSR, Leon Trotsky'[42] who attended at least one performance recalled by Yuri Annenkov:

During one of the acts, happening to glance towards the seat of Trotsky, I saw that he was no longer there. I assumed that the production was perhaps not to his tastes and that he had decided to leave the theatre. But after two or three minutes Trotsky suddenly appeared *on the stage* and, in the same setting which contained the actors, delivered a short speech regarding the fifth anniversary of the founding of the Red Army which fit [sic] right in with the action of the play. After thunderous applause the action on stage continued as if without interruption and Trotsky again returned to his seat.[43]

LEF journal, which was allied with Meyerhold, had Trotskyist connections, and Trotsky's call in *Literature and Revolution* for 'a Soviet comedy of manners, one of laughter and indignation',[44] was answered, if at all, by Mayakovsky's

6. Trotsky, as depicted by the 'left' artist, Alexander Rodchenko, 1923

The Bedbug (1929) and *The Bathhouse* (1930), staged by Meyerhold and the author together. Furthermore, Lenin's polemic against 'left-wing communism, an infantile disorder', was used against Trotsky and his followers in the 1920s – it was levelled against, for instance, Meyerhold's production of *D.E.* in 1924.

In 1921, with no theatre, no government appointment and no wife, all this lay ahead. The new start he needed came in October when he was appointed Director of the newly-formed State Higher Directing Workshop (GVYRM), which early in 1922 became the State Higher Theatre Workshop (GVYTM). Sergei Yutkevich described applying to the Workshop:

we found ourselves in the tiny hall of a mansion in the Novinsky Boulevard, which had previously been a school ... Thence a minute and creaking wooden lift led to a classroom in which were lines of plain school desks. The classroom and the small hall were the entire premises of the GVYRM. In the hall, behind the table of the admissions board, Meyerhold himself presided. He was wearing a faded pullover, soldiers' puttees over his trousers and enormous thick-soled shoes. He had a woollen scarf around his neck and from time to time would put a red fez on his head. By his side was a man who was totally bald, with a very neat red beard, piercing eyes and rapid movements: Ivan Alexandrovich Aksenov ... Next to him was another entirely bald man, ascetic and monk-like in appearance: Valery Bebutov. At the side was a Mongol, small but stocky. This was Valery Inkidzhinov.[45]

In parallel with this in December 1921 Meyerhold founded a Laboratory for the Actor's Technique, soon to become the Free Workshop of Vs. Meyerhold, for performers with a little more experience. The two groups mixed fairly freely and both provided Meyerhold with well-known protégés. From GVYTM came Sergei Eisenstein, Erast Garin, Zinaida Raikh, Nikolai Ekk, Sergei Yutkevich and others; from the Free Workshop, Maria Babanova, Mikhail Zharov, Vassily Zaichikov, Igor Ilyinsky, Dmitri Orlov, Maria Sukhanova and others. Zinaida Raikh had been married to the poet Sergei Esenin, who had abandoned her before he met Isadora Duncan. After directing a touring agitprop troupe in 1919 and working with various Moscow workers' clubs, she had met Meyerhold and she now provided him with another new start. They were married in the spring of 1922 and achieved eighteen years of warm, even voluptuous, personal and professional partnership.

Meanwhile the Zon Theatre, which had housed the First Theatre of the RSFSR, had been made over in January 1922 to the Actors' Theatre, a new grouping to be formed from actors attached to GVYRM and those of the fast-sinking Nezlobin Theatre Company, who were still performing plays from the old repertoire to three-quarters empty houses. In April, Meyerhold led his students in a commando-style raid on this theatre – typically enough, he divided them into brigades, assigned each brigade to an area of the theatre and had the whole place cleared from top to bottom. Everything – flats, scenery, props, curtains and all – was chucked out into the yard. When the dust settled there was an empty theatre which was to encompass Meyerhold's work for the next ten years. The Nezlobin actors, no longer able to present their versions of *The Two Little Orphans*, *The Madwoman*, and the rest because their costumes and scenery had all been destroyed, were stranded: Meyerhold flung together his first production in the newly-emptied theatre with them, *Nora*, from Ibsen's *A Doll's House*. It was the end for the Nezlobin company, but the beginning for the Meyerhold Workshop, who five days later made their debut with Meyerhold's production of *The Magnanimous Cuckold* by Ferdinand Crommelynck.

In the late summer of that year, 1922, GVYTM was formally dissolved and with it the Actors' Theatre, and on 17 September the State Institute of Theatre Art (GITIS) was inaugurated, with Meyerhold as director of training and research. GITIS was an umbrella organization, taking in the State Institute of Music Drama as well as Meyerhold's Free Workshop and his official acting and directing students. The Free Workshops of Nikolai Foregger and Boris Ferdinandov, Solomon Mikhoels's Jewish Studio, and the Armenian Theatre Studio, and, later, others too were also constituent members of GITIS; each retained a large measure of autonomy in what was intended to be 'a place unique on the planet, where the science of theatre is studied and drama is built. Exactly: "science" and not "art" − "built" and not "created".'[46]

Unfortunately, although Meyerhold managed to mount one production, *The Death of Tarelkin*, under the auspices of GITIS, the grandiose scheme foundered within three months of its foundation and Meyerhold's own students and collaborators founded a new Vs. Meyerhold Workshop, and a Meyerhold Theatre (TIM) to go with it. This was the name of the company when they next presented a show at the Zon Theatre, *Earth Rampant* in March 1923. Meanwhile, in December 1922, Meyerhold himself had been appointed director of the ailing Theatre of the Revolution. Though some of Meyerhold's actors went with him, they also retained an independent existence based at the Zon, so that for a year Meyerhold effectively controlled two Moscow theatres. In April 1923 Meyerhold celebrated twenty-five years in the professional theatre and was honoured with the title 'People's Artist of the USSR' − the first theatre director to receive the award, and only the sixth artist in all. Shortly afterwards, his workshop was recognized by the state and became the State Experimental Theatre Work-shop (GEKTEMAS) in the name of Vs. Meyerhold. In December, he left the Theatre of the Revolution, having presented two plays there, in order to concentrate on GEKTEMAS and the Meyerhold Theatre, which finally, on 18 August 1926, gained state subsidy and was renamed the State Theatre in the name of Vs. Meyerhold (GosTIM).

Throughout these vicissitudes, we can detect the structure Meyerhold was constantly striving to achieve for the kind of work he was pursuing. It had three tiers − a school, a 'workshop' and a theatre which presented shows to the public, with any member of the group able to pass freely between the tiers while being chiefly attached to the workshop or the school. At last he was able to work with the kind of people he sought – mostly young, and of a 'low' enough social class to have few preconceptions about theatre. 'We were mostly provincial young people', Garin explained, 'straining to get at a new art. None of us idealized the past, no-one intended to imitate already approved models, as usually happens in theatre schools.'[47] They rapidly developed a fierce loyalty to Meyerhold, whom they knew as the Master, and whose battles they waged with a will – Zharov, for instance, recalled the 'Meyerholdites' marching in a body behind their own banner to one 'dispute' in the Hall of Columns in Moscow. Yet their 'involvement with the community' (as our jargon today would put it) was enormously impressive and based in 'the Methodological Club Laboratory' of GEKTEMAS. This consisted of the same personnel now in the guise of collaborators with workers' clubs, Red Army groups, students and so forth, with two fundamental aims: 'the working out of methods and forms of artistic work in the clubs on the basis of a Marxist understanding of the clubs' work and the utilization of the achievements of Vs. Meyerhold in the theatre; and the education of new club instructors, able to answer the demands of club work.'[48] Meyerhold's students went into clubs to do practical sessions, hold seminars, give lectures and they mounted 'mass' productions, living newspapers and so on with the members.

The 'achievements' of Meyerhold in the theatre which his collaborators wished club members, amateurs and others to 'utilize' centred on an actor training based on physical skills and known as 'biomechanics', and a method of play construction which relied not on the gradual unfolding of a plot to its inevitable denouement but one focussed in a montage of attractions or sequence of theatrically exciting moments. These are discussed in detail in the following chapters of this book. Suffice it to say here that these methods produced a string of stunning theatrical triumphs – none of them without some controversial feature, it should be added – beginning with *The Magnanimous Cuckold*. There followed *The Death of Tarelkin* (1922), *Earth Rampant* (1923), *The Forest* (1924), *D.E.* (1924), *The Mandate* (1925), and *The Government Inspector* (1926), the last being the occasion for the publication of at least three books of criticisms within a year.[49] The accomplishment was so varied, so modernistic and so dazzling that the only comparison that seemed valid was with Picasso – a comparison made by Nikolai Foregger, Louis Lozowick and others.[50] When Lunacharsky promulgated the slogan, 'Back to Ostrovsky', he was countered with the riposte: 'Forward to Meyerhold!' When the Meyerhold Theatre went on tour to southern Russia in the summer of 1926, 'at the station we were met with an orchestra, and on a width of red calico stretched between two vehicles was written: "Welcome to the Revolutionary Theatre in the name of Meyerhold".'[51] It was even possible to buy in Moscow trinkets like combs with the world 'Meyerhold' engraved on them.

Yet in the last few years of the decade, life became slowly more difficult. With the failure of the world revolution to materialize, and Germany almost the only country willing to maintain, let alone increase, trade and cultural contacts, Stalin proposed a new slogan: 'Socialism in one country'. It meant self-reliance of the most strenuous kind. By 1928, production had at last largely reached the levels it had been at in 1913 – grain production in 1928 was 73.3 million tonnes when it had been 81.6 million in the exceptionally good year of 1913 (though the population was probably over 20 million more in 1928). But steel production was at 4 million tons compared with 4.2 million in 1913, and electricity generation was up from 1.9 million kilowatts in 1913 to 5.05 million in 1928. It was time to end NEP. A five-year plan for industrialization and for the collectivization of agriculture – in many ways policies remarkably similar to those of the now disgraced Trotsky – was adopted in April 1928.

Meanwhile events abroad were encouraging the Soviet Union to retreat into its own shell. The rise of Nazism in Germany was one ominous sign, the Wall Street crash in 1929 was another. In the field of culture, organizations like the Association of Artists of Revolutionary Russia (AKhRR) and the Russian Association of Proletarian Writers (RAPP) were gaining influence at the expense of, for instance, Mayakovsky's group based round his magazine *LEF* (now *Novy Lef*), with whom Meyerhold was associated. In 1928 'Artistic Councils' were instituted in each theatre to oversee the repertoire, and make those in receipt of state subsidies accountable to their paymasters. This was probably an excellent idea in most cases, but for an organization like Meyerhold's it led to difficulties. Because the main thrust of his work was pedagogical, not presentational, his company had always seemed improvident. Now the pressure on it was increased, the more so because box office receipts were falling and no new plays were forthcoming. Meyerhold wanted to present Tretyakov's *I Want a Child* and Erdman's *The Suicide*, but both were banned. The Zon Theatre was in increasingly desperate need of repair, and the polemics, whose ferocity and bitter tone Meyerhold himself had helped to set seven or eight years previously, now turned on him. He must have felt increasingly isolated as many friends and fellow artists emigrated: in 1924 Vyacheslav Ivanov and his old literary mentor Alexei Remizov left, followed by the theatricalist director of the Petersburg silver age, Nikolai Evreinov; in 1928, the director Alexei Granovsky, whom Huntly Carter described as one of the post-revolutionary theatre's 'Big Five' along with Lunarcharsky, Meyerhold, Tairov and Stanislavsky, went, as did Meyerhold's particular friend and an actor whom he greatly admired, Mikhail

Chekhov, nephew of the playwright. Furthermore, in 1929 Lunacharsky resigned as Head of the Commissariat of Education, while Stalin had his fiftieth birthday celebrated with unusual publicity and tastelessness.

There were good things, too. In 1928 the Kabuki Theatre visited Moscow, and Meyerhold's enthusiasm led him to propose taking his company to Tokyo, though this proved to be impossible. He discovered and employed a young composer, Dmitri Shostakovich, who lived for months at his flat while composing the opera, *The Nose*. When the flat was engulfed in a fire, Meyerhold saved Shostakovich's manuscripts before his own possessions, and ever afterwards kept a list of emergency telephone numbers – fire, ambulance, etc – prominent in his hallway. And best of all, Mayakovsky supplied him with two brilliant plays – both still absurdly little known in the English-speaking world – *The Bedbug* and *The Bathhouse*. These Meyerhold produced in 1929 and 1930 with a typical emphasis on spectacle and physical energy.

They caused an explosion of furious argument and denigration. A typical comment on *The Bathhouse* came in *The Workers' Gazette*: 'It is a tiring, confused show, which can be of interest only to a small group of literary fans'.[52] But Meyerhold replied energetically: '*The public* demands spectacle,' he asserted, referring to football matches and sports arenas on one hand and to the Catholic Church's processions and rituals on the other. 'The plays of Vladimir Mayakovsky and Nikolai Erdman are splendid,' he stated, for they – and he – 'reconstruct the theatre in such a way that the spectator is presented not with unadorned facts but with a revolutionary form through which he can absorb powerful revolutionary content, dazzling in its variety and complexity.'[53] Is there a hint of desperation here? Perhaps not. But there must have been more than that, an icy shiver down his spine, when Meyerhold learned that Mayakovsky had committed suicide on 14 April 1930 at the age of thirty-six. The two men embodied the same spirit, and Mayakovsky was virtually the only artist whom Meyerhold was prepared to admit was his equal – 'I simply couldn't begin to produce his plays without him', he said.[54]

DECLINE 1930–40

Bolshevism created the conditions for a popular, socialist theatre, one in which avant-garde intellectuals and common people met and mingled and struck sparks off each other, and for perhaps a decade one of those elusive 'golden ages' of the theatre existed. Meyerhold was the very heart and soul of that golden age, and its lessons for us even today are many and urgent. Unfortunately the Bolsheviks – or too many of them – remained cultural 'barbarians' (to use Lenin's term), and after engineering the upheaval, they could not sustain the excitement they had generated. Perhaps no one could have. At any rate the fifty-year-old Stalin now hustled 'class struggle' under the carpet and led a new struggle for 'national unity'.

Of course such a move was not simply perverse. The need for international contacts was both obvious and immediate, and before Hitler's accession to power in Germany in January 1933 relations between the Soviet Union and Germany especially began to proliferate profitably. In 1933 the USSR and the USA established diplomatic relations, and in the next year the USSR was admitted to the League of Nations. But the rise of fascism, and the apparent instability of the 'democracies' of the west seemed to lead to a need for ever greater national vigilance. This took two forms: first, exhortation and compulsion to increase productivity for the state – a second five-year plan began in 1932, the White Sea Canal was completed in 1933, the year when the legendary Stakhanov achieved his record output and all workers were urged to become 'Stakhanovites'; and second, by clamping down harder on political dissent, so that eventually the whole social and cultural life of the country was poisoned by more and more arrests, murders and show trials. Any intelligent observer could appreciate the need for extreme vigilance as Hitler and Mussolini strutted the world stage, and no doubt there was a good deal of devious plotting and surreptitious chicanery within the country. But to put to death a brilliant playwright and poet of the stature of Sergei Tretyakov, who supported communism wholeheartedly, or a scholar and *animateur* like Ivan Aksenov, who organized much of the Meyerhold Workshop's activity, taught there himself and translated Crommelynck's *The Magnanimous Cuckold*, almost beggars belief. Yet the executions of these and other long-standing colleagues punctuated the 1930s for Meyerhold and must at the very least have often cast him down.

To begin with, the signs were contradictory. The International Congress of Revolutionary Writers, held in Kharkov in 1930, severely condemned the avant-garde trends of the twenties, with which, of course, Meyerhold had been closely linked, and was the harbinger of the 1934 Congress of Soviet Writers. This endorsed 'socialist realism' as the only permissible aesthetic, condemned everything else, 'naturalism' as well as 'formalism' and 'petit bourgeois decadentism', and created a single acceptable line in all matters literary, cultural and artistic. On the other hand, Meyerhold's company toured Berlin and Paris in 1930, amazing and delighting most spectators, while annoying or baffling some reviewers. They also took part in a memorable workers' demonstration in Cologne on May Day. Meanwhile, Meyerhold's case for more subsidy seemed to be accepted: if it depended on his doing more productions and less teaching, he argued, he would need better conditions to work in. Consequently, in October 1931, the tatterdemalion old Zon Theatre was closed for extensive refurbishing or rebuilding. Over the next few years, slowly but certainly, a new building arose, designed expressly to meet the needs of Meyerhold's new style of theatre.

Meanwhile, the company toured extensively and used the tiny Passage Theatre as a temporary base from the summer of 1932. Meyerhold himself had lost none of his energy. Mikhail Sadovsky described how during a rehearsal

he jumped from his seat, took off his jacket, and rushed to the stage. He made a few comments, then ran back into the auditorium just as quickly, bent over someone there, and whispered something in his ear. A moment later he was at the opposite end of the auditorium and only his sharp voice was heard calling: 'All right! Bravo! Terrific!' . . . he was never still for a moment, but would appear now here, now there.[55]

Though Meyerhold had a reputation for irascibility, Filippov records that he 'frequently saw him discard the mask of peevishness and unsociability'. For instance, there was 'his amused reaction to an exhibition of humorous cartoons and caricatures by the then young Kukriniksy trio. Meyerhold laughed genuinely and most infectiously, commenting on individual drawings to Zinaida Raikh.'[56]

Meyerhold retained that supreme grace of being able to see through his own pretensions. There was the occasion when a large peasant woman burst into his rehearsal and started to berate him for rejecting her daughter's application to his school – she was 'so gifted, and sang, and danced, and had come to Moscow from a long way away, it wasn't fair, it was an insult', and so on and so on. Meyerhold shooed her away into the office, then exploded with fury – how could he rehearse when any person off the streets could burst in whenever they chose, there was a plot against him, and much more. 'And then, calming down, he scratched the back of his head and said: "But why didn't we accept her daughter? If the daughter possesses half the personality of the mother, she's certainly talented and she should be accepted."' In *The Lady of the Camellias*, Meyerhold used a live parrot on the stage. At one rehearsal, the assistant stage manager, a man named Mekhamed, had put the parrot in place but had forgotten some other prop. Meyerhold was furious and dressed him down mercilessly, ending with a yell: 'And whose fault is it?' The parrot immediately squawked: 'Mekhamed's!' The tension was broken, and Meyerhold laughed as loudly as anyone.[57]

The Lady of the Camellias (1934) was perhaps his finest production of the decade. He said he hoped that 'a pilot who attended the show would fly better afterwards', and Rudnitsky records that 'many masters of the theatre believed (and continue to believe) this production to be Meyerhold's best'.[58] Also it gave his beloved wife her best part and her most notable triumph. It

7. Meyerhold in rehearsal, 1930s

might be added, however, that Zinaida Raikh was only one of his ex-students who was fulfilling her potential. Among others, Georges Pitoëff had made an important name for himself in the Paris theatre, and those in the USSR included Nikolai Okhlopkov, now director at the Realistic Theatre in Moscow, and Sergei Radlov, whose production of *The Good Soldier Schweyk* reached its five-hundredth performance in Leningrad in 1933 and who was now moving forward to become perhaps the leading Soviet interpreter of Shakespeare.

But in January 1936, *Pravda* published a ferocious denunciation of 'formalists and aesthetes', of whom Shostakovich was a leading example, as his opera *Lady Macbeth of Mtsensk* demonstrated. This signalled an amazingly vicious campaign against any formerly avant-garde artist who would not recant and accuse other artists of formalism. It was depressingly like what was going on in Nazi Germany and, later, was to be repeated in Eisenhower's USA. Radlov and Okhlopkov rushed to denounce Meyerhold, and Platon Kerzhentsev, erstwhile Proletkult theorist but now President of the Soviet Committee for Cultural Affairs, completed the attack in an article in *Pravda* in December 1937. Meyerhold's 'systematic deviation from Soviet reality', Kerzhentsev wrote, 'the political distortion of that reality, and hostile slanders against our way of life have brought the [Meyerhold] theatre to total ideological and artistic ruin, to shameful bankruptcy ... Do Soviet art and the Soviet public really need such a theatre?'[59] Meyerhold tried to fight back – he refused absolutely to disown his earlier work, an action which would in any case, perhaps, have been anti-Marxist – but the forces ranged against him were becoming overwhelming.

In January 1938, the Meyerhold State Theatre was closed. In March, his old master, the now ailing Konstantin Stanislavsky, invited him to join the production staff at his Opera Theatre. But Stanislavsky died in August. 'Take care of Meyerhold', he is reputed to have said shortly before his death, 'he is my only heir in the theatre – here or elsewhere.'[60] In October, Meyerhold was appointed artistic director at the Stanislavsky Opera, and the same month wrote to his wife from Gorenki:

Me without you is like a blind man without his guide dog ... I reached Gorenki on the 13th, saw the silver birches and gasped ... Look: these leaves are scattered in the wind. Scattered, then still, as if frozen ... When I saw on the 13th in a legendary world the golden autumn, its miracle in all this, I babbled to myself: Zina, Zinochka, look, look at these miracles and ... don't leave me, *I love you*, you – my wife, sister, mother, friend, darling. *You are golden like this nature which creates miracles.* Zina, don't leave me!'[61]

When in June 1939 an All-Union Conference of Theatre Directors was held in Moscow, he knew what was happening. Of the list of emergency telephone numbers, he said: 'I think that this can go away, Zinochka, I am afraid that something more serious is happening to us.'[62] At the conference, Meyerhold came under scalding attack, and though he seems to have tried to defend his position and his work again, it was hopeless in that poisoned atmosphere. He was arrested as soon as the conference was over, and Zinaida Raikh a few days later. Raikh was released, but on 17 July she was found in the Meyerhold flat, with eleven knife wounds, and her throat cut. Meyerhold was brought to a secret trial on 1 February 1940, and – it is believed – shot on the following day. According to Ehrenburg, the State Prosecutor, fifteen years later, told him that in a last statement Meyerhold had said: 'I am sixty-six. I want my daughter and my friends to know one day that I remained an honest Communist to the end.'[63]

2 The fourth dimension

The fundamental cause for the split between Stanislavsky and Meyerhold at the very beginning of the century lay in their divergent views of the place of the audience in the theatrical event. Stanislavsky taught that: *'an actor must have a point of attention, and this point of attention must not be in the auditorium'* and that 'during a performance . . . it is important that the sequence of objects you focus on should form a *solid line. That line must remain on our side of the footlights, and not stray once into the auditorium.'*[1] Meyerhold always opposed this conception of the actor deliberately and unwaveringly excluding the spectator from his consciousness, and as early as 1907 posited an actor who 'stands face to face with the spectator . . . and *freely* reveals his soul to him, thus intensifying the fundamental theatrical relationship of performer and spectator.'[2] For Meyerhold, the audience was the vital fourth dimension without which there was no theatre. The other three 'dimensions' – the playwright, the director, and the actor – worked to no avail if they had no audience, for it was somewhere between them and their audience that theatre 'happened'.

Those who witnessed rehearsals and performances of the same production testify to the difference an audience made in Meyerhold's theatre. Sayler saw him at work just before the revolution: '*Don Juan* in rehearsal was antic and jolly. In performance it was sheer joy, – the joy of the theatre as theatre . . . the give and take between audience and actor [was] dynamic and almost incessant.'[3] Almost two decades later, van Gyseghem watched Meyerhold at work:

It is not necessary for an actor exactly to copy the movements of a drunk man, so long as what he does creates in the mind of the audience the image or the thought of a drunk man. It is as though from the union of two qualities a third is born. From the union of the state of mind of the audience plus the visual and actual image of certain movements is created this third quality – a drunk man.[4]

Meaning in the theatre was therefore the creation of theatre professionals and theatre spectators jointly. This is the cornerstone of Meyerhold's theatre. The ability of the theatre to 'start the spectator's brain working', to 'stimulate' his 'feelings' and to 'steer him through a complex labyrinth of emotions' was important, but

modern dramatists and directors rely not only on the efforts of the actors and the facilities afforded by the stage machinery but on the efforts of the audience as well. We produce

8. Meyerhold's production of *Don Juan* by Molière, Alexandrinsky Theatre, Petersburg, 1910

every play on the assumption that it will be still unfinished when it appears on the stage. We do this consciously because we realize that the crucial revision of a production is that which is made by the spectator.[5]

In Meyerhold's opinion, this was what distinguished the great periods of theatrical history from the mediocre: the great performances of the past 'were constructed in such a way that the conclusion had to be drawn by the spectator'.[6] And it was to the past that Meyerhold first turned in his search for a form of theatre which would enable this creative intercourse between performer and spectator to occur. The influence of Wagner on the young Meyerhold was pervasive, and at first he tried to realize Wagner's demand for 'a voluptuous mingling of all forms of art, under whose spell men would reach an emotional union'.[7]

This notion excited the Russian Symbolists, who wanted to set up a theatre of their own to be called 'The Torches', and they invited Meyerhold to be its artistic director. He accepted, but 'The Torches' never got further than a feverish 'golden dream'. Then at the Moscow Art Theatre Studio in 1905 he was able to work practically on the idea, most interestingly in the projected *Death of Tintagiles*, which however was never seen by an audience. It was at Vera Komissarzhevskaya's that he was finally able to present concrete productions designed to create the 'mystic union' of Wagner and the Symbolists, notably in *Sister Beatrice* (1906). But although this production did startle and delight its audiences — 'agitated' was Blok's word for their response, 'as though this random audience has felt the spirit of a miracle that was flowering on the stage'[8] — Meyerhold, never a mystic, drew a different lesson from it.

In the 'agitation' which Blok detected, Meyerhold sensed not a religious consummation — he agreed with Bely that if theatre was a 'temple' it was so 'without a deity', patently an absurdity — but a flow of energy back and forth between audience and performer which was uniquely of the theatre. It certainly had little in common with 'mystic communion' as his production of Blok's own *The Fairground Booth* showed. At the end of the first performance of this production, 'the tumult in the audience resembled an actual battle; reputable people were ready to come to blows; whistles and roars of hate were interrupted by reverberating shouts of mirth, challenge, anger and despair; "Blok, Sapunov, Kuzmin, M-e-y-e-r-h-o-l-d, b-r-a-v-o-o-o . . ."'[9] For the rest of his career this was the kind of response Meyerhold strove for and often evoked. 'Not only could he not abide a quiet, unresponsive audience,' wrote Sadovsky, 'he was truly frightened by it, and was prepared to break every single rule to galvanize the spectators.'[10] Meyerhold himself said: 'If everyone praises your production, almost certainly it is rubbish. If everyone abuses it, then perhaps there is something in it. But if some praise and others abuse, if you can split the audience in half, then for sure it is a good production.'[11]

Yuri Yurev, who played the eponymous hero of Molière's *Don Juan* at the Alexandrinsky Theatre in 1910, records:

When in the noisy applause at the end of the first performance, Varlamov and I went before the audience, a piercing whistle from the upper circle was suddenly heard; this served as a signal for other 'protesters'. One of them, a fairly thickset man of fifty, in evening dress (as we then recognized, it was Prince Argutinsky), whistled especially hotly right in our faces, quite unembarrassed to give himself up to such behaviour.[12]

And Lev Arnshtam records Meyerhold's reaction to such a scene after the premiere of *Teacher Bubus* at the Meyerhold Theatre in 1925:

I stood with Meyerhold in the wings. In the hall they not only applauded but whistled. 'Vsevolod Emilevich, they're whistling!' I said to Meyerhold fearfully . . . 'Whistling!' he exclaimed delightedly. 'This is wonderful! Let's go!' He drew me behind him, onto the stage, to take our bows. In the front row, demonstratively leaping to his feet and waving his hands high, Lunarcharsky was applauding. But Meyerhold bowed particularly respectfully and saluted with his arm stretched out to the corner of the hall from where the whistles clearly reached us.[13]

Meyerhold himself wrote after the commotion caused by *The Fairground Booth*: 'Maybe a section of the audience hissed Blok and his actors, but his theatre was still theatre. And perhaps the very fact that the audience felt free to hoot so violently demonstrates better than anything that the reaction was a reaction to a performance of true theatricality.'[14]

An audience which feels 'free to hoot' is of course a popular, perhaps lower-class, audience. Meyerhold's delight in and fascination for popular comedians, music hall and the circus had begun in his boyhood, and remained with him throughout his life. Tatyana Esenina, his adopted daughter, recalls that Novinsky Boulevard where the Meyerhold family lived in the 1920s, 'was a lively spot – Smolensk market place was not far away and . . . gypsies with bears and itinerant acrobats used to go up and down the boulevard',[15] and his most important essay in the pre-revolutionary period, also called *The Fairground Booth*, upholds this kind of basic entertainment as the true tradition of theatre: '"Les Clercs de la Basoche" (founded 1302) resorted to the principles of mummery and went out into the streets. It was there, in the intimate relationship between the histrion and his public, that the true theatre was created . . .'[16] But the audiences at the Komissarzhevskaya Dramatic Theatre or the Alexandrinsky were anything but street gazers, and it took a great deal of provocation to make them feel 'free to hoot'. The decorative image of an itinerant Petrushka puppet show or a fairground entertainment was one thing; the kind of disorienting theatricality or grotesquerie such exhibitions actually throve on, however, was quite another.

As for *Don Juan*, as Yurev suggests, it was 'the fact that Molière had not been presented in the traditional way' that 'angered' Prince Argutinsky and his friends. So while Stanislavsky was trying to outlaw even applause from the Art Theatre, Meyerhold was cursing 'the parterre, the silent, apathetic parterre' which was regarded primarily as 'a place for relaxation'.[17] After a group of wounded soldiers had watched one of his rehearsals in 1915, he wrote: 'in the way they responded to the performance of the comedians, they constituted the very audience for which the new theatre, the truly popular theatre, is intended'.[18] And two years later, he was urging the soldiers to come and 'liberate' the theatre from its old-style habitués.

And they did. By 1920 Meyerhold was noting that 'the audience has changed completely . . . we have a new public which will stand no non-sense'.[19] These were the people 'who only recently stormed the Winter Palace and smashed Kolchak, Deniken and Vrangel – [who] applauded the portrait of Lenin on the wall in A. Razumni's *Kombrig Ivanov* . . . [and] even the outward signs of a new revolution - the red scarves and the leather jackets' aroused them.[20] Ehrenburg remembered Meyerhold's theatre in 1920 as being 'unheated; everyone sat in overcoats, fur jackets, sheepskin coats. Thunderous words and delicate clouds of steam escaped from the actors' mouths . . . Members of the audience – Red Army men with a brass band, or workers – mounted the stage from time to time.'[21] Theatre tickets were free at this time, and the theatre became a 'meeting place'. The doors were left 'wide open and the winter's storm would blow into the foyer and corridors, making the visitors raise the collars of their overcoats . . . In the lobby, one could crunch nuts and smoke machorka (a very cheap kind of tobacco). Red Army detachments and groups of workers youth . . . filled up the theatre with clamorous and exacting throngs.'[22] Even a decade later, when spectators paid for their tickets, some of the rough, unvarnished qualities remained: 'Red lights spell out the name of the revolutionary theatre. Like pebbles on the beach we are picked up by the tide of movement and swept into the heart of the crowd that is surging into the theatre . . . They stamp their feet and shake their upturned collars so that the fur glistens in the crude light with the drops of their breath.' Though there are some of 'the old intelligentsia' here, they are mostly young people who have hurried from work to theatre, some still in their overalls, and they give an impression of strength and self confidence: 'if they are beautiful, it is that beauty which seems to come from the quality of the spirit rather than from any sheen of their skin.'[23]

Many theatres, those which had found their identities before the revolution, were disoriented by such an audience. Stanislavsky has described how the Art Theatre was 'faced by an altogether new audience which we did not know how to approach . . . We were forced to teach this new spectator how to sit quietly, not to talk, to come to the theatre at the proper time, not to smoke, not to crack nuts . . .'[24] The 'new' spectators, attitude in 1921 was reported by M. Zagorsky who found four railway employees who had been to a 'bourgeois' performance of the Art Theatre the same day as they attended Meyerhold's production of *Mystery Bouffe*: 'the difference was colossal' between the heightened temper of Meyerhold's work and the 'terrible boredom and utter disappointment' they felt in the Art Theatre.[25] Erast Garin records how M.S. Vizarov, an actor from the Nezlobin Company, which Meyerhold had taken over, playing the part of Torvald Hjalmer, in Meyerhold's production of *Nora* (his version of *A Doll's House*) in 1922, was so put off by the rowdy audience that he began to call Nora by the name of the maid, Elena. The reaction was so merciless that, Garin records drily, 'some days after the performance, Vizarov emigrated'.[26]

The Zon Theatre, formerly the Aumont, where, according to Ehrenburg, 'Muscovites had once ogled half-naked beauties',[27] was Meyerhold's company's home after the revolution, but it was never more than makeshift – 'a coat with the collar torn out',[28] Shklovsky called it. Whereas the Alexandrinsky had been huge and imposing – too much so, perhaps, for anything other than grandiose spectacle – the Zon was not only run down

but small, with a proscenium opening only a little wider than 15 metres, hard
seats and walls of peeling paint and crumbling plaster. The Passage Theatre
where Meyerhold's company was lodged for most of the 1930s was even less
imposing, yet 'the audience loves' the performance, wrote van Gyseghem;
'they follow every movement and then glance at each other and laugh'.[29]
Such a subjective impression, of people alert and responding spontaneously,
perhaps unpredictably, is endorsed by Zagorsky's investigation, discussed in
more detail below. He concluded:

different groups of spectators receive from the stage completely different impressions
and what gladdens and stimulates one, drives away and exasperates another. *There is
neither a unified audience nor a unified performance.* The revolutionary current from the stage
breaks up the audience, organizing and differentiating it into positive and negative
elements. And in its turn, the reverse current from the auditorium breaks up the show ...[30]

The elements of stimulation and fragmentation, then, were the crucial
ingredients in Meyerhold's conception of the audience as the 'fourth dimension'. His pupil, Sergei Eisenstein, asserted in 1923 that the 'basic material' of
the new theatre was the audience, who were activated by 'attractions', that is,
'aggressive moments of theatre', drawn from popular sources, especially
'music hall and circus'.[31] It was this that Gorlov noticed in 1924: 'it is not
coincidence that our only theatrical revolutionary to date, Meyerhold, bases
himself in the old popular entertainments − mystery plays, farces and
carnivals',[32] and Lozowick observed in 1930 that Meyerhold found the best
precedents for a theatre which could 'energise' its audience in 'the Medieval
theatres of Italy, Spain, England; in old Japan and China, whose actors had
been marvellous showmen, acrobats, jugglers, clowns, buffoons, entertainers
with a healthy sense of the grotesque and the ridiculous'. Lozowick adds
perceptively that Meyerhold's aim was 'to learn from these healthy traditions
without copying them but in order to turn them to account in the light of
contemporary knowledge and needs, in the light of the lessons from factory
and laboratory'.[33]

The effectiveness of this new twist to a traditional relationship between
stage and auditorium during the 1920s has been well documented. The
production of *The Dawns* for example in 1921, 'inflamed' and 'excited' and set
up 'currents of living interaction expressed in the audience's applause to
certain lines', reaching a climax when 'the entire audience and the actors
united to the sound of the "International" in a vow to build a new world'.[34]
The union at the end was not a mystic religious communion, but a turning of
old traditions to new account, the account of the factory and the laboratory.
The night when the performance was interrupted to announce the Red
Army's decisive breakthrough at Perekop, which prompted someone to sing

'As Martyrs You Fell' while cast and audience stood in silence, was the high point of this 'unification' in *The Dawns*, though, as Braun notes, 'such unanimity of response did not occur every night'.[35]

The response to *Mystery Bouffe* a few months later was comparable. Fevralsky, who was present at the premiere, recalled:

At the end of the first act, warm applause was heard. As the action unfolded, the play's success increased. The performance of the 'International' (in Mayakovsky's new version), which concluded the play, produced an ecstatic ovation from the public. The spectators threw themselves onto the stage, spontaneously uniting it with the auditorium, and literally dragged out from behind the wings the author, the directors – Meyerhold and Bebutov – the actors and even the backstage crew. Mayakovsky and Meyerhold, hands joined, were lifted shoulder high. After forty-five years it is difficult to recall another production which infected its audience with such enthusiasm.[36]

Perhaps more typical, because provoking fragmentation as well as stimulation, was *The Magnanimous Cuckold* (1922). Lunacharsky cried 'Shame on the public who screamed with raucous laughter over the slaps, tumbles and bawdy bits. Shame on the public who laughed like that not in a dive scarcely tolerated by the communist regime but at a production presented by a communist director.' But Ilinsky records that 'the premiere of *The Magnanimous Cuckold* had a stunning success . . . a success accompanied by heated arguments, by enthusiasm or utter disappointment', adding that 'such a success is especially sonorous and eloquent'. Ilinsky says that at the end 'a storm of applause burst out, the spectators, particularly the students and young people, threw themselves onto the stage and lifted us up, beginning with Meyerhold. I was never raised higher than that, even in the theatre of Meyerhold.'[37] Finally, a comment from the poet Boris Pasternak, who wrote to Meyerhold after seeing his production of *Woe to Wit* in 1928:

I remember several of Stanislavsky's productions; when I was thirteen and visiting Petersburg for a few days, I would go every evening to watch Komissarzhevskaya; I've seen Mikhail Chekhov . . . but one thing is incomparable: when I saw your work, I experienced *theatre* for the first and only time in my life. I realized what it meant, and began to believe that as an art it was indeed conceivable.[38]

Consciously, Meyerhold employed a battery of means to bring the audience to such a pitch quite apart from the acting, the *mise-en-scène*, and so on. In the foyer, there was usually an exhibition, perhaps of photographs of Soviet industrial or agricultural progress, perhaps of posters from ROSTA; in the auditorium, exhortatory or agitational placards were often hung on the walls. Meyerhold was considerably exercised by the question of the interval, which he called a 'reef' upon which the production might founder.[39] So, in *The Death of Tarelkin* in 1922, he filled it by bringing students into the auditorium, some of whom played catch between the stalls and the circle,

9. Meyerhold speaking in a debate on the theatre, 1920s

while others lowered on strings from the ceiling apples for the spectators to take and eat, and signs with legends such as 'Death to the Tarelkins! Make way for the Meyerholds!'[40] Eight years earlier, Meyerhold had tried something like this in his production of two of Blok's plays at his own Studio, when extras threw oranges to the spectators and a troupe of Chinese children jugglers whom he had come across in the street entertained – or failed to entertain, since one observer remarked that their appearance 'enraged the audience'.[41]

After the performance, Meyerhold occasionally organized discussions between performers and spectators, and these sometimes involved major figures in the cultural world like Lunacharsky or Mayakovsky. The regular Monday debates after performances of *The Dawns* became legendary:

It was at these disputes that problems about the political physiognomy of the theatre, of its reconstruction were placed before the professional theatre in a naked sharpness and manner. Moreover the inner affairs of the theatre were placed before the public . . . 'The Mondays' were the first open social tribune from which basic charges were made at the bourgeois theatre. The very principle of these gatherings undermined the professional seclusion, the caste of the theatrical environment.[42]

There were more formal debates, too, like the one on *The Government Inspector* (1926), when 'thousands gathered in a great hall . . . [and] followed the dispute with every fibre; between speakers they shouted, applauded, screamed, whistled'.[43] For, as Alpers understood, 'these debates were the arena on which battle was going on; the battle for a new conception of theatrical art'.[44]

Meyerhold developed a number of devices to encourage the fragmentation and stimulation of the mass of spectators during a performance. Frequently, as in *Don Juan* and *The Dawns*, for instance, the auditorium lights were left on, in an attempt both to prevent the spectator's cosy acceptance of what he was watching and to encourage the actor to draw energy from specific audience members. More important, Meyerhold abolished the front curtain. He first did away with this in 1906 in Poltava for his productions of Ibsen's *Ghosts* and Dymov's *Cain*, and though it was regarded as peculiar, and even shocking, the local newspaper reporter admitted that 'the elimination of the curtain . . . reinforces the distinct impression obtained from the drama'.[45] This, together with the equally revolutionary elimination of the footlights, threw a new emphasis onto the forestage, the area where contact between performer and spectator was at its most unpredictable. In his contribution to *The Theatre: A Book on the New Theatre*, a collection of essays by various hands published in 1907, Meyerhold was already making this point, and when he collected his own essays for publication in his book *On Theatre* in 1912, he felt constrained to note in the introduction: 'Despite the fact that in not one of the articles set out here is the theme of the forestage highlighted in detail, the reader will easily notice that all the threads of the different themes in this book are drawn together in the question of the forestage.'[46]

In practice his attention to the forestage could be seen, for instance, in *Don Juan* (1910) in which, 'above the forestage were three chandeliers; the forestage itself was lit by two huge candelabras; there were no footlights at all'.[47] And in *The Dawns*, staged before Meyerhold had had time to get rid of the orchestra pit at the Zon Theatre, '"in the orchestra stood the chorus of the tragedy" . . . this chorus was necessary to the director because they connected "the action of the tragedy on the stage to the reception of the action in the auditorium"'.[48] The changing of scenery before the audience's eyes was a natural corollary to all this, and it should perhaps be emphasized that these devices, commonplace enough now, were extraordinarily radical then.

The result, wrote Bakshy before the 1917 revolution, was 'to destroy the opposition between the spectator and the object observed'.[49] Wagner had thought to create his 'mystic union' by increasing the gulf between the two, and the naturalistic theatre, too, presupposed an invisible 'fourth wall' keeping one from the other. Meyerhold's arrangement, by breaking the frame created by the proscenium arch, unsettled the spectator–object relationship and implicated the audience member in the dramatic action in a new way.

The logic of Meyerhold's vision, of course, required a new theatre building. Even in his most triumphant days after the revolution, his working-class spectators were making comments like 'the theatre needs renovating'

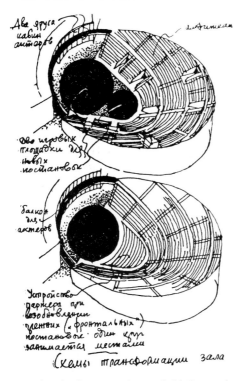

10. Plans for the projected Meyerhold Theatre: the steeply raked amphitheatre

and 'the arrangement of the hall is not in keeping with the performance'.[50] At
the beginning of the century Fuchs had argued for a theatre with a steeply
raked auditorium and a wide stage with a shallow forestage, and steps to a
recessed area. The Symbolists' dream for the Torches Theatre was more
fantastic, a circular space surrounded by the audience and reached by three
walkways. It was to be 'the navel of the Universe' reflecting the cosmos, with
astral, universal and socially functional planes.[51]

In 1931, Meyerhold's company left the Zon Theatre to enable it to be
reconstructed according to plans he had worked out in conjunction with the
architects Mikhail Barkhin and Sergei Vakhtangov, and it was this project –
never completed – which contained the most impressive monument to
Meyerhold's vision. In style, it was to be an amphitheatre, steeply raked,
which gave spectators an axonometric view of the stage, from above and
from an angle, so that, he said, the patterns of the actors' movements could
best be appreciated, but also of course to unsettle the customary spectator–
object relationship. The stage itself incorporated two revolving stages, a
smaller one downstage of and at an angle to the larger, jutting out well into

the auditorium. The inspirations for this were the Greek and Elizabethan theatres, which Meyerhold contrasted with the Roman, and Roman-derived, frontal stages which had dominated most periods of theatre history. The revolves could be lowered out of sight for scene changes, and indeed the front revolve could accommodate seats to provide a sort of proscenium arrangement, and other platforms could be lowered from above. The stage floor was to be on a level with the auditorium floor to allow for the passage of processions, motor vehicles and the like, and also to allow spectators to walk there rather than in the foyers during intermissions. For the theatre was democratic in its unification of auditorium and stage, and there were no boxes or balconies, no best seats or cramped accommodation. At the back of the stage, a semicircular corridor, out of light but not out of view, contained doors to the dressing rooms so that the actors could step straight from them onto the stage, again unsettling expectations brought from conventional theatre-going. The orchestra was housed above these dressing rooms, and there was a mobile, revolving projection booth able to focus on a screen placed anywhere on the stage or in the auditorium. The ceiling was a massive glass dome to let in daylight, retractable to create an open-air theatre on suitable summer days. There was even a 'Tower of Creativity' with rooms for the director, designer, composer and others to work in. It is a brilliant conception which one can only regret was never completed.[52]

Meyerhold's work demonstrates how this theatre would have been used, for not only did he, even in the buildings he did work in, do away with such trappings as the front curtain and the footlights, he also encouraged the actor to make direct contact with the spectator. Varlamov, as Sganararelle in *Don Juan*, for instance, walked along the front of the forestage, shining a lamp at the dignitaries in the front rows of the stalls and making not-too-offensive humorous comments about them. Blok found this objectionable, but to others, like Wladimir Weidlé, is was 'expressive and extremely amusing'.[53] And in *The Mandate*, the wedding feast extended beyond the edge of the stage in an attempt to implicate, or challenge, the audience.

Meyerhold frequently used the auditorium aisles for exits and entrances even in conventional 'frontal' theatres. His use of the technique in Sologub's *Death's Victory* in the provinces as early as 1908 caused some controversy, but after the revolution the new audiences readily accepted it and clearly found it exciting. In *Earth Rampant*, bicycles, motor cycles and, in the final scene, when the hero's body is brought in, an army vehicle entered down the aisle, while in *The Last Fight*, as in several other productions, the central characters, in this case a group of sailors, made their first entry through the auditorium, so that their identity with the spectators themselves should be recognized. More decisive action in the auditorium required space, which a frontal theatre lacked, though in one version of *The Fairground Booth* (1908), the Author was seated in the front row, and in *The Last Fight* a 'weeper' was placed in the stalls. In Meyerhold's pre-revolutionary productions in experimental spaces where the seating arrangements could be more flexible, he was able to use, for instance, a dramatically grotesque exit through the audience, as at the climax of *Columbine's Scarf* (1910), as well as, earlier, staging the sinister polka among the spectators sitting at their tables. In Znosko-Borovsky's *The Transfigured Prince* (1910) Meyerhold went further: not only was there dancing in the auditorium and on stage at the same time, not only were there 'plants' in the audience, but at one point an actor crawled out from under the scenery to describe a battle, ending by fleeing into the audience, where he hid under a table.

The relationship between actor and spectator is well described by Houghton as 'self-conscious'.[54] The audience knows, and is constantly reminded, that it is in a theatre: the prompter in *The Fairground Booth* crawls into his box and lights his candle in full view of the audience; Harlequin leaps through a window, revealing the sky to be no more than blue paper stuck inside a window frame; when the clown dies 'a stream of cranberry juice squirts from his head';[55] and of course at the end the scenery is whisked up into the flies. In *Don Juan* there were two prompters in wigs and costumes who took their seats behind ornate screens and who were plainly noticed among the screens' curtains from time to time. For Zamyatin, Meyerhold's theatre was 'a game with the spectators, based on the unmasking of theatrical illusion . . . [and] allowing every kind of anachronism, eccentricity, dissonance'.[56] Thus, in *D.E.* (1924), 'Mikhail Zharov played the master of ceremonies . . . When Zharov found himself bored by his role, he recited foreign movie titles with no special meaning as asides to the audience',[57] and when Ernst Garin performed 'The Reception of the Inventors', 'so that the audience knew that all seven inventors were played by one actor, Meyerhold arranged that in one of the moving screens, which served as the set for the show, a large hole should be cut. Consequently, the spectators saw the way the transformations worked.'[58] Meyerhold often emphasized that many spectators enjoyed the performer as performer, and by 'baring the device' (to use the terminology of the Formalists), the director enabled them to see the show as a show and also forced them to examine rather than simply accept 'The Project of the Grandiose Ruination', as the episode was entitled. As he himself remarked, half humorously, 'We have to protect the interests not of the author but of the spectator.'[59]

Given such an emphasis it is not surprising to learn that Meyerhold was probably the first theatre director to try systematically to measure audience response, and he persisted with experiments to do this over nearly two

11. 'Outsiders' at a rehearsal of Meyerhold

decades. His purpose was practical, not academic: it was to discover moments where the two-way communication was happening so that he could use the information to improve his own directing. He experimented with different methods at different times. Probably the most obvious means of testing reaction was to invite people into rehearsals. Mikhail Sadovsky records:

Virtually from the first rehearsal, Meyerhold built the production on the audience. He always had present at rehearsals twenty or thirty 'outsiders', that is, people he knew. And the audience did not trouble Meyerhold, or disturb him, on the contrary it stimulated him. Meyerhold was always moving about, always bustling between the stage and auditorium. Often his figure could be discerned leaning over one of the seated spectators. He was asking him something. He consulted everyone. The person who polished the floor might come into the auditorium, snatching a minute from his work. Meyerhold bore down upon him and his questions could be heard: 'Well, did you like it? Did you understand it? What did you understand from it?'[60]

In 1921, Meyerhold tried issuing audiences to *Mystery Bouffe* with a brief questionnaire, which asked for comments. A sample of 187 of these provided the data for an article by his literary manager, Mikhail Zagorsky, published in *LEF* in 1924. This showed that nearly seventy per cent of those questioned liked the play. When the total was broken down into class groupings – workers, peasants, intelligentsia and Soviet office workers and *haute bourgeoisie* – it was found that in each of the first three groups the number of those who enjoyed the play was also about seventy per cent; but among the *haute bourgeoisie* the figure was considerably lower. The very class differences, as well as the fact that no class responded as a homogenous unit, is clear evidence of the fragmented nature of the audience, which Zagorsky himself commented on.

Other comments are worth noting in passing. A trade union delegate 'liked the originality of the performance and the destruction of the mystery of the wings. Especially the closeness of the stage to the audience.' Another worker thought 'the music sometimes hinders the acting', while a third thought 'the Menshevik should be less comic'. One peasant spectator commented that 'The bourgeoisie didn't like it, they grumbled and even walked out, insulted, but the young lasses and lads thought it was fine.' 'The son of a laundress and a man-servant' wanted to know why no copies of the text were available; for him, 'the Menshevik is splendid, just like in life', though he found Mayakovsky's verse 'somewhat fanciful' and difficult to get used to. 'With me', he continued, 'were about ten workers, and we exchanged opinions, and I came to the conclusion that in general they were enjoying the play though they did not understand some details.'

Of the minority who disliked it, some did so because they disliked the revolution; others because they saw the play as offensive propaganda. A few disliked the 'futurism' of the production, and a few the style: 'An anti-artistic outrage, just like a fairground show', commented one, which may have pleased rather than dismayed Meyerhold. Finally, and most numerously, were those audience members who took exception to the blasphemy in the play, or to its mockery of Tolstoy, who clearly retained a considerable following even at this date.

The whole discussion clearly vindicates Zagorsky's contention that Mayakovsky and Meyerhold's work was not, as some critics objected, beyond the comprehension of the 'new' audience.[61] A mere 187 responses is hardly a basis for significant conclusions, and a questionnaire completed after the performance can only record a generalized judgment, not the fleeting impressions of the moment-by-moment experience. Nevertheless, Zagorsky's article seems eminently sensible and surprisingly revealing so that it may be regretted that the experiment was not much repeated and that where it was – for *The Dawns* (1920), *The Forest* (1924) and *Woe to Wit* (1928), for example – the results were never published.

More widely used in the Meyerhold Theatre during the 1920s and into the 1930s was the 'Record of Spectators' Reactions' kept by the 'laboratory assistant' (trainee director) on duty for that performance. This consisted of a large chart with spaces for recording the play, the date, the cast and the running time, as well as comments on the type of audience, how full the house was, and so on. The chart itself was arranged in a series of columns, each column representing a small duration of time – not more than two minutes.

Down the left-hand margin was series of possible reactions. Any audience reaction was then noted in the column indicating the time it occurred. The complete list of types of reaction to be noted was: 1. Silence; 2. Noise; 3. Loud noise; 4. Reading in concord (i.e. following the text as the actors spoke it); 5. Singing; 6. Coughing; 7. Stamping; 8. Fidgetting; 9. Exclamations; 10. Weeping; 11. Laughter; 12. Sighing; 13. Hubbub; 14. Applause; 15. Whistling; 16. Hissing; 17. Walking out of the auditorium; 18. Standing up; 19. Throwing things onto the stage; 20. Climbing onto the stage. Not surprisingly, only a few of these were often used, and some, such as 'Noise', seem alarmingly vague. Nevertheless it was easy to extract certain kinds of information from a completed chart, and thereby make some sort of judgment about the particular performance. And comparisons between performances could be made less vaguely than is usual in theatrical circles.

For instance, two charts completed by laboratory assistant M.M. Korenev allow us to compare the reception of two performances of *Earth Rampant*,[62] the premiere and the performance a week later. Many columns were of course left blank when no audience response was discernible, but added up scene by scene, the following reactions were noted:

4/3/23	11/3/23
Scene 1 (20 mins) coughing; noise	laughter; noise
Scene 2 (6 mins) laughter	laughter ($\times 2$); noise ($\times 2$)
Scene 3 (15 mins) noise	noise
Scene 4 (8 mins) laughter ($\times 30$); standing up; applause (at end)	laughter ($\times 32$); noise; applause (at end)
Scene 5 (20 mins) laughter ($\times 4$); silence	noise; silence
Scene 6 (2 mins) laughter ($\times 3$)	laughter ($\times 2$)
Scene 7 (12 mins) silence ($\times 3$); laughter (x 2)	noise; laughter ($\times 3$)
Scene 8 (14 mins) laughter; coughing; silence ($\times 2$); applause (at end)	silence ($\times 2$); laughter; applause (at end)

In conjunction with this chart, there were further forms to be filled in at each performance, though they seem not to have been consistently kept up, recording: 1. account of the work of the staff on duty in the theatre for the particular performance; 2. the timing of scenes, scene changes, intervals, etc; 3. account of the intervals; 4. account of the performances of the actors; 5. account of the backstage staff's work; 6. account of the box office's work. Such a comprehensive attempt to understand the theatrical process is almost certainly unique in theatre history. It would probably require a full-time research team with a modern computer to keep it going properly and to analyse its results fully. Nevertheless, it shows the seriousness with which Meyerhold addressed the question of the 'fourth dimension' in his theatre.

However, a moment's reflection suggests several questions. For instance, is the quantifying of reactions commensurate with a commitment to fragmenting rather than unifying the audience? The charts aimed to measure audience reactions, but made no attempt to address the question of the quality of different reactions. And Zagorsky, in his article on the questionnaires, at least focusses the problem on why particular spectators react in particular ways: the 'Record of Spectators' Reactions' cannot significantly approach that question.[63]

Moreover, it is difficult to assess what effect, if any, all this research actually had on Meyerhold's own work. Though *Earth Rampant*, for instance, was initially adapted to bring it 'closer to the understanding of the audience',[64] there is little evidence that the production was modified in the light of the laboratory assistant's charts. Meyerhold did claim that his production of *The Forest* was built 'on a strict computation of the reactions of the theatre audience', which was why he employed 'well-tried devices from all the epochs of the theatre'.[65] It is hard to resist the conclusion that Meyerhold is being disingenuous here. Perhaps this is too harsh. He certainly taught his actors to be aware of how certain 'signs' were an 'infallible' guide to the spectator's attitude to the performance,[66] and Hedgbeth has asserted with regard to *D.E.*: 'Throughout its run, the play was often revised because of the reaction and suggestions of spectators.'[67] Certainly, this was Meyerhold's ideal.

The point is that like any genuine artist, perhaps particularly one claiming to be Marxist in his approach, Meyerhold was interested not merely in the work of art as an object in itself, he was equally interested in its 'means of production', which in terms of theatre includes the collaboration of the 'consumers' or audience. 'We intend the audience not merely to observe,' he wrote in 1907, 'but to participate in a *corporate* creative act.'[68] For thirty years and more, that was the intention he strove to fulfil.

3   The actor's business

Meyerhold stressed throughout his career that it was the actor upon whom the audience was dependent for its entry into the theatrical experience. 'The actor is left *alone*, face to face with the spectator, and from the friction between these two unadulterated elements, the actor's creativity and the spectator's imagination, a clear flame is kindled.'[1]

Consequently, it is hardly surprising that Meyerhold's most intense endeavours were directed at what he called 'the theatre's most complex area: . . . the art of the actor and the system of his playing'.[2] Meyerhold loved actors, prized their individuality and above all cared for his students. Garin recalled him sitting by the fire of the rehearsal room while his students were going through their exercises, watching over his 'brood'. 'He was like a kind of grey wolf – grey eyes, grey hair, grey service jacket.'[3] The myth of Meyerhold repressing actors, put about in the 1930s to justify the repression of him, is categorically denied by virtually all who worked with him. Maria Sukhanova, an actress at the Meyerhold Theatre for eighteen years, wrote that such an idea was 'incorrect': 'A creative relationship with him was a great joy.'[4] For Mikhail Zharov, 'this opinion is profoundly mistaken and false',[5] and almost all his other actors – Garin, Ilinsky, Pluchek, Sadovsky, and many others, not to mention collaborators like Mayakovsky, Vakhtangov, Shostakovich, and more – endorse this emphatically. Yuri Yurev, a major star of the Imperial stage before he ever met Meyerhold, wrote that he would 'always remember with delight and great gratitude working with V.E.'[6] and he gave a lecture on 'The Contemporary Theatre' at the Theatre Club before the First World War which was a virtual 'hymn to Meyerhold'.[7]

Meyerhold not only inspired actors, he was a superb actor himself – 'the greatest in Russia today' according to Houghton in the mid 1930s.[8] No wonder his rehearsals were, as Shostakovich remarked, 'thrilling'.[9] He tended to work without notes (though not without preparation), letting his imagination be fired by the particularities of the actors he was working with. 'The director only punctuates, the actor writes in blood', he said.[10] Yet rehearsals – and the final production – were only genuinely fruitful, as Meyerhold realized very early in his career, when the actors understood their part in the 'kindling' of the 'clear flame' of theatricality. It was this at bottom that he worked to help his actors acquire, both in his rehearsals and for most of his career in his own stage school. Understanding the 'actor's business' and training young performers in it became perhaps the main labour of his life.

Probably Meyerhold's earliest attempt to teach the art of acting was in 1904 when with the Comrades of the New Drama he recruited nearly sixty young extras for crowd scenes and then invited them to come to classes on speech and movement. The following year Stanislavsky described the new 'Theatre Studio' as 'not a finished theatre and not a school for beginners, but a laboratory for the experiments of more or less experienced actors'.[11] This was probably the ideal working situation for Meyerhold, one which he strove to repeat through the vicissitudes of Dr Dapertutto's Studio, the Meyerhold Free Workshop, and his other pedagogical establishments. Blok called the Theatre Studio 'a new theatre and at the same time a school for actors; having acted, they must learn . . .'[12] For Meyerhold, the alternation between performing or producing and teaching or learning was crucial to his development as an artist: the two kinds of activity, publication and research, existed in a dialectical and interdependent relationship; and paradoxically he often found that through the public production he was learning and the training exercises were becoming self-contained entities of achievement. This ability to make two kinds of activity cross fertilize one another is one reason why Meyerhold's pedagogical work was as important as his actual directing.

As soon as he was appointed to the Imperial Theatres in Petersburg, Meyerhold set up a 'theatre studio' with the musician Mikhail Gnesin, in which various kinds of gymnastics and movement were taught, as well as speech and voice production. Even in 1908 the bases of both these courses was their relationship to music. By now Meyerhold had realized that to create a 'theatrical' theatre, he must address the central 'question of the forestage'.[13] And just as the Wagnerian or Stanislavskian actor required a specialized technique, so the actor on the forestage needed certain distinctive skills. What anchored the forestage performance in Meyerhold's system was its rhythmical base, rooted in a musical conception of both the role and the play. But it manifested itself most immediately in the actor's ability to 'play', and this was what Meyerhold's pupils had first to master.

The *commedia dell' arte* formed an appropriate model, for the forestage was a kind of equivalent of the old strolling players' travelling stage. The colourful and amusing *commedia* also provided a useful counter to the ponderous sincerity of so much serious drama on art theatre, Imperial Theatre and boulevard theatre stages. But Meyerhold stressed the necessity for technical excellence in the *commedia*-based player: 'the duty of the comedian and the mime is to transport the spectator to a world of make-believe, entertaining him on the way there with the brilliance of his technical skill . . .

the improvisations of the *commedia dell' arte* had a firm basis of faultless technique.'[14] So that when he was able in September 1913 to open his own permanent Studio, Gnesin's course in the music of stage speech and Meyerhold's own in stage movement were supplemented by a course by Vladimir Soloviev in 'the history and technique of *commedia dell' arte*'. The content of Meyerhold's own classes skirted deliberately closely round *commedia dell' arte*, concentrating on elements drawn from nineteenth-century French vaudeville, from the theatre of the Spanish golden age, and from contemporary drama by writers such as Blok, Sologub and Maeterlinck. He also had a 'grotesque group' who not only made up their own scenarios but performed, for instance, three-minute versions of *Othello* and *Antony and Cleopatra* with 'three actors and four proscenium servants'. Mostly, however, he concentrated on the specifics of movement: 'Movement is the most powerful means of theatrical expression', he wrote in 1914. 'The role of movement is more important than that of any other theatrical element. Deprived of dialogue, costume, footlights, wings and an auditorium, and left with only the actor and his mastery of movement, the theatre remains the theatre.'[15] The essence of theatre, therefore, to Meyerhold was pantomime, for in pantomime the audience is primarily arrested by the actor himself and his skill in movement. This was what was meant, properly, by 'playacting', utilizing those 'means which are exclusive' to the art of theatre, and which achieved their finest flowering in the great periods of theatrical history.

Consequently, when the students gave a public demonstration of their work on 12 February 1915, the relation of each item to a moment of the theatre's past was important. The programme was:

1. Two Baskets, or Who Got the Better of Whom. An *étude* composed of 'antics appropriate to the theatre'.
2. Two Jongleurs, an Old Woman with a Snake, and the Bloody Climax Under the Canopy. Pantomime composed by Meyerhold and Soloviev.
3. Ophelia. An *étude* of the mad scene from *Hamlet*.
4. The Story of the Page who was Faithful to his Master and of Other Events Worthy of Presentation. An étude treated in the style of a sentimental, late-seventeenth-century story (performed on the main stage; training in slow motion.)
5. Harlequin, the Vendor of Bastinadoes. A pantomime in the style of the French Harlequinade of 1850 ('antics appropriate to the theatre').
6. Fragment of a Chinese Play – 'The Catwoman, the Bird and the Snake'. A pantomime by Meyerhold and Soloviev (use of Chinese scenic conventions as might be interpreted by Carlo Gozzi; use of *mise-en-scène* to create illusion of more characters than actually appear).
7. The Two Esmeraldinas. A sketch from a *commedia* scenario.
8. Collin Maillard. An étude performed in profile in the manner of Lancret's paintings.

9. The Street Jongleurs. A pantomime in the style of the popular performances of late-eighteenth-century Venice (use of stage audience to guide emotions of real audience; acting on two levels; 'antics appropriate to the theatre').
10. From Five Chairs to a Quadrille. An *étude* by Meyerhold and Soloviev in the manner of the 1840s.
11. The Baker and the Chimney-Sweep. An *étude*.
12. The Loss of the Handbags.
13. The Cord.
14. Three of Them.
15. Three Oranges, the Astrological Telescope, or What One's Love for the Stage Masters May Lead To. A circus buffoonade (use of trick properties; 'antics appropriate to the theatre').
16. How They Carried Out Their Intentions.[16]

Each item had its own self-contained aim – a different kind of movement, working with props, and so on – and a contemporary description gives a good idea of the impression made:

Seats were arranged in a half-circle with a centre and two aisles through which in the course of the evening players entered, sometimes running or even carrying each other on their shoulders. There was no stage in the accepted sense; in its place was a quite high platform with a white silk curtain closing off a narrow entrance in the middle. In front of the platform was a forestage carpeted in a semi-circle with navy blue cloth. The players jumped constantly from stage to forestage and back, performed clown tricks or did resounding falls, crawled, climbed under the platform, or even feigned to pull out each other's teeth. All this either at unusually high speed or with the slow stateliness of a funeral march (Hamlet, the madness of Ophelia) to the accompaniment on the piano of classical music by Mozart and Rameau or the improvisation of the pianist.[17]

Two years later the 'Studio Programme' had been somewhat refined and now consisted of five areas of practical work:

1. The technique of stage movement. Members of the Studio must aim at perfection in dancing, music, athletics and fencing (the Studio director will recommend specialist instructors in these fields). Recommended sports: lawn tennis, throwing the discus, sailing.
2. Practical study of the technical aspects of production: stage equipment, decor, lighting, costumes, hand-props.
3. The basic principles of Italian improvised comedy (*commedia dell' arte*).
4. The application in the modern theatre of the traditional devices of the seventeenth and eighteenth centuries.
5. Musical recitation in drama.[18]

And, as an indication of what Meyerhold was looking for at this time, there were seven areas in which students were examined before they were awarded the title of 'Comedian':

1. Musical proficiency (as instrumentalist or singer).
2. Physical agility (gymnastic or acrobatic exercises; improvised pantomime extract containing acrobatic tricks).

3. Mimetic ability (performance of act without words on command: a *mise-en-scène* and the basic devices will be demonstrated by the director).
4. Clarity of diction (reading from text).
5. Familiarity with theories of prosody.
6. Knowledge (if any) of other art forms (painting, sculpture, poetry, dance) and own work if available.
7. Knowledge of dramatic history within limits of higher school course (questions and answers.)[19]

It is an extraordinarily comprehensive and progressive package for its time, one which few of today's higher institutions of drama can match.

Nevertheless, it is in a sense a *cul de sac*, too dependent on historical models, and when the Bolshevik revolution flung Meyerhold into the present, he was glad to modify his approach to actor training to make it more compatible with the stirring times in which he lived. Consequently, the syllabus he drew up with L.S. Vivien for a new acting school and workshop in November 1918 was, at least in aim, both more businesslike and more precise. It is assumed that 'the theatre is a self-contained art form, which requires the subordination of each individual component of the theatre to the one law of theatre'. Its tasks were threefold – to create versatile actors, to raise the level of acting throughout the country, and to spread knowledge of the specific techniques of acting much more widely. Its programme of work fell into three parts, here labelled 'Preparing – Individualizing – Perfecting', but corresponding remarkably closely with Meyerhold's consistent emphasis on three tiers of work in a school, a 'workshop' and a theatre.

The programme for the first stage, 'Preparing', covered four areas:

1. SPEECH: Breathing; Voice production; Treatment of speech defects; Articulation of words; Poetic rhythm (exercises);
2. MOVEMENT: Gymnastics and sport; Fencing; Juggling; Dance; Stage movement;
3. SUBSIDIARY SUBJECTS: Music (elementary course); Playing a musical instrument; Rhythmic gymnastics; Singing (sol-fa, choral, solo and duet); Drawing;
4. THEORETICAL AND RESEARCH SUBJECTS: Anatomy and physiology; Drama study and stage study; The art of theatre and other art forms (analogies); Pantomime; Dance (general consideration); Prosody; Psychology of the feelings (basic principles).

'Individualizing' was expected to last for three terms, each of which covered different ground. Term 1:

1. SPEECH AND MOVEMENT: The emotions (a selection of exercises derived from the work of playwrights who are able to co-ordinate clearly particular emotions with specific forms);
2. DEVELOPMENT OF THE IMAGINATION: Images (a record of the impressions of specifically theatrical moments in novels or stories); Masks (traditional Italian masks);

3. SUBSIDIARY SUBJECTS: Dance; Singing; Make-up; Fencing;
4. THEORETICAL AND RESEARCH SUBJECTS: Theatrical styles; Methods of
    stage playing (a) according to historical period and country (b) according to
    author; Costume; Aesthetics (basic principles).

Term 2:

1. PRACTICAL EXERCISES (within the limits of what has been done in previous
    terms): Pantomime; Interludes; Vaudeville; Improvisations using speech and
    movement;
2. SUBSIDIARY SUBJECTS: Dance; Singing; Make-up; Fencing;
3. THEORETICAL AND RESEARCH SUBJECTS: Theory of stage composition;
    Playing and experiencing (two systems); Mimesis (the lowest rung on the
    ladder – imitation with no creative input; the highest – masks, the grotesque);
    Analysis of the actor's playing; Methods of playing (theatricality, naturalism;
    types of theatrical presentation; playing in a theatrical manner; different
    historical periods; stage designers; *mise-en-scène* and its problems).

Term 3:

1. STYLES OF THEATRICAL PRESENTATION (and the peculiarities of theatres
    which develop from the peculiarities of playwrights): Theatres of Greece,
    Rome, Italian Renaissance, eighteenth-century Italian (Gozzi, Goldoni), Span-
    ish golden age, French classical, German, Shakespeare; Russian theatre
    (Griboyedov, Pushkin, Lermontov, Gogol, Ostrovsky); exotic theatre (Indian,
    Japanese, Chinese); contemporary theatre;
2. SUBSIDIARY SUBJECTS: Make-up; Fencing.
3. THEORETICAL AND RESEARCH SUBJECTS: Style; Theatre architecture;
    Playwriting; History of the theatre; History of costume; History of make-up.

It should be stressed that section 1 of each term's work is designed to be
practical, not academic. The course is completed in the third part of the
programme, 'Perfecting', which simply involves performance work 'under
the direction of masters of theatre art'.[20] (Who these are is not divulged!)

This programme is amazing for its breadth and scope, and it is only to be
regretted that circumstances prevented its ever being more than a paper
project. By the time Meyerhold was able to set up a school and workshop in
post-revolutionary Russia, his ideas had moved on again. Nevertheless, even
here his conviction is plain, that the dominant styles of acting – declamatory
or naturalistic behind the proscenium – were irrelevant to the theatre, for the
theatre had now to enter a new demystified age. He dreamed of 'tracking
down a "genuine actor" among the Red Army men or in a factory; he thought
that the "heart of today will only be grasped by an influx of newcomers", and
the playing of the actor had to come from the "I" of the citizen'.[21] The new,
young, proletarian, wildly enthusiastic and committed student revitalized
and redirected Meyerhold's work: in GVYTM in 1922, 'the work was
completely saturated in physical training: gymnastics, boxing, fencing,

acrobatics, vaulting, classical dance, folk dance, rhythmic gymnastics and, finally, "biomechanics"'.[22] This last was the pivotal course around which the others revolved, and its significance and the exercises it involved are discussed below. It should be noted, however, that despite the 'saturation' of physical work, the course also included a good deal of work on speech and voice. There were lectures and seminars on politics, philosophy and Marxist aesthetics from Larissa Raisner, where arguments apparently burned passionately, and visits from progressive artists and poets. Lyubov Popova, the Constructivist artist, was on the staff of GVYTM at this time, teaching stage design, and the poet and dramatist Sergei Tretyakov taught 'word movement'. The atmosphere was intense but extraordinarily buoyant, so that while the students got through enormous quantities of work, they were quite capable of the kind of joke Sergei Eisenstein played in the practical dance examination, when he transformed 'the embodiment of haughty pride' into 'something very reminiscent of Toulouse-Lautrec', which set everybody 'rolling about with laughter'.[23]

The course evolved and changed as time went on: by 1927, Andrei Bely was teaching the course in poetics; in 1928, the Mongolian specialist in oriental theatre, Valery Inkizhinov, had gravitated to the cinema and was soon to emigrate; and by the 1930s the course included some study of Stanislavsky's system. By then of course the Zon Theatre was being destroyed and recreated and Meyerhold's company and school were virtually homeless – van Gyseghem watched them doing a movement workout in the foyer of the theatre they were appearing at. The basis of the work was still biomechanics, however, and some words must be said on this widely misunderstood subject.

BIOMECHANICS

The problems with understanding biomechanics seem to spring, first, from the fact that it was a means to an end, not an end in itself, and second, as Ilinsky points out, it was never fully explained or codified by Meyerhold.[24] In the early 1930s Meyerhold seems to have claimed that biomechanics would create not only the 'new actor', but actually the 'new man' in line with the now disgraced Trotsky's earlier prescription (which still held good, even if its author was unacknowledged) that 'one of the ultimate aims of the Revolution is to overcome completely the separation of . . . intellectual work, including art, from physical work'.[25] Though biomechanics as such seemed to spur Trotsky to anger – 'When the passionate experimenter, Meyerhold . . . produces on the stage a few semi-rhythmic movements . . . and calls this biomechanics, the result is – abortive'[26] – yet his vision of communist society seemed remarkably close to Meyerhold's vision of the biomechanical actor: 'Man at last will begin to harmonize himself in earnest. He will make it his business to achieve beauty by giving the movement of his own limbs the utmost precision, purposefulness and economy . . .'[27] Biomechanics was not so much a set of exercises or a style of performance; rather, it was what bound the elements of acting together philosophically, psychologically and physically. In the end, it was what gave Meyerhold's productions resonance, why they were satisfying rather than merely showy.

As Gorelik noted, biomechanics first aimed to give 'decision, grace and authority to the actor's movements'.[28] As a minimum training, it taught the actor self-awareness in three-dimensional space, the need for efficiency as well as expressiveness in movement and the essential rhythmic and dynamic qualities in stage movement. But there was more than mere physical training in it, both for students like Valentin Pluchek, who called it 'a system of training the psycho-physical apparatus of the actor',[29] and for observers like Louis Lozowick, who said 'biomechanics . . . meant the study of the physiologic and psychologic laws that govern the actor's body as a normally functioning mechanism so that its every gesture and movement might be employed with the greatest efficiency'.[30] And indeed this quasi-scientific approach to the inclusion of the actor's mind as well as his body was endorsed by Meyerhold himself, who wrote that 'the formula for acting may be expressed as follows:

$$N = A_1 + A_2$$

(where N = the actor; A_1 = the artist who conceives the idea and issues the instructions necessary for its execution; A_2 = the executant who executes the conception of A_1).'[31]

In his acting classes, Meyerhold was less opaque. He quoted Coquelin's 1895 formulation from which the cryptic algebra derived:

The arts differ according to the nature of their medium; well, the actor's medium is – himself. His own face, his body, his life is the material of his art; the thing he works and moulds to draw out from it his creation. From this it follows the existence of the comedian must be dual. One part of him is the performer, the instrumentalist; another, the instrument to be played on.[32]

Meyerhold called this duality variously the 'first I' and the 'second I', the 'creative process' and the 'technique', or – and this implies a possible definition of biomechanics itself – 'imagination' and 'biomechanics'.

In the early days of 'biomechanics', Meyerhold attempted to relate it to 'Taylorism', named after the inventor of time-and-motion studies, Frederick Winslow Taylor, whose theories acquired an ardent following in the infant Soviet Republic. His ideas, even as synthesized by his followers, may seem crude to us when compared with later movement analyses such as Laban's, yet at the time they were clearly an important advance. Thus, 'smooth, continuous, curved motions of the hands are preferable' in the Taylor canon 'to straight line motions involving sudden and sharp changes in direction; ... motions of the arms should be made in opposite and symmetrical directions, and should be made simultaneously; ... rhythmic movements are generally the most efficient' and so on.[33] The efficiency of movement advocated by the Taylorists was obviously close to Meyerhold's own long-standing commitment to efficient stage movement: 'the spectacle of a man working efficiently affords a positive pleasure', he argued.[34] And just as Taylor broke down the movement he studied into *working cycles*, so Meyerhold broke down stage movement into *acting cycles*, which consisted of three parts — intention, realization, reaction. Yet here the blurring of Meyerhold's thought is most apparent, because this cycle, as Meyerhold uses it, refers not just to the A_2 part of the equation, not just to the 'second I' or the actor's 'technique', but involved also, through the intention, the 'first I', the 'creative process' as well.

In fact, Meyerhold dealt with this confusion by changing the scientific location of his theory to chime now with Pavlov's reflexology and the 'acting cycle' became the 'playing link'. Now, the stimulus (A_1 in the previous equation) triggers a reflex action, which is the realization. When the realization is done, it comes to rest prepared for a new intention, and this comprises the reaction. The aim of training is now to prepare the actor by creating in him a state of 'excitability' which can provoke the correct reflex action: the 'point of excitability' is the period of receptivity and rest. An actor at a 'point of excitability' is like a car whose engine is idling: press the accelerator and the car 'realizes' the action, it moves forward. If the actor is without this 'excitability' he is like a car whose ignition is switched off: press its accelerator, and nothing happens. So biomechanics comes to include the creation of 'states of excitability'. Most obviously this is seen in the creation of plastic stasis, which evokes the desired 'reflex excitability'. Igor Ilinsky reported one of Meyerhold's explanatory examples: 'If I sit you in the posture of a sad person, and sad phrases come out ... this is the external conception, the "idea" part of the acting link. The idea forces the actor to sit in a sad posture, but the posture itself helps to make him sad.'[35]

Externally provoked behaviour, the motivation for which was derived from sources other than personal emotion, was related by Meyerhold to the dynamic popular theatres, west and east, which he quoted as his models. In this he was echoing the Formalist proposition that popular techniques rejuvenate high art. Where they quoted the devices of the detective story as invigorating Dostoievsky's *The Brothers Karamazov*, Meyerhold held up the 'cabotin' or strolling player as the instrument needed to energize the Russian

12. Mei Lan-fang, the famous Chinese actor whose work Meyerhold profoundly admired, here dancing with pheasant feathers in a demonstration of 'lightness and gaiety'

theatre: 'Most important ... is a mask, then a few rags to brighten his costume, a little braid, a few feathers, a few bells, a little of everything to give the performance plenty of glitter and plenty of noise.'[36]

Russia's geographical position between Europe and the orient put Meyerhold in a position to use not only the cabotin tradition of the *commedia dell' arte*, but also the external techniques of Japanese and Chinese theatre. He may have first seen Japanese theatre as early as 1902 when Otodziro Kawakami's troupe toured Russia:[37] in April 1935 he hosted the guest appearance of Mei Lan-fang at the Central Art Workers' Club in Moscow (the

visiting Bertolt Brecht was in the audience), and all his life he preached the
need to learn from the east. To begin with, in the Japanese Noh theatre, the
actors used the forestage – they are 'close enough to the spectator for their
dances, movements, gesticulations, grimaces and poses to be clearly visible'.[38] It was the rhythmic movement, the calculated gestures and the explicit
theatricality of oriental theatre which Meyerhold valued most highly. In the
conventional language of Chinese classical theatre, for instance, an actor
repeatedly shrugging his shoulders indicates weeping, and if a character
enters carrying a lantern, this tells us it is night. In the Japanese Noh theatre,
which begins 'where the spoken word fails',[39] Meyerhold pointed to the fact
that the 'actor is both acrobat and dancer'[40] and wanted his own students to
emulate this virtuosity. Primarily, this focusses attention on the actor's body,
which he wanted to become a 'word-equivalent',[41] 'the main transmit-
ter of the invigorating shock',[42] a 'poetic' force rather than an 'everyday'
assemblage of limbs and trunk and head.[43]

'A theatre which relies on *physical elements* is at very least assured of
clarity', Meyerhold wrote, and 'every movement is a hieroglyph with its own
peculiar meaning. The theatre should employ only those movements which
are immediately decipherable; anything else is superfluous . . .'[44] Thus, the
actor's art was demystified, as the Japanese Noh player's was, and 'put, as it
were, on a research footing'.[45] But in a production like *The Magnanimous
Cuckold* it was 'academic without inverted commas' for though it 'stated and
solved important problems for the actor and director: the problem of
traditional popular entertainment and contemporary production; the grotesque and realism; comedy and the psychological situation'[46] yet more
importantly, in Fevralsky's memorable phrase, 'the acting was full of life's
juices'.[47]

THE ELEMENTS OF ACTING

The product of biomechanics was therefore convincing, even if the theory
was less so. In Meyerhold's usage, 'biomechanics' was often little more than a
compendium word to cover all the elements of acting which he taught and
wished to utilize in productions, and this rather loose usage has made it seem
more formidable – and perhaps more comprehensive – than it may ever have
been. Thus, *The Magnanimous Cuckold* was presented by the Meyerhold Free
Workshop, where students were trained through exercises and methods
devised or at least adapted by Meyerhold, and known by the blanket term
'biomechanics'. Really, however, the term is better understood as a kind of
philosophical underpinning of the actual programme.

In essence, Meyerhold's exercises concerned stillness, or movement, or the interaction of the two ('reflex excitability'); most simple exercises had more complex, more advanced developments, which in turn shaded into self-contained *études*, 'antics appropriate to the theatre' or full-blown pantomime scenarios, which can often be exemplified in productions; and finally Meyerhold was careful to distinguish between solo exercises, and exercises to be executed with one or more partners.

The first and simplest element for the actor was the 'silhouette', a concept which Meyerhold probably took from painting very early in the century. Certainly a vivid example of it occurred in the 1906 production of *Hedda Gabler* when Lovborg and Hedda 'throughout the entire scene sit side by side, tense and motionless, looking straight ahead. Their quiet, disquieting words fall rhythmically from lips which seem dry and cold . . . Not once throughout the entire long scene do they alter the direction of their gaze or their pose.'[48]

At the same time as he was creating this production, Meyerhold was also working on *Sister Beatrice*, the central role of which was presented by Komissarzhevskaya as a series of silhouettes. And though these productions came from Meyerhold's Symbolist period, other later works, such as *Teacher Bubus* (1925) and the *The Second Commander* (1929) were noteworthy for the way one tableau seemed to give way to another. Meyerhold's acting exercises relevant to the silhouette include the 'profile' *étude* taken from the paintings of Nicolas Lancret which was one of the items in the Studio's February 1915 presentation mentioned above, and the exercise known as 'The Patient Endurance of Blows' in which the actor remains calm under a hail of mimed blows. For a time in the revolutionary period, the 'silhouette' gave way to the 'poster':[49] in *The Dawns*, for instance, an actor took up and held the pose of an orator, but not to great effect, for whereas the silhouette is motivated from within the action of the play, the poster is not.

A more provocative development out of the 'silhouette' was Meyerhold's notion of the 'reject', an action which usually involves a pause, and which contradicts the flow of the scene – Othello's showing of immense love for Desdemona before he strangles her could be played as a 'reject', for instance. Meyerhold's exercise, 'Shooting from the Bow', involved several 'rejects', as the detailed description below will make clear, for as Meyerhold himself often said: 'You can't shoot from a bow without drawing back the string.'

The 'reject' is further modified by the 'retard' and the 'negation'. The 'retard' is a slowing down of the action precisely at the moment when the audience feels it should speed up – Desdemona's singing of the 'Willow Song' in *Othello*, for instance. It was a feature much acclaimed in poetry by the Formalist critics and developed by Meyerhold into a particularly effective theatrical device. Already in the *Hedda Gabler* production mentioned above he was using something of the technique:

13. Vera Komissarzhevskaya in *Sister Beatrice* by Maurice Maeterlinck, 1906

In order to look through the bulky manuscript more comfortably, Lovborg comes forward to rest it on the table and after the words 'This contains all of me', he lapses into a thoughtful silence, straightening up and placing his hand on the open manuscript. After a few seconds' pause he starts to turn over the pages, explaining his work to Tesman who had now joined him. But in those motionless few seconds, Lovborg and the manuscript have impressed themselves on the spectator and he has an uneasy presentiment of the words' significance, of what Lovborg is really like, what links him with the manuscript, and what bearing it has on the tragedy of Hedda.[50]

More brilliant, perhaps, was the moment in *The Mandate* when Gulyachkin

suddenly surprised himself . . . by saying majestically: 'I am a Party man,' [and] this fatal phrase immediately terrified and froze him and those around him. The boarder Ivan Ivanovich, at whom the threat was directed, curled up in fear and crouched on the ground. Gulyachkin's mother and sister froze, mouths open. Gulyachkin himself, crazed by his own heroism, stood petrified in an unnatural, simultaneously proud and frightened pose.[51]

At this moment the revolving stage began to turn and the whole immobile silhouette was borne away.

14. Chatsky and Mochalin in *Woe to Wit*, 1928

The 'negation' was somewhat akin to Lenin's idea of 'Two steps forward, one step back.' It was exemplified by Meyerhold in the Japanese theatre's 'hanamichi' or 'flower walk' down which the actor entered while gesturing away from the stage. As a silhouette it is an expressive pose, like the mystics in their cardboard cutout suits in *The Fairground Booth* (1906) or the warriors with their 'strange pensiveness' in *The Second Commander* (1929).

Finally, there is a kind of silhouette which Meyerhold developed which might be called the 'pose-pause', a moment which is expressive but not necessarily dynamic. In *Woe to Wit* (1928), for instance, there are moments of calm where the silhouette tells all – the moment when Sophia and Mochalin return from the tavern, pause and look at each other delightedly; or the moment when Chatsky and Mochalin meet, gauche idealism and worldly wisdom summed up in two almost identical poses.

The pause, the silhouette, is vital to biomechanics precisely because it is a system based on movement. It is like the punctuation mark, without which the sense is lost. Close to the silhouette, but moving out from it, is the gesture, which Meyerhold considered almost as important. Gesture can clarify an intention, can qualify it or contradict it; but whatever purpose it served, gesture in Meyerhold's theatre was marked by three traits. First, it was never casual or spontaneous, but always deliberate and significant; it partook of the nature of a *rhythmic* contribution to the performance (a secret learned when

Meyerhold played Pierrot in Mikhail Fokine's 1910 production of *Carnival*); and finally it was a movement which reverberated through the whole body. When this last idea was queried, Eisenstein demonstrated how balancing a billiard cue on one's nose does not *apparently* involve the whole body; but if one balances, say, a teaspoon, it soon becomes apparent that the whole body is involved. Examples of the reverberative gesture were the 'abrupt, puppet-like' movements Meyerhold insisted the Mayor produce in *The Government Inspector*[52] (1926), the religious open palms of the nuns in *Sister Beatrice* (1906), and the way Liza scratched herself on waking in *Woe to Wit* (1928): 'The scene with the scratching begins so that it will be noticeable. If your hand was here on your chest (he demonstrates), then the first scratch must be as far away as possible so that the public sees it. And then the second must be near the knee or a little lower so that each movement appears distinct.'[53] The hands were used in Japanese theatre as agents of expressiveness, and Meyerhold sought to do the same. Several observers noticed how expressive his own hands were[54] and he himself found Mei Lan-fang's hands 'miraculously' communicative.[55] Meyerhold's simplest exercise for the hands was called 'Pandora's Box' in which various objects in a box – 'bits of metal, bits of silk, matches, cigarette papers, feathers, fluff, little shells, nails, pebbles, glass'[56] – are simply sifted, sorted, grasped, felt; then many items can become objects for simple play with the hands – 'little canes, lances, small rugs, lanterns, shawls, mantles, weapons, flowers, masks, noses, etc.'.[57] Beyond this, Meyerhold's actors also learned to juggle, with balls, with sticks, with clubs, with knives. This led to some memorable scenes in production, as in *The Forest* (1924), when Ilinsky mimed hooking a fish, taking it off the hook, fluttering his hand to give the impression of holding the flapping creature, and then placing it in a teapot! Or in *The Mandate* (1925), when Sergei Martinson's 'long apelike hands jump high into the air' to complete the comedy of a body 'all hinged' as he plays the piano.[58]

Meyerhold worked on the actor's head, neck, eyes and mouth, too. He had his actors move their eyes in a particular direction, then the head; he had them turn the head fast, then slow; he made them balance a ball on the nape of the neck. As for the eyes, 'the good actor knows the value of his gaze. With only a shift of his pupils from the line of the horizon to the right or the left, up or down, he will give the necessary accent to his acting, which will be understood by the audience. The eyes of poor actors and amateurs are always fidgetty, darting here and there to the sides.'[59] Thus Meyerhold's transformation of the corpulent Varlamov, usually a braggart in home-spun Russian drama, into Molière's Sganarelle in *Don Juan* (1910):

Everything that went on inside him was reflected in his eyes. Up to the end, it saturated his whole being and increased the vitality of even such a bulky, slow-moving figure as his was at that time. He conveyed everything to the spectators through his eyes and the general expression of his face. There was so much *joie de vivre* in it, comicality, naive good nature and ready animation . . . that from his first appearance on the stage his face served the public like a playing card of Sganarelle.[60]

Varlamov could never have been more than an occasional actor for Meyerhold, however, because of his lack of movement. For Meyerhold, as for Wagner, 'the ground of all human art is bodily motion',[61] but in practice, whereas 'Wagner employs the orchestra to convey spiritual emotions, I employ *plastic movement*.'[62] Van Gyseghem explains this clearly:

Biomechanics teaches the actor to use the space about him on the stage three-dimensionally, as a definite measurable commodity. Just as his feet measure distances on the floor of the stage as he walks, so the rest of his body is made to use the air about him for a specific effect. Through exercises he is taught to achieve the feeling of the place of the actor in space, time and rhythm.[63]

Practically, the exercises and *études* aimed to develop consciousness of the centre of balance, to enable the actor to adapt the same movement patterns to different spaces, to help him to manage transitions from large to small movements, to enable him to 'freeze' in any position and to leap from stillness into intense action.

The simplest exercises were to some extent like scales for a pianist. They included deep knee bends, with spine erect, stretching and contracting in various planes and at various tempi. More characteristic, perhaps, were the walking and running exercises, particularly those employing smooth, loping steps so that a cup of water held in the hand or balanced on the head would not spill, or those where direction, speed and so forth had to be changed instantaneously in response to external stimuli like claps of the hands. There were also various falls, backwards and forwards, and the 'fall and recovery' based on circus techniques. And lastly, mention should be made here of the 'dactyl', a preparatory exercise often used before other more complex exercises or *études*. In this, the actor stands relaxed, arms down, on the balls of the feet which are placed one in front of the other as in a boxer's stance, with the toes pointing slightly inwards. Leading with the hands, which describe a wide semi-circle as they move upwards through 180°, clapping twice sharply as they go, the whole body is brought to a position stretching upwards, with the heels raised off the ground and the head thrown back. Then the hands describe a downwards semi-circle, clapping twice, ending flung backwards behind the actor; the arms again lead the movement – when they are parallel with the ground, the knees begin to bend and the head is flung forward. The knee of the rear foot is no more than an inch off the ground, the back is bowed, the head beside the forward knee. By swinging the arms forward, enough momentum is created to return the actor to the initial standing position. The

15. The dactyl, a preparatory exercise in biomechanics

dactyl, like other biomechanical exercises, was done staccato, legato, and in various rhythms, while, again like other exercises, it might include a cry – 'Aahh!' – at key moments to encourage reflex action.

Biomechanics also involved a good deal of gymnastics, acrobatics and the like: actors did somersaults, rolls, leaps and leapfrogs; they learned to tap dance, charleston and fox trot, to do some eurhythmics and some ballet. Specific exercises included the Bridge or Crab (hands and feet on the floor, stomach uppermost), and 'Leg thrusts from a squatting position' as in the Cossack dance. Martinson's fourteen-second dance in *The Last Fight* (1931) –

'a parody of an American sailor . . . [with] a spit to the side, a gesture with the thumb, and an eyelid pulled down'[64] – and Garin's fifth inventor in *D.E.* (1925) – 'whose crippled leg – a character unto itself – inadvertently kicks the millionaire interviewer'[65] show these exercises transferred straight to productions. The chase sequence in *The Magnanimous Cuckold* (1922), with something like thirty performers doing leaps, somersaults, leapfrogs and so on, was probably the single most exhilarating example.

Other exercises for simple movement included watching the movements of animals as models, particularly members of the cat family, and this, too, was often transferred to specific roles. In episode 12 in *Woe to Wit* (1928), Meyerhold wanted the granddaughter to 'show her tail . . . when I say that she shows her tail, I have in mind a female turkey that is flirting with a male turkey. The actress who wants to learn to give such a performance will go to a poultry yard.'[66] Actors were also encouraged to learn from the work of painters such as Daumier or Callot, and to learn from the puppet which, despite its unchanging face, has enormous expressive powers. More obviously theatrical were the exercises based on work actions – hammering, scything, sawing – or sports activities – throwing the discus or putting the shot. Conventional Chinese actions suggested small *études* – walking with high steps to signifiy going upstairs, or walking in decreasing circles to signify climbing a hill. More complicated was an exercise like going through a door from the Chinese theatre: touch the fingertips in front of the chest to signify a door, open the hands and extend the arms to signify opening it, take two or three steps forward to go through it, and bring the fingertips together again to signify closing the door.

Probably the two best-known biomechanical *études* are 'Shooting from the Bow' and 'Throwing the Stone' and both involve combinations of exercises already described to produce increasingly complex variations. 'Shooting from the Bow' is a mime, involving holding the imaginary bow in the left hand in front of the actor, running towards the quarry with smooth, loping strides, and jumping two-footed to a halt when the quarry is sighted; there follows a sequence of 'forward' actions balanced by 'rejects' as the actor draws an imaginary arrow from a quiver on his back ('reject'), loads it in the bow string, draws back the string ('reject'), fires and leaps forwards to land two-footed with a cry. This was developed into a complex *étude* called 'The Hunt'; more important for the beginner was the rhythm of the movements and the need to feel each gesture reverberating through the whole body, as the centre of balance changed and the weight was transferred from front to back, and forward again. 'Throwing the Stone' is at its simplest very similar. The actor runs, halts, crouches and leans back to pick up the imaginary stone, rises and leans forward to aim, takes the stone around in a wide arc backwards,

16. 'Shooting from the Bow', a widely-known biomechanical exercise

poises, throws, leaps forward to land two-footed with a cry. Again, increasingly complex variations were added, one of which, involving twenty units of action, van Gyseghem noted in the 1930s.

It was exercises of this kind that helped Nikolai Okhlopkov to amaze audiences to *D.E.* (1925) by acting in different rhythms with different parts of his body – jerky hand rhythms contradicted by languid leg movements or a foot tapping swiftly against a slowly drawled speech. And these techniques were behind the much-discussed but not especially significant concept of 'pre-acting'. Because this was closely identified with one of Meyerhold's least successful productions, *Teacher Bubus* (1925), it has been taken as a self-indulgence on his part; yet it is, as he himself pointed out, an old device of the oriental theatre, one which prepares the audience for what is to come, and directs their attention to its significance. It has been constantly employed in the theatre, and Meyerhold was grappling with it as early as 1905.[67] As he pointed out in 1936, Charlie Chaplin, too, used it: 'His so-called "momentary pauses for aim", that peculiarly static style of acting, the freeze – it all comes down to the expedient concentration of action. Observe how Chaplin deploys his body in space to maximum effect: study, as we do, the movements of gymnasts and blacksmiths.'[68]

More problematical, and more significant, was Meyerhold's concept of the actor's 'self-admiration', the 'mirroring of the self'. In the first instance, this meant a sharp awareness of the actor's own physical presence, and with each movement a knowledge of 'how I look'.[69] 'Meyerhold called this "mirror-gazing", meaning the actor's ability to see himself from the side, as it were, and thus make his playing more simple and natural.'[70] But simplicity and naturalness were only a beginning: Meyerhold then used the exercise which was also employed by Mikhail Chekhov and others of encouraging the actor to perform an action 'with the quality of' rather than 'with the feeling of': walk across the room *with the quality of* anger, pick up a book *with the quality of* fear, sit down *with the quality of* humility.[71] This induces not only a detached but also an ironic attitude to the part in the actor. It also assists the *yuan*, a Chinese term denoting 'the actor's self-admiration in the process of playing'[72] a quality very evident, for example, in Yuri Yurev's performance as Don Juan in 1910. He was 'very young and handsome', Golovin wrote, 'he wore a magnificent, large wig with ringlets of a golden hue. Ribbons, bows and lace quivered on him like flames. He wore his costume with uncommon, even exquisite, perfection, and was charming, affected to a degree, and modishly urbane.'[73] Equally striking, though to quite opposite effect, was Igor Ilinsky in *The Magnanimous Cuckold* (1922):

Bruno . . . pale, stiffened face, his redundant monologues [delivered] in the same monotonous declamatory manner with the same intonations, and the same gestures of his

17. 'The Stab with the Dagger', biomechanical exercise

hands. Then the same Bruno would be burlesqued by the actor who would perform acrobatic stunts in the most pathetic passages of his speeches, and who would belch or roll his eyes humorously in the midst of the hero's dramatic experiences.[74]

So far the work described has all been concerned with the individual actor. Equally important for Meyerhold was the work he devised for pairs, to develop mutual co-ordination, trust and responsiveness. One-against-one sports like boxing, fencing and tennis were useful in themselves, and also as exemplars. Meyerhold extolled tennis's 'changing rhythm, attack when the ball is smashed going over into defence, changing the tempo-rhythm in a way reminiscent of an actor's encounter on the stage'.[75]

There were consequently many biomechanical exercises for pairs in the Meyerhold Workshop, such as the 'Stab with the Dagger': the first actor leaps towards the second, draws an imaginary dagger from his belt, reaches up above his head with it; as he brings it slowly down, the second actor arches slowly backwards, arms perpendicularly down, shoulders parallel to the ground; when he can go no further, the second actor utters a cry and jerks upright, and the first actor leaps backwards to his original position. Or, the 'Slap in the Face', a well-known acting exercise in which the slapper appears to strike his partner's face while the partner actually claps and jerks back his head at the supposed moment of impact, but characterized in Meyerhold's version by shifts backwards and forwards in the centre of balance of both actors, and the wide sweeps of the hands.[76] The 'Boxing Match' was more dance-like, co-ordinating movements of 'give and take, thrust and guard'[77] between two partners, while the 'Foot Strike' is much jerkier, involving one actor kicking at the nose of the partner who recoils from the foot. The 'Trip', in which the actor pulls his partner over his thrust out foot, and the 'Take by the Throat', a self-explanatory exercise, were slap-stick or clown-like, while more concerned with balance were the 'Tower', one actor standing on his partner's shoulders, and the 'Foot on the Back', in which the actor makes a low, leapfrog-type back and his partner steps up onto it; the first actor now walks until at the end of the exercise the partner leaps or somersaults off.

These exercises involve carrying the partner. The 'Fireman's Lift' is another such exercise, which Meyerhold often preceded by the 'Stab with the Dagger' and followed by a run using long, sweeping steps. 'Dropping the Weight' involves one partner standing in front of the other, facing the same way; the two take a handshake grip (i.e. two right hands, or two left hands), the actor behind places his other hand on the partner's waist and his same-side foot sideways and forwards, and lets the front actor fall gently towards the foot. Then there is the 'Leap on the Chest': the actor whose chest is leapt upon must put one arm behind the knees of his partner the instant they land on his chest, and then the exercise may develop into a version of the 'Stab with the Dagger' to demonstrate and practice co-ordination as the centre of balance shifts.[78] Then there is the 'Pick-a-Back', when one actor leaps onto his partner's back and the partner runs off with long sweeping strides, and the 'Horse and Rider', the same exercise only now the actor leaps onto his partner's shoulders from behind.

Rarely were any of these exercises transferred intact to the stage, though in *The Magnanimous Cuckold* (1922) the Cooper leapt onto Bruno's chest, and Stella's final elopement began when she leapt onto the Cowherd's shoulders and they left as Horse and Rider. Rather, we should see them complementing other, more overtly theatrical, exercises with the partner to widen the creative options available. Thus, there were exercises in 'Taking the Partner Aside', leading him decorously, pushing him roughly, and so on; the 'Chase', two actors running in time on the spot, varying the style in synchronization and smiling all the time at the audience; or 'Throwing the Spear', based on the Chinese convention in which if the target actor caught the spear his death was signified. 'The Challenge', striking the rival across the face with a glove, was a stylized Western theatrical convention; the 'Flower Offer', when the beloved is offered a flower, 'torso swaying, head turning and slightly inclining, arms gracefully outstretched first to the left, then to the right',[79] was a Japanese convention. These exercises inform moments like the chase with bladders on sticks or on the trapeze in *The Death of Tarelkin* (1922), or the opening of *The Magnanimous Cuckold* (1922) when Bruno runs up to the top of the 'construc-

18. 'The Leap on the Chest', biomechanical exercise

19. 'The Horse and Rider', biomechanical exercise here executed by Maria Babanova as Stella and Nikolai Losev as Volopas in *The Magnanimous Cuckold*, 1922

tion', turns to catch the pursuing Stella by the shoulders, and together they slide down the chute, crying 'Wheee!' They inform sequences like those in the ballroom scenes of *The Fairground Booth* (1906) and *The Queen of Spades* (1935) which involve intimate momentary interchanges between couples. They inform fleeting moments of fleeting significance, as in *Crimes and Crimes* (1912): 'Maurice was sitting at a small table, a bottle of champagne before him. Henriette was behind Maurice's back: her suddenly extended hand took a glove from the table and with a slow movement of the fingers stuffed the glove into the glass. The result was an intense dialogue between eyes and hand.'[80]

The bottle, the glove, the glass were the kind of items Meyerhold liked to give his student actors to improvise with – 'Playing with Props' he called it.

The 'play' invests the objects with unexpected significance, as when Boris Zakhava summoned the deputies to the Parliament in *D.E.* (1925) with a silver bell which expressed his character's feelings towards the different parties by the way he rang it; or when Zinaida Raikh, as Aksyusha in *The Forest* (1924) beat the clothes she was washing to convey her scorn for Gurmyzhskaya. Before the revolution, the contents of Meyerhold's props cupboard were likely to be less political and less utilitarian: a 1914 list includes 'a magic wand, a flying butterfly, a golden orange, a magic veil, a collapsible stick, a tambourine, two plates, a little violin with a long bow . . .' and so on[81] while the actor has to learn, for instance, how 'to strike a tattered tambourine not merely to make a noise, but to convey through that one gesture all his skill and refinement, to strike it in such a way that the spectator forgets that it has no skin'.[82] 'Playing with Furniture' has the same potential to make inanimate stage decorations into direct contributors to the meaning, as with the revolving door in *The Magnanimous Cuckold* (1922), when the Mayor bows goodbye and his backside hits the door which flies round and strikes Peter who is knocked forwards into Estrugo who falls to the floor; or the seesaw in *The Forest* when Schastlivtsev, heavier than Ulita, sits pensively smoking at his end while she is left stranded in the air.

'Play with Costume' should be mentioned here, too. 'The Master did not recommend training in tights. Better was a loose costume. Then the student would learn to sense the lines and folds of the clothes.'[83] Before the revolution in the Meyerhold Studio these took the form of Russian blouses with belts and loose, tapering trousers, 'wine red with gold for men and dark blue with coloured belts for women'.[84] After the revolution they became more utilitarian in cut and colour, though the need for awareness of the fold and fall of the costume was still stressed. Meyerhold began with hats: 'the headgear as a motive for the stage bow',[85] noted Sayler about the exercise which taught the actor 'to doff a beggar's cap as though it were pearl-encrusted'.[86] Early in his career Meyerhold knew how to make a costume speak. Here is a description of his Pierrot in *The Fairground Booth* in 1906:

On the stage direction, 'Pierrot awakes from his reverie and brightens up', Meyerhold made an absurd wave with both his sleeves, and in this movement was expressed the suddenly dawning hope of the clown. Further waves of his sleeves conveyed various different things. These stylized gestures were inspired by the musical conception of the character; they were eloquent because . . . they were prompted by the inner rhythm of the role. The gestures always followed the words, complementing them as though bringing a song to its conclusion, saying without words something understood only by Pierrot himself.[87]

'Play with Costume' provided a striking silhouette in *The Storm* in 1916: 'when Katerina Roshchina . . . fell on her knees in ecstatic rapture before the

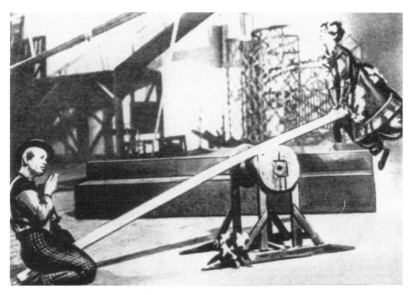

20. The seesaw in *The Forest*, 1924

images, she spread the folds of her heavy silk dress artistically and with a graceful motion raised her thin arms, pausing for a moment as though on the canvas of an exquisite artist.'[88]

A cloak provided the finest opportunities for 'play'. Before the revolution Meyerhold was teaching the actor 'to hitch up a tattered cloak with the flourish of a *hidalgo*'[89] and in the 1930s he demonstrated its use in what was effectively an infinitely variable *étude*:

Vsevolod Emilevich went up onto the stage. He ordered the carpet to be spread out in the middle of the stage. He put on the hat and took the cloak out of my hand. He smoothed it and threw it over his right arm. With an elegant gesture of his left hand, he took the top part of the cloak and drew his left hand aside, but not very far, so that all the lower part of the cloak fell beside his left leg. He put his right hand on the cloak and with his other hand spread it out like a fan in front of his leg. The cloak lay beautifully and free. Then his right hand gathered the upper part of the cloak, threw it over his right shoulder, and thus, holding it back, he walked the stage with a smooth gait, making a figure of eight and turning to the audience first his face, then his back . . . He again took the cloak in his left hand, again spread out the upper part near his leg, flung it up to his right and then over his left shoulder and head, and clasped it at his throat. Turning round, he went to the back of the stage. The cloak unfolded behind him, covering him from the back and making a long train on the floor . . . Then he drew himself up, stood erect and with a quick movement of his right hand threw the right hand edge of the cloak over his left shoulder and, proudly, with his head held high, looked sternly into the auditorium. Then with his right hand he folded back the edge of the cloak from his left shoulder, threw this edge over his right arm and, slightly bending his head, he went quickly out into the wings . . . He ran out again

21. Bruno and Estrugo reach down to Stella and the nurse in Act 3 of *The Magnanimous Cuckold*, 1922

onto the stage, extending his right hand and holding the edge of the cloak in it. His whole figure was in profile, hidden from the spectator by the cloak, but the left edge was quivering from the rapid running and was dragged along the floor. The impression was of a bird with dark wings flying past. Finally, he turned to face his audience and, falling on one knee, but leaving his right hand holding the cloak up, he covered his bowed head.[90]

The description is worth quoting at length as it shows how endless were the variations that Meyerhold worked out with almost every exercise he used.

The last group of exercises in the biomechanical system concerned groups

22. Meyerhold's production of *A Profitable Post* at the Theatre of the Revolution, 1923: Yusov about to 'break' over Zhadov

of actors working together. Biomechanics was supposed to be a collective, not an individualistic, training and the idea of the actor fitting into a group was seen by Meyerhold to be healthily creative, in the way a musician's work in an orchestra was. In fact, in *The Magnanimous Cuckold* (1922) the teamwork of the leading three performers – Ilinsky, Babanova and Zaichikov – was apparently so synchronized that the trio came to be known by the abbreviation Il-Ba-Zai. Meyerhold developed specific exercises for small groups like the 'Pyramid', a traditional circus turn, and the 'Triangle', one actor 'riding' two others, mounting the back member of the pair as in the 'Horse and Rider' exercise and adopting different postures as the two bearers jogged along. And he made great use of 'multiple uniformity', groups acting in unison, particularly effectively playing the group and the individual off against one another, as in the scenes of Beatrice and the nuns in *Sister Beatrice* (1906), the bribes scene in *The Government Inspector* (1926), or the scene of the meeting on the steppe in *The Second Commander* (1929) when the individual voice was constrasted with choral speech using megaphones. Finally Meyerhold used exercises based on the traditional circus 'parade' opening (such a 'parade' was staged in *The Forest* in 1924) and the comic curtain call, to develop creative and comic group work. Consequently some of the photographs, posed as they are, of group scenes from Meyerhold's productions are extraordinarily rich, like the famous shot from *The Magnanimous Cuckold* when Bruno and Estrugo lean down from their balcony to Stella and the nurse, just unable to reach them, their bodies echoing the inhuman geometry of the 'construction', a great gaping hole at the centre of the composition, yet Bruno's raised leg and the fact that he is lying on top of Estrugo suggesting the naiveté and rough-and-tumble of childishness in the world of adult sexual desire; or the scene from *A Profitable Post* (1923) where Yusov, the quintessential NEPman, dances a bureaucrat's version of the 'Russly', egged on by the drunken minor officials and almost in the teeth of the solitary Zhadov, the composition arranged round the dynamic energy lines flowing through the officials to rear up at Yusov like a breaker about to cascade over Zhadov.

CHARACTERIZATION

All Meyerhold's work was based on the primary necessity that every action and every speech had to be 'justified' in Stanislavsky's sense. Nothing, no matter how fantastic or grotesque, could proceed without that. Nevertheless this did not imply the necessity for a psychologically consistent or even convincing character. Meyerhold's theatre was always much closer to those Formalist prescriptions in which character was seen as little more than an action-function: one of the Formalist school's best-known critical works, Vladimir Propp's *Morphology of the Folktale*, is a deliberate attempt to analyse the significant workings of the folk tale without recourse to the romantic conception of character rooted in a constant psychology. Actually, this rejection coincides with a dialectical materialist view of stage life and real life: *dramatis personae* are not real people, and to suppose they are is to misunderstand the very basis of art.

Characterization in Meyerhold's theatre, therefore, was a vehicle for (in Formalist terms) 'deformation' and 'estrangement', which often revealed social rather than personal meanings. Thus, Tarelkin, the minor bureaucrat, become 'estranged' when seen as a jester–acrobat, flying across the stage on a trapeze to escape the police; in *The Forest* (1924), a series of wigs 'deformed' the truthfully conceived characters of Ostrovsky – 'the leading lady's lewdness was emphasized by her burning red wig and sentimental whining voice, the unctuous priest had a gold wig and beard, a young sap wore green hair, etc.'[91] The wigs function slightly as the costumes of the characters in *commedia dell' arte* do: Pierrot's floppy white suit and Harlequin's multi-coloured lozenges are a convenient shorthand for the audience but to the performer they are useful because they give a specific 'centre' to his work.

Meyerhold here was again close to Coquelin, for whom 'the creation of living *types* . . . constitutes the art of the theatre'.[92] Coquelin discussed the actor's *emploi* or 'business' which Elsie Fogarty emphasized 'was not strictly typecasting, rather a practical anticipation of the possibilities of the student's future career, based on his physical characteristics, vocal quality, height, mental affinities, etc.'[93] The similarity of this approach to that of the Meyerhold Workshop, which in 1922 published seventeen 'set roles of the actor', is obvious. The roles were:

	MALE	FEMALE
1.	Hero	Heroine
2.	Lover	Young girl in love
3.	Mischief maker	Mischief maker
4.	Clown, Fool, Simpleton, Eccentric	Female Fool, Simpleton, Eccentric
5.	Villain, Intriguer	Villainess, Intriguer
6.	Mysterious Stranger	Stranger (as if from another world)
7.	Outsider, Renegade, Unbeliever	Outsider, Renegade, Unbeliever
8.	Fop	Courtesan
9.	Moralist	Matron
10.	Guardian (Pantalone)	Guardian
11.	Friend (Confidant)	Confidante
12.	Braggart (Miles Gloriosus)	Matchmaker
13.	Guardian of the Law	Guardian of the Law
14.	Scientist (learned doctor, wise man)	Scholar, suffragette
15.	Messenger	Messenger
16.	Men in women's parts	Boys in girls' parts
17.	Walk-ons	Walk-ons[94]

The list is slightly odd − 'Men in women's parts', for instance, seems different in kind from 'hero' or 'lover' − but should be regarded, first, as a series of initial stimuli for student-actors and, second, as providing a basis in a particular type which the actor can then embroider. This was certainly how the actors approached their roles in *The Magnanimous Cuckold* (1922), beginning from a 'set type': Bruno − 'simpleton'; Stella − 'young girl in love'; Estrugo − 'fool'; Count − 'fop'; and so on. 'Typing' roles in this way carries with it the danger of abstraction, but without 'typing' Meyerhold felt that acting carried the greater danger of becoming merely anecdotal and irrelevant.

The idea was clearly extracted from the *commedia dell' arte*, in which character, rooted in type, was yet both socially specific and at the same time more subtle than merely a 'set role':

Arlecchino, a native of Bergamo and the servant of the miserly doctor, is forced to wear a coat with multi-coloured patches because of his master's meanness. Arlecchino is a foolish buffoon, a roguish servant who seems always to wear a cheerful grin. But look closer! What is hidden behind the mask? Arlecchino, the all-powerful wizard, the enchanter, the magician; Arlecchino the emissary of the infernal powers . . . The two aspects of Arlecchino represent two opposite poles. Between them lies an infinite range of shades and variations. How does one reveal this extreme diversity of character to the spectator? With the aid of the mask.[95]

Meyerhold himself had demonstrated what this meant in practice as early as 1906 when he played Pierrot in Blok's *The Fairground Booth*: 'He was not at all like the familiar Pierrots, sickly sweet and sobbing beautifully. Rather he presented sharp contradictions, at one moment speaking words of unearthly sorrow in a muffled whisper and at the next being full of gibes and insults.'[96]

23. Igor Ilinsky's 'mask' as Bruno in *The Magnanimous Cuckold*, 1922

For the actor, the actual creation of the part proceeds from the 'establish-ment of the emploi'.[97] This may be the typical gesture, such as close-up photographs of Ilinsky and Babanova demonstrate in *The Magnanimous Cuckold*, or may be something closer to a mask, as Zaichikov's unchanging expression and forward-pointing hair were. In a series of scenes, a series of such 'masks' may be developed, as Garin did for Khlestakov: in different scenes he played the mask of the dandy, the mask of the liar, the mask of the glutton, the mask of the opportunist, and so on – a grotesque gallery, in other words, centred on Garin's own spindly physique. However, the fact that each scene had its own mask enabled the actor to remain emotionally detached from the part as such and to display a range of ironic comments on the character he was playing. Garin himself pointed out that the actor must be technically equipped to do this, and insisted that his technique had been developed through the exercises in biomechanics he had had in the Meyerhold Workshop.[98]

Two further comments may be added to these. First, after the Bolshevik revolution, Meyerhold's conception of the mask types became much more sociological in orientation: the remarks about Arlecchino quoted above could not have been written after 1917. The principles of the 'set roles' remained more or less constant throughout Meyerhold's maturity, but there is little doubt that the system is more convincing when based on identifiable types from the contemporary, observable world – which, of course, Arlecchino himself was originally in Italy. It was this social awareness as the basis of characterization that led Lunacharsky to coin the term 'sociomechanics'.

Secondly, one should note Meyerhold's thoughts on the casting of actors for it has relevance to his notions of interpreting dramatic characters as types. He remarked to Gladkov in the 1930s: 'I need to know who is the juvenile lead in my theatre so as never to cast him as a juvenile lead. I have often noticed that an actor blossoms out quite unexpectedly in a part where he has to struggle to subdue his natural characteristics.'[99] Most interestingly to us in an age of feminism, perhaps, this led him to propound that 'women should take over "men's roles" on stage, as well as in real life, by acting parts written for male actors'.[100] How serious he was in this is unclear, but he himself was not averse to cross-sexual casting, both for comic effect, as when the lithe and youthful Mikhail Zharov played the washerwoman in the Death of Tarelkin (1922), and for more serious purposes, as in his film of the Picture of Dorian Gray (1915), when Varvara Yanova played the part of Dorian, and in his production of Calderón's The Constant Prince (1915), when Nina Kovalenskaya played Prince Fernando.

SPEECH

From the foregoing it is clear that speech as such assumes a different, perhaps less important, place in Meyerhold's theatre than in many others. It becomes an illustration of action, a decoration or commentary on it. Though by no means a hard-and-fast rule, speech tends to be separated from movement, so

24. Mikhail Zharov (inside the cage) as Brandakhlystova the washerwoman in *The Death of Tarelkin*, 1922, with Nikolai Okhlopkov

that the actor has to learn to do one thing, then the other, rather than blur the two together as in most systems. In this way, speech becomes less a tool for psychological characterization and more an element in the rhythmic texture of the scene. The remark recorded during a rehearsal of *The Government Inspector* is typical of Meyerhold throughout his career: 'The dialogue should have a kind of beat to it . . .'[101] Garin remembered a speech exercise which concentrated on the rhythmic elements of Brutus's oration in *Julius Caesar*:

25. Varvara Yanova as Dorian Gray in Meyerhold's film, 1915, with
Meyerhold as Lord Henry

Conducting with the hands to the count of 'four', the student simultaneously pronounced
the speech:
    'Romans' — one, pause — two.
    'Countrymen' — three, pause — four.
    'And lovers' — one, pause — two, three, four, etc.[102]

Mikhail Gnesin, Meyerhold's most constant collaborator on speech training courses before and after the revolution, spent a good deal of time attempting to notate speech by quasi-musical means.

By 1905 Meyerhold had virtually worked out what he wanted speech to contribute to the theatrical experience, and he later expressed it thus:

1. What is needed is the cold minting of words, completely liberated from the tremolo and the weeping of the actors' voices. Never tenseness and gloominess of tone.

2. The sound must always have support, and the words must fall like drops into a deep well. In stage speeches there must be no howlings of the endings as if one were reading decadent verses.[103]

In 1923 Sergei Tretyakov defined the problem as being 'to teach the actor–worker not to converse and not to declaim, but to speak'. This he attempted to do by shifting the emphasis away from the melodic elements in speech, the vowels, onto the 'articulatory–onomatopoeic (the consonants)', and away from 'conversational intonation (usually unreal anyway, since real conversation accumulates verbal rubbish as well as all sorts of drawings in of breath, hiccoughs, clearings of the throat and other messy noises)' onto 'rhythmical configurations' which were 'crystallized from examples of common phraseology'. Speech then took on the quality of 'verbal gesture' and the actor's task was to create a 'vocal mask' analogous to his 'set role' and presumably with the same qualifications and possibilities.[104] Thus we find Meyerhold instructing Starkovsky, as the Mayor in *The Government Inspector* (1926), in rehearsal: 'Since you're young . . . forget about that senile voice. Enunciate every word perfectly clearly.'[105] And Yurev describes his voice work in *Don Juan* (1910) as 'a quick, headlong speech, almost without a rise in tone. All my attention was focussed on the changing tempi and the quick, bold switches from one rhythm to another, on precision of diction, and on the different "typefaces" – this in italics, that brevier, that nonpareil, and in bolder type only in a few instances.'[106] Thus, twelve or more years before Tretyakov attempted to codify the practice, Yurev was breaking down the speech content of his role into a series of more or less self-contained 'verbal gestures'.

A CONSTRUCT OF ACTION

For Meyerhold's actor, this ability to create a sequence of self-contained entities is the secret of creating a part. It is perhaps a little like building a wall. Each individual entity is a brick in that wall, a self-contained combination of movements or a piece of action, long or short but complete in itself. Each such entity is then added together, and the result is not a character in the conventional sense, rather the role as a whole is seen as a construct of action.

An example of a piece of action which works initially as a self-contained entity is this from *Thirty-Three Fainting Fits* (1935): Igor Ilinsky

breaks off his speech, clutches his heart with one hand, his coat lapel with the other. The father rises, steps back a pace and holds out both his arms, as though Ilinsky were about to swim to him. The maid in the background raises her broom and holds it poised in mid-air over her head. There is a pause. The Chopin music begins to play. Ilinsky, still holding his lapel, reaches out with the other hand from the glass on the table. He holds it at arm's length from his mouth; his eyes grow bigger; the music plays louder. The father and the maid stand motionless. With a quick jerk Ilinsky draws the glass to him and downs the water. The music stops, the maid returns to her sweeping. Ilinsky carefully smooths his lapel and returns the glass to the table. The father continues with the next line.[107]

The whole vignette is an almost perfect example of the interplay of stillness and movement which characterized Meyerhold's work at its best.

The danger with constructing a performance by such a method is obvious: it can get out of hand and destroy the integrity of the play. In one scene in *Woe to Wit* (1928) between Famusov and Chatsky, Meyerhold had the characters playing billiards, intending to use the clicking of the balls, the chalking of the cues, and so forth, as punctuation marks in the action. Actually, the audience became more involved with the game itself, applauding good shots and so on, until the interesting idea became quite self-defeating. The problem with the billiards, a perfectly good example, it might seem, of a self-contained action vignette, was actually twofold: first, it was superimposed on the scene, and second, it was an 'antic' which was not particularly 'appropriate to the theatre'. It suited the billiard hall, not the stage. The best examples of self-contained entities of action were those which consisted of antics appropriate to the theatre which were yet able to express in their action the 'idea' of the scene or the character, as happened for example in *Krechinsky's Wedding* (1933) when the two women who were both in love with Krechinsky were seen, Lidochka running hither and thither, embracing Atueva, overflowing with excitement and nervous laughter, and Atueva standing rigid, tense and unresponsive; or in *The Government Inspector* (1926) when Khlestakov regaled the Mayor's Wife with tales of his Petersburg triumphs and absent-mindedly drew her little finger to his lips on his teaspoon.

Sometimes the stage furniture opened possibilities for such moments – the giant stride and the seesaw in *The Forest* (1924), for instance, or the 'sausage machine' which devoured Mikhail Zharov in *The Death of Tarelkin* (1922). In this production, one of the exploding stools provided the actors with an 'antic' that was 'appropriate to the theatre': Raspluyev sits on it, it explodes under him. He jumps up and his first clerk picks it up to inspect it. He sees nothing, shakes his head, passes it to the second clerk, who inspects it, sees

26. The giant stride in *The Forest*, 1924

nothing, shakes his head, passes it to the third, and so on down a line of seven clerks. Famusov's chase of Liza in *Woe to Wit* (1928) provided another 'antic' of the *commedia dell' arte* type: she leaps away from him, cowers behind the pedestal. Famusov throws himself at her, she runs behind the armchair. He stands on the chair: '"Oi, rascal", (a blow on the cheek) "scamp" (a blow on the other cheek) ". . . and nothing but" (a blow on the back) "mischief and whimsies in your empty head" (a blow on the head)'.[108]

The overt theatricality or 'staginess' of such moments show the actor 'baring the device' (in the Formalists' phrase). The 'device' itself, deforming the subject matter, comes to form the material, as Meyerhold had found happened in the popular theatres of the past, where such moments 'force the spectator to recognize the actor's performance as pure play-acting'.[109] The final 'baring of the device' was to put the actor in an empty space, or a space with a few platforms, a slide, some stairs, a swing door, and let him create. This was the method of *The Magnanimous Cuckold* (1922) as a precise description of a small section of the action between Ilinsky and Zaichikov will show.

Bruno (Ilinsky) is sitting astride the bench, staring down at it, gloomily preoccupied with his jealousy. Estrugo (Zaichikov) enters, sees Bruno, looks over his shoulder onto the bench to see if he can see what Bruno is looking at. He sees nothing. He steps up on the bench, looks again, sees nothing. He goes round in front of Bruno, bends down to look again, but Bruno sees him and peremptorily points to him to be seated. Estrugo, not understanding, now

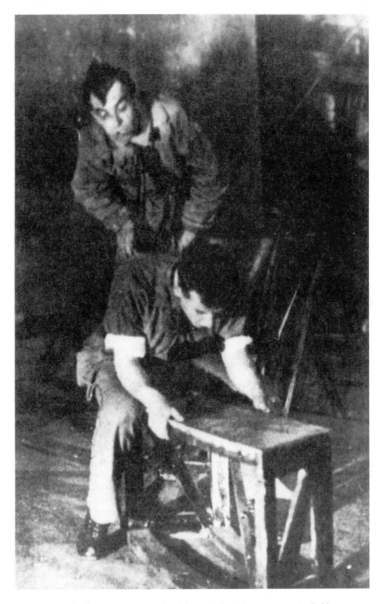

27. Estrugo looks over Bruno's shoulder, in *The Magnanimous Cuckold*, 1922

looks at the place Bruno is pointing at. He is baffled, seeing nothing. Bruno slaps the bench: 'Sit down, Estrugo.' Estrugo bends, imitates sitting just beyond the end of the bench, facing Bruno. 'No, here', Bruno says. Estrugo sits on the very end of the bench. Bruno moves back, as if making more room. 'Closer', he says. Estrugo moves closer. This action is repeated. Then, the third time Estrugo moves up, Bruno suddenly shakes his fist at him, he ducks down and covers his head with his hands. 'Be quiet! Shh!' Bruno shouts.

Slowly, Estrugo raises his head and peers timidly at Bruno. 'Will you be quiet?' screams Bruno. He thrusts Estrugo's head back down on the bench, then, more reflectively, traces a question mark with his finger on Estrugo's back, murmuring, 'Is Stella true to me, or not?' As his soliloquy proceeds, he builds up more speed and ends by whacking Estrugo on the back. 'So she's faithful, is she? Prove it!' Estrugo timidly raises his head. 'You can't', yells Bruno, thrusting Estrugo's head down again. 'Will you swear she's true?' he asks. Estrugo raises his head again. 'You won't'. says Bruno. He wags his finger at Estrugo, haranguing him, and ends by pushing his head down between his own knees. Estrugo waves his arms madly in protest. Bruno grabs them and forces them against his back. Estrugo's hands waggle in protest. Bruno holds them down. Estrugo's fingers wave, till they, too, are restrained, down to the last little finger.

And so the action – quintessential Meyerhold, we may say – proceeds. And if it seems laboured or pedantic when spelled out like this, for the audience in the theatre it was precisely the opposite: it displayed

the lively, mischievous, and unbridled gaiety of the comedians who enacted *Le Cocu Magnifique* with a controlled virtuosity over their bodies. It was as if a band of comedians had just raced out of a sunny square into the gloomy theatre, had joined in tossing all the trashy rags out into the street, had taken the stage in battle, and, in unrestrained happiness at having the space of an open stage under their control, had given themselves up to the most 'crazy jokes of the theatre'. It furnished clear and convincing proof that the actor himself contained the magic power of transforming the wasteland of the stage and the abstract constructions into something living.[110]

4   The *mise-en-scène*

For the action construction centred on the forestage, the usual type of theatrical *mise-en-scène* is unsatisfactory. Meyerhold spent much creative energy trying to find an alternative, trying in effect to resolve the reverse side of the 'problem of the forestage' from that which affects the actor.

His first solution utilized Wagner's theoretical discussions and Appia's practical advocacy of an approach which treated the stage as a three-dimensional cube of space, wherein different planes, levels and angles could be deployed. 'The greatest obstacle is the flat surface of the stage', Meyerhold wrote in 1909. 'If only one could mould it like a sculptor moulds his clay, the broad expanse of floor could be transformed into a compact series of surfaces on varying levels. Lines would be broken up, characters could be grouped more closely in delicate curves, beautiful chiaroscuro effects could be achieved...'[1] As the conditional tense implies, he had not solved this problem yet, though he had identified it. It sprang from the relationship between the spectator and the observed object again: if the actor, in order to encourage the audience's active participation in the creation of the work, was going to emerge onto the forestage, then a type of *mise-en-scène* had to be devised to complement rather than negate this. The old decorative or illusory set was unacceptable: the *mise-en-scène* needed the capacity for independent intervention.

Already in *The Fairground Booth* (1906) the Mystics had been placed behind their table parallel with the proscenium, clothed in cutout cardboard suits, and when Harlequin jumped through the window, this too proved to be cardboard. The *mise-en-scène* thus made a direct – even crude – comment on the cardboard sham of contemporary life. The effect was as striking as that achieved perhaps more subtly over twenty years later in the banquet scene in *Woe to Wit* (1928), when the rumour-mongers were seated behind another long table, also parallel with the proscenium: 'Someone spears his fork into some kind of food, puts it in his mouth; or he takes a goblet, drinks without any toasting of his neighbour. He simply takes the glass, drinks, then sets down the glass and, after a few moments, drinks again.'[2] The guests all listen guardedly, tensely, when Sophia remarks casually that Chatsky is 'not in his right mind', and this 'news' ripples out both ways to the ends of the table. Then Chatsky enters. 'There he is' – 'There he is' – 'There he is' – rolls along the line. The guests hide their faces with their napkins, only their eyes peep

28. *The Fairground Booth,* with the Mystics behind the table and Pierrot to the right

out. 'Shh!' the Granddaughter hisses. The others take up the noise which swells as Chatsky moves across the stage, and dies as he says in despair: 'No, I can stand no more, after a million torments . . .'[3] Many of Meyerhold's *mise-en-scènes* were similarly effective: *The Government Inspector* (1926), for example, provided 'innumerable ensembles and designs', according to Huntly Carter,[4] while *The Lady of the Camellias* (1934) gained effect from the unexpected angle of the setting, and the action, to audience.

Many of these scenes were drawn from paintings, which Meyerhold responded to particularly readily. Carter noted how 'Meierhold composes scenes in black and white with great skill. By means of the bare walls of the stage and the limited light at his disposal he sometimes achieves Rembrandtesque effects',[5] and Markov recorded how his 'compositions' were 'suggestive of an old masterpiece' and how 'with exquisite taste Meyerhold builds up *mise-en-scènes* which recall the great traditions of painting'.[6] More precisely, the *mise-en-scène* of the first act of *Sister Beatrice* (1906) was modelled on Domenico Veneziano's 'Martyrdom of St Lucy',[7] the banquet scene in *Woe to Wit* (1928) already described, owed much to Diego Rivera's painting of a group of bourgeois gorging themselves at a dinner,[8] and scenes in *The Lady of the Camellias* (1934) were inspired by Manet.[9] In *Roar China!*, the staging of the Chinese boy's struggle was 'in harmony' with the frescoes of Giotto which Meyerhold held in particular esteem: 'as in

29. *Woe to Wit*, with the guests behind the table and Chatsky about to enter from the right

Giotto, the frontally-constructed *mise-en-scènes* profoundly affected the spectators'.[10] The scene of the meeting on the steppe in *The Second Commander* (1929) was modelled on Velasquez's *The Surrender of Breda* and a comparison between this painting and a photograph of the scene indicates how Meyerhold followed his model, notably in the positioning of the horse and the use of a forest of spears to create the impression of vast numbers. But it also shows how he diverged from it: the semi-circular staircase changes the impact, adding tension and claustrophobia as well as plasticity to the composition. The great painter shows us the world afresh; Meyerhold uses this vision creatively to show us his own, equally fresh vision.

Meyerhold's, of course, is a theatrical vision. Because rejection of the illusionist theatre involved the setting becoming part of the action, Meyerhold went radically further than almost any other theatre practitioner in redefining the stage space, ridding his theatre of all those items which conventionally define it, such as the proscenium arch, the borders, the wings and so on. For almost every production, Meyerhold evolved a new shape to the space he worked in, sometimes using a created backdrop, like the polished redwood in *The Government Inspector* (1926), sometimes leaving the bare brick walls of the theatre and placing a construction – or several constructions – in the space, as with the scaffolding in *Earth Rampant* (1923). Sometimes the construction had moving parts, as with *The Magnanimous Cuckold* (1922), sometimes the whole was mobile, as it was in *D.E.* (1924).

30. Velasquez, *The Surrender of Breda*

But whatever the particulars of any specific use of stage space, the frame of the proscenium arch, which divided the dramatic from the 'real' world, was to be destroyed. Van Gyseghem described the Meyerhold Theatre in the 1930s as having not so much a stage as 'what one might call an "action-space" at one end of the theatre'.[11] Gregor explained the 'extraordinary sensation' made by Meyerhold's production of *Don Juan* (1910) by the fact that it was 'the first occasion on which the division between the stage and the auditorium was done away with. The colour-scheme of Golovin's scenery harmonized with the rest of the interior, so that the stage seemed merely a continuation of the "house", and the actors made their entrance and exit straight through the audience.'[12] And Znosko-Borovsky recalled how the spectators at Meyerhold's production of Pinero's *Mid-Channel* at the Alexandrinsky in 1914

were astounded by what appeared to be a 'cubistic' decor, a semicircle which was broken up by a repeated design of yellowish squares each with a gold fillet. But it was worth returning to the auditorium to understand the idea of the director and the designer, A. Ya. Golovin: the decor repeated that of the lower wall of the auditorium, where the boxes had been before they were done away with, but the many doors of which had remained. The

31. The meeting on the steppe in *The Second Commander, 1929*

way they were painted with the fillet, their arrangement, everything was repeated on the stage, which architecturally was thus merged with the auditorium.[13]

This solution, which created an effect not unlike theatre-in-the-round (though of course in this case the audience only half encircled the performer) had grown from earlier experiments. In the early years of the century, Meyerhold had caused an outcry by removing the front curtain. In *Sister Beatrice* (1906), the action was staged in front of a flat backdrop on what was in effect a shallow strip of forestage. The lack of depth in the acting area aimed to force the production to do without wings, which Meyerhold considered to be merely devices to conceal things from the spectator. The lack of depth in this arrangement, however, denied the actor and director the full scope of the stage, and was abandoned in favour of the arrangement which unified auditorium and stage through the decor.

The chief effect of this, perhaps, was the challenge which it presented to conventional illusionistic theatre and this was reinforced by the use of 'proscenium servants'. These were first widely seen in the production of *Don Juan* (1910). Znosko-Borovsky recalled how when 'an actor had to sit down, a flunkey in livery pulled up an armchair. Little negroes ran onto the stage to help with props and accessories, and when the stone guest appeared, they hid in horror under the table.'[14] They also spread a luxurious perfume in the auditorium and rang little silver bells to recall the spectators after the interval. In fact, Meyerhold had experimented with this convention previously, for instance at Vyacheslav Ivanov's Tower in his production seven months earlier of Calderón's *Adoration of the Cross* (1910) when 'at the end of each scene two little blackamoors would draw the curtain from opposite sides'.[15]

Meyerhold had discovered these characters in the oriental theatre – the Chinese 'props man', for instance, who, all in black, is on stage throughout the play, arranging the costumes, furniture, cushions and so on. He gives the actors tea after their scene is over, and holds up strips of painted silk to indicate the location of the action. The Japanese theatre, too, had

special stage assistants, known as 'kurogo', clad in special black costumes resembling cassocks . . . When the costume of an actor playing a woman's part became disarranged at a tense moment in the drama, one of the kurogo would quickly restore the graceful folds of the actor's train and attend to his coiffure. In addition, they had the task of removing from the stage any objects dropped or forgotten by the actors. After a battle the kurogo would remove fallen helmets, weapons and cloaks. If the hero died on the stage, the kurogo would quickly cover the corpse with a black cloth, and under the cover of the cloth 'the dead actor' would run off the stage. When the course of the action required darkness on stage the kurogo would squat down at the hero's feet and illuminate his face with a candle on the end of a long stick.[16]

An oriental audience simply overlooks these extraneous attendants as a modern western audience ignores an usher showing a latecomer to his seat. But Meyerhold knew his audience in Petersburg would not ignore the 'proscenium servants'; they were a vital part of his strategy to disrupt the audience's expectations, to challenge its relationship to the stage, and to prevent the performance from being a closed entity. This is perhaps best exemplified in his production of Blok's *The Unknown Woman* (1914) where the 'proscenium servants' were dressed in grey uniforms, and all their movements as they shifted props or furniture were done with rhythmic grace. They held high on bamboo poles a green curtain behind the action till at the end of the scene they came forward and lowered it in front of the actors.

From either side were rolled out the halves of a very sharply humped bridge, and on it appeared the astrologer, observing a shooting star. One of the attendant props men raised high to the ceiling a burning flame on a thin bamboo cane, described a semicircle with it in the air, and finally lowered it to where another props man extinguished the flame in a cup of water. All the action on this bridge proceeded in a manner consistent with this spirit, and when for example one of the characters was caught in the snow, he was simply wrapped in a white muslin shawl.[17]

This was a theatre which defied and bewildered the canons of accepted criticism. The only critics likely to be able to elucidate what Meyerhold was up to were the Formalists, but they seem never to have made a systematic attempt to produce theatrical criticism. This may be regretted, for the key to the *mise-en-scène* in a production like *The Unknown Woman* is the Formalists' favourite element in any work of art, the device. The devices here operate on two levels. First, those like the muslin snowstorm, the firework star, and so on, 'make strange' the subject matter. They deform reality in order to force us to see that reality afresh, in what is, according to the Formalists, the chief function of art – to restore to us a 'fresh, child-like vision of the world'. Art exists 'in order to restore to us the perception of life', wrote Shklovsky at about the same time as Meyerhold was presenting *The Unknown Woman*, 'to make a stone stony'.[18] This is what Meyerhold was doing with the star, for instance: it was not a particular star, but it did make its audience reflect on the qualities of 'starriness'. Second, the device operates at another level when it is perceived as a device, in other words when it does not conceal what it is. In Meyerhold's case, this 'baring of the device' meant drawing attention to the theatricality of the presentation, thereby effectively demystifying the theatre and focussing precisely on the tension between the form (actors, *mise-en-scène*, and so on) and the materials (action, setting, and so on). Our recognition of this tension, and our ability to keep the different elements which create it in mind simultaneously, not only gives pleasure, but also gives us the wherewithal to make meanings.

All this was firmly embedded in Meyerhold's armoury by 1917, but it was only after the revolution that it was in any sense systematized. Then, the movement of the actors as it affected the *mise-en-scène*, for instance, became known as 'scenometry', 'a new subject for academic study', according to Garin, 'which created our antipathy to "literature" on the stage, that is, to theatre in which movement and physical expressiveness become subordinate to the insouciance of literature, narrative, the theatre of discussion'.[19] Sayler described the effect of this before the term 'scenometry' had been minted:

In Don Juan's scene with the peasant girls . . . Meyerhold has developed the amusing series of asides first to one girl and then the other in such a way that Juan describes a kind of fantastic geometric figure in his dual conversation. It is all highly artificial, just like Molière's language in the scene, but it is also highly amusing and even mildly exciting in its stimulus to our sense of gesture.[20]

This is a precise, if unconscious, description of 'baring the device'. Van Gyseghem, on the other hand, felt baffled and uncertain how to react (a response which would not necessarily have dismayed Meyerhold): 'As the play progresses, a tapestry of fantastic devices is woven by these living puppets; a theatrical tapestry which is composed not of colours and emotions or beauty but of geometrical designs, which fascinate the brain, but never touch our emotions.'[21]

Meyerhold's explorations of the problems of the *mise-en-scène* were considerably helped by the fact that as a Russian he inherited a tradition of stage design far in advance of that achieved anywhere else in the world. From 1881, Stanislavsky's cousin, Savva Mamontov, had used leading painters to design and execute theatrical settings, first at his own house, then at his 'Private Opera' which introduced the work of Rimsky-Korsakov, Borodin, Mussorgsky and other composers, as well as the singing of Fyodor Chaliapin, to the public. His first production here was of Rimsky-Korsakov's *The Snow Maiden*, designed by Victor Vasnetsov, and Mamontov went on to use Levitan, Roerich, Alexander Golovin and others. This work was developed by Sergei Diaghilev, whose presentations took Europe by storm in the first years of the twentieth century at least as much by their designs as by anything else. These ranged from Leon Bakst's riotous fantasies to Natalia Goncharova's Russian peasant style for the 1914 production of *The Golden Cockerel*, and again included work by Alexander Golovin, probably most notably for the first production of *The Firebird* in 1910.

Golovin became perhaps Meyerhold's most stimulating collaborator in the years before the October revolution. Their first joint work was the 1908 production of Hamsun's *At the Gates of the Kingdom*, and in 1910 Golovin designed the brilliant *Don Juan* in which 'stylization' of a period – that is, the reproduction of the essence of its style – replaced the conventional insistence on a literal and detailed recreation of specifics. Thus, the huge chandeliers and candelabras, the designs and patterns on the walls and panels, the rich drapery, the furniture and the carpets, in reds, browns, golds and purples, evoked the period of 'Le Roi Soleil' rather than copied a particular portion of it. Even so, the painting, for such in a sense this setting was, proved that it could act on an audience itself and not be mere background: it was uncurtained and brilliantly lit as the spectators entered the auditorium, thereby not only creating the mood Meyerhold desired but also stimulating the 'theatre-in-the-round' effect of unifying the whole of the theatre's interior.

Nevertheless, such a *mise-en-scène* was still at bottom painterly. It was the latest in the line of development from the time of the Renaissance when the discovery of perspective had led the theatre to borrow a pictorial conception and then to frame it with a proscenium arch. Meyerhold's own dissatisfaction with this tradition had been expressed in 1906 or before: 'The hills on the battlefield in *Julius Caesar* may be constructed so that they decrease in size towards the horizon, but why don't the characters become smaller, too, as they move away from us towards the hills?'[22] The relationship between auditorium and stage, spectator and actor, was still obstructed by the picture frame, and even in Golovin's most brilliant work we tend to see a *mise-en-scène* which 'houses' the action but is not a dynamic part of it.

The revolution seems to have liberated Meyerhold to take the further step

32. *The Death of Tarelkin*, 1917, designed by Boris Almedingen

needed for the *mise-en-scène* to become a full participatory member, if one may so express it, of the production. Where before he had worked for a *mise-en-scène* which had the primary function of changing the audience–stage relationship, now he saw that it could become an active component in the mechanism of the production in its own right. Just as stage wings were a means of deception, so was even the most masterly of painted sets. By removing the paint and exposing the bare wood, by tearing down all the decorations and leaving only a 'machine for acting', Meyerhold tried to create a new kind of stage action. This can be seen by comparing the distorted, closed-in world of Almedingen's designs for Meyerhold's 1917 production of *The Death of Tarelkin* with that presented by Stepanova for his production of the same play five years later. Almedingen, a former student of Golovin, created an expressionistically nightmarish world reminiscent of some film sets of the time – *The Cabinet of Dr Caligari*, for instance. But therein lies its weakness for Meyerhold: it is the face of the nightmare, its inescapable shell, but no more. Stepanova's set actually contributes independently to the action, with the chairs exploding and a mincing machine which 'devours' Mikhail Zharov's Bradakhlystova. The *mise-en-scène* plays an active part in the events of the nightmare. The contrast is equally stark between two productions Meyerhold presented within a week in 1922. *Nora* (*A Doll's House*) represented a rejection of the old: for it, he placed the old theatre's flats with their faces to the wall like a 'house of cards';[23] and five days later presented *The Magnanimous Cuckold* in a set which was, as Meyerhold desired, a 'machine for acting', and whose component parts whirred and turned explosively. The rejection of stage painting was therefore crucial, for

33. *The Death of Tarelkin,* 1922, designed by Varvara Stepanova. Note the bare brick walls at the rear

it was this which enabled Meyerhold not only to focus on the forestage as he desired but also to create a completely new dynamic factor in the production of the drama.

He discovered the key to constructivist art. According to the First Working Group of Constructivists in 1921, this aimed to 'realize the communist expression of material structures'.[24] As Christina Lodder has pointed out, it was really closer to industrial design than conventional art, and arose in part as a response to the call by Trotsky and others for a fusion of art and technology. Its creations tended to use wood, steel, wire and similar 'industrial' materials which were utilitarian, hard and clearcut, so that they often resembled objects, as sculpture usually does, but were in fact only themselves. The artists were concerned with the relationships between textures, planes and angles and so on, particularly as they reflected a contemporary and future industrial world. Its appeal to Meyerhold lay in its functionalism: it did not aim to reproduce an everyday environment, but nor was it in any sense decorative. As early as 1907, he advocated the replacement of 'the unsightly clutter of the naturalistic stage . . . by constructions'[25] and in the 1920s he claimed that the bridge in *The Unknown Woman* (1914) had been the first stage construction. Whatever the truth of that, a constructivist stage set's non-naturalistic, non-painterly qualities gave it the strengths possessed by the bare stage – throwing into relief the reality of objects and

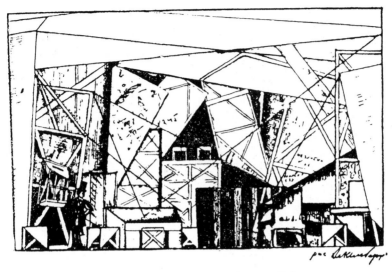

34. *Nora* (*A Doll's House*), 1922. Sketch by Boris Kelberer

people, focussing attention on essentials, and compelling the spectator to extend in his imagination what is only suggested to him by the action. At the same time, constructivism had the potential of unexpected spatial configurations: because it represented nothing, the construction offered actor and director new and unlimited challenges for working in and moving through space.

These qualities were first and perhaps best exemplified in *The Magnanimous Cuckold* (1922). The set for this was originally commissioned from the Stenberg brothers and Konstantin Medunetsky, the founders of constructivism, and contained elements from an idea worked out by Meyerhold's student Vladimir Lyutse, but in the end the construction was Lyubov Popova's. One of the most impressive of the many artists of revolutionary Russia, Popova had previously only designed theatrical costumes, for a children's play and for the 1921 Korsch Theatre production of Lunacharsky's *The Locksmith and the Chancellor*, and an unrealized mass spectacle in collaboration with Vesnin and Meyerhold. The attraction of theatre to such an artist was that here the total environment was controllable whereas in the real world any creation had to exist in conventional pre-existent surroundings. The theatre could give a glimpse of a totally transformed environment.

Popova's construction consisted of two platforms of differing heights, each reached by its own staircase and joined by a ramp. From the lower platform a slide descended and both platforms surmounted boxes constructed with vertical, horizontal and diagonal wooden slats, which made a

35. Model of the set for *The Magnanimous Cuckold*, 1922

series of panels a few of which were filled in. Behind the construction were a large trellis, three wheels, one of which was painted with the consonants of the play's author's name, and a propeller-like device pointing diagonally upwards. In front to the side was a curving, sloped bench. The woodwork was left largely bare, though some pieces were blackened with boot polish and others reddened with rouge. Popova's aims, stated a few days after the opening, were, first, 'the organization of the material elements of the spectacle as an apparatus ... utilitarian suitability must serve as the criterion'; and, second, 'to introduce material elements' which would co-ordinate the action: 'to this end the movement of the doors and window, and the rotating of the wheels were introduced into the basic score of the action; by their movement and speeds these were to underline and intensify the kinetic value of each movement of the action'.[26]

The kinetic quality of the set — the wheels and propeller whirled round with increasing speed to chime with the accelerating emotional climaxes — made it particularly dynamic and exhilarating to watch. E. Rakitina wrote: 'We will never understand [the set] correctly if we regard it statically. It is not a picture to be admired. Rather, it is a kind of machine which takes on a living existence in the course of the production.'[27] The construction is first and foremost, then, a thing in itself, a concrete object of wood and metal with its own shape, its own contribution to the action, its own challenge to the director and actor, as well, of course, as the spectator. It can be walked round, entered, bumped into, climbed on. But it also clearly evokes the windmill in which the play is set – it is a 'synthesis and interpretation of the mechanical elements' of the windmill.[28] And on another level, already hinted at in the previous chapter, it suggests a child's playground, with elements of the climbing frame, the slide and so on, a toy propeller which can never hope to lift the machine off the ground, but is fun in itself.

Yet these allusive qualities, which are in fact part of the fascination of Popova's construction, did not appeal to the artist herself who, before her tragically early death, designed one more production for Meyerhold, *Earth Rampant*, in 1923. Huntly Carter called this an 'agitational' set[29] because it involved not the cleverly synthesized creations of her earlier work, but real objects which were really utilitarian. Popova's notes for the production demonstrate this:

1. Basic structure
2. Details: a. car
           b. tractor
           c. a three-dimensional screen
           d. continual agitational slogan attached to the structure
           e. a slogan on the tractor
3. A film projector, film camera, films, slides, *Cinema Truth*
4. Objects: a coffin
           a red pall
           a small machine gun
           bicycles
           weapons
           a field kitchen
           3 field telephones
           one camp bed
           one field pack
           one large table
           maps
           2 typewriters
           2 aeroplanes (Godunov's system)
5. Lighting by searchlights. Coloured bulbs for Burbus's lantern
6. Noises
7. Music. A military orchestra
8. Parade (military section)
9. Pyrotechnics
10. Costumes: peasant group 70
            his highness 1
            Burbus's staff 13
            group of civilians: men 7 women 3[30]

36. *Earth Rampant*, 1923. The construction. Note the screen for projections and the bare brick walls at the rear

The basic structure (number one above) was a reproduction of an actual gantry crane on wheels, on which were hung the screens for projections. The rejection of any form of aesthetic consideration was made plain by Popova who declared that the props were 'taken from surrounding reality and introduced onto the stage in their normal form . . . The objects are chosen in line with relating the play's plot to the present tasks of building the republic.'[31]

Nevertheless, this design no less than that of *The Magnanimous Cuckold* made its own independent and dynamic contribution to the drama, for not only did the car and tractor drive onto the stage, but the projections changed, the fireworks exploded and so on. Moreover, the use of real objects in an artificial setting increases inevitably the tension between the materials and the form, and thereby compels the audience to question its understanding of both revolution (the subject of the play) and theatre. In Eisenstein's terminology, the *mise-en-scène* itself becomes an 'attraction', that is, 'an independent and primary element in the construction of the performance'.[32]

Eisenstein was Meyerhold's 'laboratory assistant' on the production of *The Death of Tarelkin* (1922), which came chronologically between *The Magnanimous Cuckold* and *Earth Rampant*. The setting here consisted of several freestanding constructions, each made of slats of wood painted bright white. It was designed by another constructivist, Varvara Stepanova, whose first theatre design it was. It was intended to be utilitarian to the point where the function of each piece, its responsiveness to the actor, was paramount. Each was to be comparable to a piece of gymnasium equipment, though the famous 'sausage machine' which swallowed Zharov at the top and spewed him out below, and the tall Jack-in-the-box-like construction from which actors appeared, were perhaps more ambitious than anything to be found in a gym. They also worked less satisfactorily, as did the other furniture which was frequently booby-trapped, though precisely how on any particular night even the actors did not know in advance. 'When an actor sat on the constructivist furniture, he would either be tossed into the air by a spring in the seat or a torpedo would go off under him, the chair would somehow turn into a board, a policeman would jump out like a Jack-in-the-box . . .'[33]

The 'active' furniture contributed to Meyerhold's meaning, which involved the transformation of Tarelkin the minor official into Tarelkin the fool and fooler of bureaucracy. From the Soviet side of the 1917 revolution, tsarist gloom and bitterness could be seen as funny and its stern upholders as buffoons and eccentrics. The constructions, however, were as devoid of realism as Stepanova and Meyerhold had hoped. To different spectators they conjured up ideas of prison, hospital, garden furniture, surgical machinery and rat traps. Not that such connotations were wrong. On the contrary they suggest the power the constructions had to stimulate the imagination, and in this sense they certainly contrast favourably with the sinister expressionism of the set of Meyerhold's 1917 production, which ultimately was empty of such resonances. And as a means of stimulating and fragmenting the audience, clearly they were more successful.

A year and a half after the 1922 *Death of Tarelkin*, Meyerhold attacked – and solved – the problem of making 'flats' as dynamic as his constructions had

37. *The Death of Tarelkin*, 1922. 'Boxing – Biomechanics – Constructivism'

been. In *D.E.* (1924), a series of screens, the largest about twelve feet long and nine feet tall, on small wheels and each with a self-lighting device, formed the set. Painted dull red, they had stage hands concealed behind them to push them into different positions on stage to represent different locales. They moved swiftly and unobtrusively, and formed a vital contributory part of the production, most notably in the chase scene. Here, as the fugitive ran, the walls moved to cut off his exits. Spotlights dashed wildly over the scene as the tempo increased till the runner got between two screens just as they came together and seemed to disappear. This was clearly an 'attraction' – one of the rare occasions in theatre history when stage 'flats' have played a dynamic part in stage action – and was one of the things uppermost in John Dos Passos's mind when he wrote that 'if there is going to be any more theatre, the future of it lies in that production'.[34]

D.E. was one in a series of experiments with dynamic decor. Others which might be mentioned included *The Mandate* (1925), where two revolving stages carried actors, furniture and props on and off in unexpected and provoking groupings, and *Lake Lyul* (1923) which developed from *The Death of Tarelkin* the use of slatted furniture; here it could be reassembled in different ways for different purposes. More interesting in this production was the central construction, a scaffolding three storeys high, with a lift running between them. In *The Government Inspector* (1926), the stage was backed by a semi-circle of fifteen doors of polished redwood and many of the scenes came onto the stage on small trucks, pre-set with furniture, props and even actors.

38. Model of the set for *D.E.*, 1924

The tiny space available on one of these wagons was a useful contrast to the huge expanse of stage available in the few scenes when they were not employed. Walter Benjamin commented:

The guiding principle of this production, the concentration of the action into an extremely restricted area, creates an extraordinarily luxurious density of dramatic values, without however neglecting the acting dimension. The high point of all this came in a party scene, which was a masterpiece of staging. There were about fifteen people huddled on the tiny performance area, grouped between barely suggested pillars made of paper... On the whole, the effect is like the architecture of a cake (a very Muscovite simile – only the cakes here could explain the comparison), or better yet, like the grouping of dancing puppets on a musical clock . . .[35]

After seeing *The Forest*, he noted: 'For the first time I clearly grasped the function of the constructivist use of the stage; it had never been this evident to me at Tairov's in Berlin and even less so in photographs.'[36]

The designer of *Lake Lyul* had been Viktor Shestakov, at that time a member of the First Working Group of Constructivists, who joined the Meyerhold State Theatre to design the 1928 production of *Woe to Wit*. This set, though in a sense a 'construction', was more architectural than a 'machine for acting'. A central acting area was flanked at the back by a high semi-circular platform, reached via a special staircase, and at the sides by galleries with steps down to stage level. The silver metal of this construction set off the orange and red of the moveable screens which were used to change the shape of the acting area. Though the construction at the rear evoked associations

39. The moving screens for *D.E.*

with the world of radio, the only strong connotation this set possessed, apart from its seeming modernity, was of the entrance hall of a nineteenth-century mansion. Architecture is more precise, less allusive then even the most utilitarian construction, and after this Meyerhold's most constant designer (usually working to Meyerhold's own rough plan) was Sergei Vakhtangov, who had trained as an architect, not an artist.

The progression of Meyerhold's work is clear: from the bas-relief of his early years (*Sister Beatrice*) to the luxurious all-enveloping painting of his period at the Imperial Theatres (*Don Juan*) to the revolutionary constructions after 1917 (*The Magnanimous Cuckold*) and then on to the architectural approach (*Woe to Wit*). Unfortunately this last phase was never properly worked out: by the time Meyerhold reached it, around 1930, he was moving out of his own theatre and thus depriving himself of the opportunity of pursuing it successfully. Nevertheless, as research work, a sequence of investigations as to what the *mise-en-scène* can contribute to a modern theatre dedicated to popular theatricality, Meyerhold's achievement is extraordinarily impressive. And the fact that so much of it is now common currency in the theatre is evidence of its influence.

The same is true of his experiments with the other elements of the *mise-en-scène*. In the matter of stage furniture, for instance, he early discovered the value of using a minimum amount and that often exaggerated as a means of focussing the spectator's eye: the stage in the projected production of *Schluck und Jau* (1905) was dominated by the vast royal bed and canopy, that in his production of Schnitzler's *The Cry of Life* (1906) by an absurdly long divan.

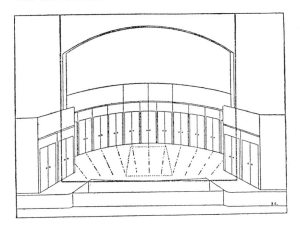

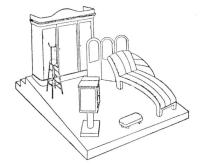

40. The set for *The Government Inspector*, 1926. General plan and two 'inset' scenes on trucks

And even at the height of his career Meyerhold used the same technique. In *The Government Inspector* (1926) much of the furniture was stylized, highly curvacious and slightly too sensual, while in *Woe to Wit* (1928), the billiard balls no less than the banquetting table were oversized. But the furniture not only impinged on the eye, like the 'scenery' it was capable of its own dynamic. In *The Mandate* (1925), says Huntly Carter,

The furniture moved about like, and with, the actors . . . Take scene 2 . . . An armchair enters, followed by a velvet stool and a small graceful pedestal. These cross the stage, actorwise. Then enters a large trunk with a woman seated on it. The accessories meet and make a design . . . In one scene there was only a couch. It was an essential actor in a piece of comedy. It concealed the players, it enabled them to do their business in many ways. It took part in the action as much as the players did.[37]

Meyerhold's approach to props on stage was similar. He usually tried to fix on a few props which were typical of the situation and ruthlessly to discard all others. As he put it himself: 'A single characteristic object replaces many that are less characteristic.'[38] Props thus become – again, rather like the stage constructions – something more than simply the things they are but less than merely symbols of something else. This can be seen in Meyerhold's use of flowers, at least before 1917. In 1906, his *Hedda Gabler* set was suffused in white chrysanthemums, to reinforce the cold, regal tone of the production, whereas the pot of geraniums on stage in *The Fairground Booth* (1906) was incongruous and ironic. In *Crimes and Crimes* (1912), Meyerhold wanted Henriette's first appearance 'to predict the outcome to the audience. She entered in a looping path, without looking at Maurice, who was standing by the counter and looking at her. Meyerhold told me [the actress playing Henriette] at the rehearsal: "This way you draw Maurice into the noose immediately." In my hands I held large red flowers on long stems.'[39]

Having chosen the typical or significant prop, Meyerhold then frequently exaggerated it, aiming to achieve something of the effect of a film close-up. One of the most famous examples of this was in fact never seen by an audience, the scene in Hauptmann's *Schluck und Jau* which Meyerhold rehearsed for the Moscow Art Theatre Studio in 1905 when the ladies-in-waiting all sit round the edge of the playing area embroidering the same ridiculously long scarf with large ivory needles. In justification for this kind of grotesquerie more than thirty years later, Meyerhold quoted a story Eisenstein told of a child illustrating 'lighting the stove' by drawing firewood, the stove and a chimney. 'But in the middle of the room there was a huge rectangle covered with zigzags. What was it? Matches, apparently. The child drew the matches on a scale appropriate to their crucial role in the action he was depicting.'[40] And the effect Meyerhold achieved, at least at his best, may be gathered from the impression left on Sergei Radlov's memory by *The Government Inspector*:

A silver bowl filled with pieces of fat, succulent watermelon. Enchanted objects, wobbling slightly, float from hand to hand, passed by servants in a trance. Huge splendid divans, like elephants carved from mahogany, stand poised in majestic slumber. What is this – *Caligari* in slow motion by some lunatic projectionist?[41]

Robert Wiene's film, *The Cabinet of Dr Caligari* (1920), in fact derived much of its strength from its use of light, a factor which Meyerhold showed he understood when he made his first few films in the immediate pre-revolutionary years. Light in film, particularly in black-and-white film, is not just a naturalistic accompaniment, but inevitably makes its own contribution, and Meyerhold's stage work has that kind of sensitivity. His two favourite states of lighting were an even, overall wash effect, and sharp directional lighting. Examples of the first were *Sister Beatrice* (1906), where the flat unvaried lighting complemented the two-dimensionality of the compositions, and, after the revolution, *The Dawns* (1920) and *The Death of Tarelkin* (1922), when

41. *Prelude*, 1933. Nunbakh with the bust of Goethe

the harsh white light emphasized the utilitarian, and perhaps the circus, characteristics of the productions.

More striking perhaps was Meyerhold's use of directional lighting, which he was among the earliest directors to exploit. In *The Life of Man* (1907), each scene used a single source of light, 'sufficient only to illuminate the furniture placed about it and the actor who is near the light source',[42] while in *Spring Awakening* (1907), each individual episode was picked out like a miniature in a single beam which cut through the darkness. The same device, perhaps with greater sophistication, was used in the productions of *Lake Lyul* (1923), where the multistorey tower construction lent itself particularly well to such an effect, and *The Forest* (1924), which Meyerhold had split up into thirty-three tiny episodes from its conventional five-act structure. In *A List of Assets* (1931), he used a thin beam to highlight, for instance, Tatarov's shaking hand as it tore out the page of Goncharova's diary, while in *Prelude* (1933) a single projector picked out the despairing face of Nunbakh and the peaceful bust of Goethe.

At best, Meyerhold was able to use the lighting as another creative, contributory element in the whole. In *D.E.* (1924), there was general, even lighting for much of the time, which showed what was happening without trying to create a 'mood'; suddenly this gave way at particular moments to flickering, stroboscopic effects of waving spotlight beams to add dynamism to the action construct. Quite different, though probably as successful, was the stylized light from the chandeliers, candelabra and candles in *Don Juan* (1910), when even the auditorium remained illuminated. A note from Meyerhold to Golovin asked for 'a genuine "Schattenspiel" after the manner of the old travelling theatres' at one moment in Act 3[43] – a rare glimpse of his desire to use lighting, as he did every theatrical device, to heighten the popular-grotesque element in the work.

Meyerhold's refusal to conceal the source of lighting is less well known than Brecht's similar refusal, which however it considerably predates. The same is true of his 'literarization of the theatre' which, Brecht wrote in 1931 after he had become acquainted with Meyerhold's work, 'needs to be developed to the utmost degree'.[44] In fact, Meyerhold had begun to do this as early as 1906 in *Sister Beatrice* when the initial letters 'BVM' (Blessed Virgin Mary) were projected onto the backdrop. By the 1920s, he not only used captions to announce the scene to come, as with the thirty-three episodes of *The Forest* (1924), he was experimenting with much more sophisticated uses of literarization.

In *The Magnanimous Cuckold* (1922), one of the 'mill wheels' had painted on it, broken into three pieces, the consonants of the author's name in roman, not cyrillic, script. To the average Moscow theatregoer, this could have meant little. Only when the wheel whirs round, do the meaningless letters blur into a unified colour pattern, reflecting the production's dynamic concern with meaning produced through movement. *D.E.* (1924), on the other hand, capitalized on cinema practice, particularly the silent cinema's use of captions, with three separate screens which aimed to create a dialectical interplay relevant to the action. The large centre screen provided not only information about the scene but also ironic comments, while two smaller screens carried political appeals, propaganda slogans, quotations from speeches by Lenin and others, as well as pictures of various kinds.

Perhaps the most interesting and impressive of all were the projections

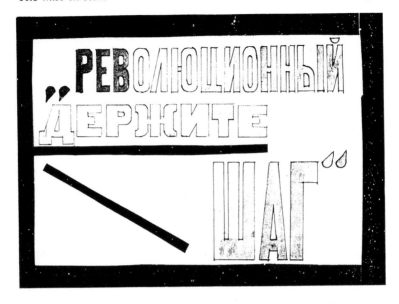

42. Slogans for projections in *Earth Rampant*: 'Keep up the revolutionary pace' (red letters, black outline); 'Episode 7: Shearing the Sheep'

used in *Earth Rampant* (1923). Unlike the usual projected titles, even those we see today, Popova's designs and lettering themselves contribute to the meaning of the play. Thus, in episode 1, there are slogans like 'Knock off the crowns of the last of the tsars' and 'The machine has conquered water, air, underground: the mechanization of agriculture will conquer earth.' The second half of the play begins with the projections: 'Education is the sword of revolution' followed by 'The struggle against counter-revolutionary speculation and sabotage.' Episode 7, 'Shearing the Sheep', includes the attractive 'Keep up the revolutionary pace', while the last episode, 'Night', ends with the rousing slogan: 'Long live the union of workers and peasants.' The modernistic lettering, in yellow and black or red and black, and the frequent changes of slogan, together with the interspersed sequences of film on another screen (there were thirty-two of these altogether) add a dialectical zest to the presentation. The contradiction between screen action and live action, words spoken and words read, doing and writing, and so on, make for a peculiarly dynamic excitement.

Meyerhold never quite achieved such an impact with costume, which at least before the revolution tended towards the fantastic and the decorative. At their best, the costumes in Meyerhold's pre-1917 productions served the identifying functions of the *commedia dell' arte* mask, recognizable but exaggerated. But already by 1917, for instance in his studio presentation of 1915, he had used a uniform costume for all his students, and it was this strand, focussed increasingly in the constructivists' utilitarianism, that was to be developed most interestingly after the revolution.

For *The Magnanimous Cuckold* (1922), Popova designed a blue *prozodezhda*, or work outfit, consisting of a loose shirt and jodhpurs for men and three-quarter-length skirts for women. The geometric pattern was intended to enhance the human form; characterization was indicated only by a suggestive adornment such as Bruno's pompoms or the mayor's coat like a laboratory assistant's. For Popova, the *prozodezhda* represented a prototype of an actor's working clothes; the actor gained freedom of movement in it, but could not hide from an audience as many costumes permitted. Perhaps inadvertently, these costumes helped the intention of the production: the actors' work clothes suggested that the stage was a workplace, and the construction a machine, while the geometrical distortion they gave to the actor's movement resembled futurist pictures, dynamic but generalized rather than idiosyncratic of individualistic. This connotation was emphasized by the vague echo of the contemporary pilot or motorist.

The clothes Stepanova designed for *The Death of Tarelkin* (1922) were meant to capitalize on the success of Popova's *prozodezhdy*. They were yellow with dark blue patterning intended to emphasize the formation of the body's

43. 'Prozodezhda', or work costume, for actor number 5, by Lyubov Popova

movements, as well as to give each character an appropriate measure of individuality. Unfortunately, it seems that these aims were not fulfilled, since the looseness of the costumes actually concealed the movement of the limbs, and under the monochrome brightness of the lighting design the subtleties of the individualization in the costumes was lost.

After this, Meyerhold did no more notable experiments with *prozodezhdy*, work clothes, as such, considering them more suitable for training and

БРАНДАХЛЫСТОВА

44. Costume for Brandakhlystova in *The Death of Tarelkin*, 1922, by Varvara Stepanova. See illustration 24

rehearsal work, and for the overtly agitational theatre of the Blue Blouse troupes. The effect of uniformity, however, continued to interest Meyerhold. Valentin Pluchek recalled how, in *The Second Commander*, 'we, the young people who appeared as the partisan masses, took up positions along the whole circumference of the structure. Meyerhold dressed us in sheepskin coats, felt boots and fur caps. These coats, hats and boots in combination with the grey background of the structure created a single colour.'[45]

This kind of contribution to the *mise-en-scène* was not newly discovered by

45. *The Government Inspector*, 1926. Episode 14

Meyerhold in the 1920s. In 1907, Alexander Benois wrote of Meyerhold's production of Sologub's *Death's Victory*: 'One wants to take a pencil and sketch those balanced clusters of people, those combinations of gestures and expressions, those beautiful lines.'[46] It was a device used most strikingly, perhaps, in *The Government Inspector* (1926) in, for instance, episode 14. What is apparent in such scenes is a visual rhythm created by the actors' bodies. Often in Meyerhold's productions, gestures or poses repeat of complement or contradict the patterns in the set, as the mystics did in *The Fairground Booth* or the characters in *The Magnanimous Cuckold*, to create a dynamic and complex *mise-en-scène*. Its importance was summarized by Meyerhold himself when he remarked: 'Acting is melody, and *mise-en-scène* is harmony.'[47]

5   Rhythm

Melody and harmony, to which Meyerhold compared acting and the *mise-en-scène*, mean nothing without rhythm. And attention to rhythm was perhaps Meyerhold's chief guiding principle throughout his career. 'A performance of a play is an alternation of dynamic and static moments, as well as dynamic moments of different kinds', he said in the 1930s. 'That is why the gift of rhythm seems to me one of the most important a director can have.'[1]

Meyerhold's preoccupation with rhythm had by then been evident for over thirty years. In 1906, he had written that 'the secret of Chekhov's mood lies in the *rhythm* of his language',[2] while Vera Verigina, an actress at the abortive Theatre Studio of 1905, described Meyerhold using an externally-imposed rhythm as the means of controlling the performance: 'It was essential to keep that rhythm all the time so as not to be seized by personal emotion.'[3]

Rhythm was seen at this period as an expressive element in its own right. Later, in the years after the revolution, Meyerhold came to think of rhythm in the theatre rather as the Formalist critics thought of it in poetry: a major means by which the artist 'deforms' his subject matter. Each component is subjected to the rhythm, which is thus not merely an organizing agent but has a direct impact upon the meaning as well.

This began with the *mise-en-scènes* themselves. In *The Forest* (1924), for example, the stage was dominated by the long, curved, descending walkway. The action cut rapidly between the gradual, unhurried approach of the two strolling players down this walkway, and the contrasting comings and goings in the country house represented on the main stage. The stage set itself was thus a factor in the creation of the dramatic rhythm. This was even more evident with the moving screens of *D.E.* (1924) or the turning wheels of *The Magnanimous Cuckold* (1922). In *The Government Inspector* (1926), the contrast between the scenes played on the cramped trucks and those on the open stage linked the dramatic rhythms closely to the spatial rhythms.

The actors were also used rhythmically. The use of a group or crowd of actors as a unit of rhythmic space was commented on by Sollertinsky with reference to Meyerhold's pre-revolutionary opera productions: 'Rhythm . . . could be sensed not only in the movements but also in the frozen immobility; the chorus . . . he breaks up into stylized, sculpted groups, only all of a sudden – in a mighty contrast – they erupt in a quick, agitated movement, which,

46. The set for *The Forest*, 1924

however, is still rhythmic.'[4] In *The Magnanimous Cuckold* (1922), this happens not only in 'crowd' scenes such as that when the men dance the 'Chechotka' while waiting to enter Stella's bed, but also in scenes like that of Bruno and Estrugo leaning down to Stella and the nurse.

Meyerhold distinguished 'rhythm' from 'metre'. He wanted 'not metre, but rhythm, rhythm and again rhythm',[5] he told the pianist, Arnshtam, and by way of explanation contrasted the circus performer with actor. Where the circus artist needs music of a strict metre, based on a metronome, perhaps, the actor should learn to work rhythmically within musical phrases.[6] 'The rhythmical background of the music helps the actor to play his part with greater precision', he told Gladkov.[7] This did not represent an oppressive control. On the contrary, the 'free movement of the actor' should 'be laid out over an entire musical phrase. A slice of scenic action had accordingly to be subordinated to an entire musical period. However, he did not like the word "subordinate". Not to be subordinate to the music, but to breathe it, to live it – repeatedly he reiterated this.'[8]

The stage movement in *Columbine's Scarf* 'lost its arbitrary character' through the use of music.[9] In *Teacher Bubus*,

the performance began with the tense opening bars of Chopin's Twelfth Étude. The clamour and noise of a crowd in the street outside also wafted in. Well-trained flunkeys rushed anxiously about, conveying their anxiety to the spectators. The hasty appearance of each of the characters through the bamboo curtain was accompanied by the characteristic jangling of the bamboo rods against each other . . . To the music of Chopin's Fifth Étude, Baron Feuervary entered. He had the brittle composure of an extremely refined parasite. Top hat, gloves, short cloak, walking stick. 'What's happening?' he asked in a

47. *The Magnanimous Cuckold*. The men dance the 'Chechotka'

high voice, with rhetorical haughtiness. 'The unemployed are demonstrating, Herr Baron.' Valentine's replies are precise, deferential, and imperceptibly ironic. Valentine's movements are dynamic – Figaro in the twentieth century. The rhythm of the Chopin Étude gives the opportunity for completely different, free, rhythmic configurations of movement and speech to each character.[10]

A performance of this kind could only be the product of intense training and this, of course, is what Meyerhold's biomechanics provided. N.F. Chuzhak pointed out in 1923 that 'Constructivist gestures, movement and pantomime (Vs. Meyerhold's "Biomechanics")' meant 'the rhythmical organization of the actor',[11] and Garin has described

working on movement strictly accompanied by music . . . Beginning with elementary movement according to the laws of nature, we proceeded to more complicated problems: on a canvas of metre, we mastered free rhythmical movement, and finally mastery of free movement according to the laws of unrestricted counterpoint. After this we apprehended without difficulty the tempi and character of movement though music: legato, staccato, etc. Movement to music was for us connected to yet another problem: the coordination of the self in time and space. Coordination demanded great precision, an absolute feeling for time, and precise calculation – to count in fractions of seconds. Then, having mastered the coordination of the self with partners, with objects and props, we proceeded in earnest to the basis of a composition.[12]

Many of Meyerhold's productions, particularly those with the biomechanically-trained actors, had a dance-like quality, and he had himself gained some experience in dance, most notably when he appeared as Pierrot

48. *Columbine's Scarf,* 1910, designed by Nikolai Sapunov. Note the grotesque figure of the conductor at the rear

in Mikhail Fokine's ballet, *Carnival,* with Nijinsky as Florestan and Karsavina as Columbine. Of course, Fuchs had argued in *The Stage of the Future* that rhythm was the basis of the actor's art, since that art had evolved out of dance. But for Meyerhold the key was much more precise. It lay in his understanding and use of the pause – the rhythmic counterpart of the actor's 'negation'.[13] In oriental theatre, the pause is regarded as the repository of true imaginative beauty: 'In a moment of pause a landscape may touch your heart or a warrior display his military value.'[14] It is an attitude rooted in traditional Chinese philosophies: emptiness is the highest achievement of Lao-tse, it signifies harmony between heaven and earth in Chuang-tsu, it conveys the greatest emotional tension in Po Tsui-i. From this, perhaps, comes Meyerhold's belief in the eloquence of the pause – in *Crimes and Crimes* (1912), to pick just one example, several commentators noted how the pauses were fraught with almost unbearable emotion – as well as his ability to use it as a structuring device – in *Sister Beatrice* (1906), 'the group of nuns often spoke in whispers, carefully graduating and measuring pauses. It was through precise execution of the diverse pauses that Meyerhold created the rhythm of the production. It was by the pauses that the movements and gestures were cued.'[15]

The use of the pause, then, allowed the performance to be controlled rhythmically without it becoming dance. In *Don Juan* (1910), for instance, 'the most important thing, and that which above all struck the public and provoked the most argument, was the dance rhythm which characterized each part. But the actors were not transformed into dancers.'[16] In *Columbine's Scarf* (1910), the tempo throughout was controlled by the grotesque conductor and his band. In *Teacher Bubus* (1925),

Meyerhold finds in the mournful melodies of Chopin a fit expression of doomed Western Europe. There is a sort of decadent morbid beauty in the outward appearance of the piece ... The actors are surrounded by a lattice-work of bamboo poles which emit a weird and doleful note when touched. The languid dancing movements of the actors, combined with the unexpectedness of the *mise-en-scène*, supply a rhythm of hopelessness and of dead beauty.[17]

In *Woe to Wit* (1928), each episode was marked off by the sounding of a gong. Individual scenes were rhythmically structured round some action, as in episode 11 when Sophia and Chatsky engage in bitter exchanges in a shooting gallery, their remarks punctuated by gunshots.

The rhythmic structuring and significance were frequently the first impression a production by Meyerhold made on an unsuspecting spectator. Thus, *The Forest* (1924) began when

suddenly on the back wall of the stage an announcement of the play and place are flung in cinematic form, then several figures run on; they are priests and choirboys bearing aloft church banners and icons, the priests have caricaturish noses and straggling beards. They go off by a door in front of the would-be proscenium. The lights on the stage go up, hard glittering lights which reveal every corner of the stage space in all its crudeness of brick and metal, paint and canvas.[18]

The Lady of the Camellias had a not dissimilar opening: 'Suddenly there was a crash on a huge gong and the lights flashed out – another crash and on the stage lights snapped up and the play began.'[19]

Some endings, too, made their mark largely by rhythmic means. In *The Mandate* (1925), there was a gradual freeze and then the bearing into oblivion on the revolving stage of the 'former people', causing Stanislavsky to say that 'Meyerhold had achieved in this act what I have only dreamed of'.[20] His most famous finale was undoubtedly that of *The Government Inspector* (1926). Here the news of Khlestakov's imposture reduces the mayor to gibbering idiocy and he is removed in a straitjacket while his wife swoons and is borne away. The church bells ring out dementedly, joined by police whistles and the music of a wandering Jewish band whose playing spurs the town officials into a mad gavotte through the audience. A screen rises at the front of the stage, with the legend: 'The Goverment Inspector from Saint Petersburg has arrived, with instructions from the Tsar. He demands your immediate attendance at the Inn.'[21] The screen continues to rise, and as it disappears into the flies above, it discloses on the stage waxwork models of the town bureaucrats in grotesque attitudes, literally petrified. Almost as effective was the end of *The Last Fight*

49. *The Government Inspector, 1926.* The final tableau

(1931), when the twenty-seven Soviet servicemen faced an imaginary enemy. As the guns and cannon boomed from all parts of the theatre and light
beams wavered, a 'plant' in the audience began to weep. Then a Maurice
Chevalier *chanson* blared out, and the last surviving sailor crawled to a
blackboard where he scrawled the number of Soviet citizens left to fight after
the deaths of his contingent:

$$\begin{array}{r} 162{,}000{,}000 \\ -27 \\ \hline 161{,}999{,}973 \end{array}$$

He died. Then he stood up and said: 'Comrades! All who are prepared to
defend the Soviet Union! Please stand up!' Everyone always did.

Even so brief a description of the finale of *The Last Fight* shows how it was
structured musically around the booming of the guns and the relaying of the
Maurice Chevalier song. In other words, it is a musical conception.
Meyerhold was himself an accomplished musician and in a production like
Teacher Bubus (1925) took immense trouble over the music. He made his
pianist play almost all the piano works by Chopin and Liszt through to him,
finally choosing over forty for incorporation into the production. For two
months, he and Arnshtam, the pianist, worked together, Meyerhold 'composing' the production while Arnshtam played over the pieces.[22] Though he
often used period music like this, Meyerhold also collaborated with contem-

porary composers such as Mikhail Kuzmin, whose 'tender, languorous music'[23] was so evocative in *The Fairground Booth* (1906) and Sergei Prokofiev, to whom he gave the scenario for *The Love of Three Oranges*.

Meyerhold's use of music was central to his organization of rhythm. Music was a constant feature virtually throughout every production – there was hardly a Meyerhold production without a vast amount of 'incidental' music, from his 1904 production of *A Midsummer Night's Dream*, which used Mendelssohn's score. The decisive influence here was probably Wagner, with his notion that the subtext of the drama is revealed in the music, but Meyerhold was also struck by the Lao-tse concept that music penetrated the realm of the spirit and pervaded inanimate nature. And once he had been faced with an opera (Wagner's *Tristan and Isolde* in 1909), he realized that treating a play as a musical score rather than as a libretto opened new windows on the practice of theatre.

The variety of uses to which Meyerhold put music demonstrates this. In *Teacher Bubus* (1925), it was a means of revealing the unspoken: 'when Stefka says: "Why? Well, because . . ." and then falls silent, the music speaks for her. Music reveals the inner essence.'[24] In *Woe to Wit* (1928), it served for a more subtle shading of emotional or psychological background, using different pieces of music to highlight different aspects of Chatsky: a piece by Beethoven reflected his sympathy with the Decembrist reformers, one by Mozart his romantic melancholy, one by Field his love of Sophia, and so on. Less personalized comment came in *The Forest* (1924) in the use of the folk-like tune, 'Kirpichiki', to accompany Aksyusha and Pyotr as they swung on the giant stride and as they left for greener pastures at the end of the play. Music was also used to create the impression of a period or a mood, the music of Rameau in *Don Juan*, for instance. In fact Meyerhold's productions always had a more or less complex sound score which served as a major means of organizing the rhythmic structure of the performance. *D.E.* was notably eclectic in this respect. A smoochy foxtrot was contradicted by a vigorous march. There were excerpts from several different symphonies, as well as snatches or verses from popular songs, including the Internationale. There was also a good deal of jazz – for a few weeks, Sidney Bechet's Quintet, then touring the USSR, played every night. And in the overall pattern, there were also gunshots and explosions, and the roar of a real motorcycle. The 'sound pattern of the performance' may have been, as Golovashenko says, 'loud and harsh';[25] it was also responsible in large measure for weaving the disparate elements of the piece together.

D.E. consisted of fifteen episodes, related by theme and to some extent by but not by the conventional means of continuing characters running he plot. It was a sort of cross between a drama and a review, and

50. A scene from *D.E.*, 1924

probably the most fragmented in that sense of all Meyerhold's productions. But to break down the given script was his deliberate practice. The three scenes of Schnitzler's *The Veil of Pierrette* became the fourteen mordant episodes of *Columbine's Scarf* (1910), and the conventional act and scene structure of *Woe to Wit* (1928) was disrupted to form seventeen summary episodes. Perhaps most interesting was Meyerhold's reconstruction of the naturalistic, slow-paced *The Forest* (1924) into thirty-three episodes, arranged on the principles of Eisenstein's 'collision montage', 'each one conflicting with the next'.[26]

Such an arrangement serves on a simple level as an example of the 'grotesque'. Meyerhold seems to have first used this term in 1911, long before the concept of 'montage' was formulated, but as early as 1904 he had written to Chekhov that Act 3 of *The Cherry Orchard* contained 'merry-making in which were heard the sounds of death',[27] indicating his fascination with such contradictions. His production of *The Fairground Booth* two years later may be seen as an early attempt to realize this on the stage. The real cranberry juice which the clown bleeds, the figure of the beautiful Columbine as Death, the fact that a crude fairground farce is used to voice the purest, most romantic yearnings, all these show Meyerhold expressing the 'sounds of death' in the 'merry-making'. They conform to Bakshy's definition of the grotesque as 'a perpetual play of contrasts following upon each other. Sublimity and triviality, beauty and ugliness, joy and sorrow, courage and cowardice, are all interwoven in a fantastic pattern as were the flowers and human figures on the walls of Roman grottoes.'[28]

By the time Bakshy wrote this, however, Meyerhold's own view of the grotesque had become more sophisticated. In 1912 he had quoted approvingly Wolzogen's definition of the grotesque as implying 'something hideous and strange, a humorous work which with no apparent logic combines the most dissimilar elements by ignoring their details and relying on its own originality, borrowing from every source anything which satisfies its *joie de vivre* and its capricious, mocking attitude to life'.[29] *Columbine's Scarf* (1910) may be said to be the incarnation of this kind of grotesque, since, as Meyerhold intended, its very rhythms jangled and disorientated the spectators. But in the years immediately after the revolution, though Meyerhold still saw the grotesque as 'the basic characteristic of the theatre', he found increasing difficulty in distinguishing it from surrealism and parody: the grotesque, he wrote in 1922, was

intentional exaggeration and distortion of nature and the combination of objects which neither nature nor our daily experience combine, along with the insistent underlining of the material and ordinary sense of the form thus created. The absence of such insistence transfers the manner of distorting and combining into the realm of surrealist play of fantasy, thus transforming the grotesque into the fantastic. In the realm of the grotesque when ready-made composition is replaced by its exact opposite or when known and esteemed methods are applied to the representation of objects the opposite of that which established these methods – this is called parody.[30]

Earth Rampant (1923), in which 'the heroic and the fairground show were oddly combined [and] tragic motifs alternated with vulgar farce',[31] was largely grotesque, but contained elements of fantasy and parody, too, and showed that by then the 'grotesque' was too limited as a description of Meyerhold's work.

The importance of 'underlining' insistently the 'material and ordinary sense of the form' put him remarkably close – once again – to the Formalists, and his method of constructing plays through a series of 'alienating devices' put together as a sort of collage of episodes is almost one which might have been promulgated by an orthodox Formalist. He admitted using 'devices'[32] (a key Formalist notion), estranging the play, particularly by breaking up its flow and recreating it in short episodes, and revealing the theatricality or make-believe of the entertainment, for instance by not attempting to conceal the pianist from the audience in *Teacher Bubus* (1925). It was Eisenstein's essay on 'The Montage of Attractions', published in 1923 in *LEF*, the journal most clearly promoting Formalist views, that crystallized what Meyerhold was actually doing.

In essence, Eisenstein argued that a production should be built as a sequence of independent, arbitrarily-conceived 'attractions', 'jolts' to the spectator, artistic, emotional, psychological or whatever, which, when correctly arranged, would inevitably lead him or her to certain conclusions. The correct arranging of the 'jolts' was the montage. It bears a striking similarity to the theory of the Opoyaz group of Formalists that the plot of a work is 'an artistically ordered presentation of motifs,'[33] and indeed a number of artists seem to have reached a similar point in the development of their work around this time. Lev Kuleshov, whose film studio was on the floor above Meyerhold's theatre workshop at GVYTM, and some of whose students also and simultaneously attended Meyerhold's courses, came to the conclusion that the order in which pieces of film were joined (the montage), not the apparent 'content' of the shots themselves, made the primary impact upon the spectator, that in fact it was in the montage that the core of the meaning resided. Kuleshov's student, Vsevolod Pudovkin, worked out a theory of 'link montage' where the 'attractions' did not collide with each other, as in Eisenstein's theory, but were linked as in a chain. Meyerhold himself felt that the theory of the montage of attractions had much in common with that of cubism, and in practice, and perhaps pragmatically, based much of his work on it.

Certainly one can analyse his productions and note the barrage of arbitrarily-chosen 'attractions' they seem to contain – the circus props, bladders on sticks, trapezes of *The Death of Tarelkin* (1922) for instance. Van Gyseghem, having watched Meyerhold rehearse a tiny self-contained sequence, wrote that on stage it would only last 'a second or two and will pass without arousing any particular comment, but a momentary impression will have been made and registered. Each tiny scene of this kind is a brick in the

51. An 'attraction' from Eisenstein's *The Wise Man*, 1923

building of the edifice which is the whole play.'[34] To continue the metaphor, where Meyerhold's method involves, as is implied here, placing a number of separate 'bricks' together, the usual naturalistic method of play construction is to erect a seamless edifice of concrete or plaster or anything which tries to conceal the 'joins'. In Meyerhold's theatre, each episode was complete in itself and was played as an independent turn. The actor used the principle of the mask or the 'set role' because in a turn he had no time, even if he had the inclination, laboriously to build a character. Each 'brick' or turn is a rhythmic element, and the composition is thus fundamentally a rhythmic construction.

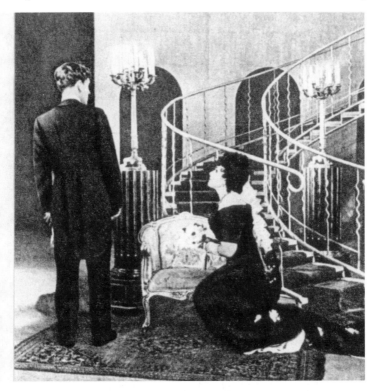

52. *The Lady of the Camellias*, 1934, with Zinaida Raikh as Marguerite Gautier

From this, the near-Formalist approach seems to slip almost inadvertently into something closer to a Marxist one. Andrei Bely, after teaching poetry for a year in Meyerhold's Workshop, wrote in 1929 his essay 'Rhythm as Dialectic' in which the equivalent of Meyerhold's ideas of 'reject' and 'negate' are interpreted as a contradiction or antithesis of the flow of the movement, and are thus inherently dialectical. Meyerhold, of course, drew inspiration from diverse intellectual traditions – film theory, Formalism and Marxism, certainly, but also the tenets of Chinese philosophy, Wagner, Fuchs and others mentioned earlier. Though his work seems to indicate the relevance of Formalism to a genuine Marxist aesthetic (as opposed to the bogus one of 'socialist realism'), he was in no sense in the business of demonstrating or signifying particular theoretical positions.

Nevertheless, it should be noted that Eisenstein's theory of the montage of attractions was worked out while its author was working in the closest collaboration with Meyerhold, and the latter certainly clung onto it. In 1936 he wrote:

When we come to examine Eisenstein's pronouncements we shall see how he divides up everything into 'attractions' – that is, into episodes, each with an unfailingly effective conclusion. He constructs these episodes according to musical principles, not with the conventional aim of advancing the narrative. This may sound rather abstruse unless we understand the nature of rhythm.[35]

That Meyerhold was writing of himself as much as of Eisenstein is demonstrated by the plan Houghton obtained of *The Lady of the Camellias* (1934), in which the left-hand column listed the titles of the episodes and the right-hand column the rhythm of the action:

ACT I

1. After the Grand Opera and strolling at the Fete — Andante / Allegro grazioso / Grave

2. One of the Nights — Capriccioso / Lento (trio) / Scherzando / Largo e mesto

3. The Meeting — Adagio / Coda. Strepitoso.

ACT II

1. Dreams of a Rural Idyll — Allegretto / Tenerezza / Intermedietto

2. The Money of the Count de Girey — Moderato. Secco / Agitato

3. Confusion of a Courtesan — Lamentoso / Molto appassionato

ACT III

1. Bougival — Giocoso

2. Bourgeois Morals — Freddo / Dolce / Impetuoso / Lacrimoso

3. Shattered Dreams — Leno con dolore / Inquieto

ACT IV

1. Olympe's Feast — Tempo vivo / Tempo di ballo

2. Again in the role of a Courtesan — Tempo di valse / Allegro agitato

3. Parole d'honneur — Espressivo / Piu mosso / Lugubre

ACT V

1.	Abandoned	Tempo commodo
		Largo e mesto
2.	A late returning	Amoroso
3.	'And life goes on'	Coda. Spianato.[36]

There is here a plainly dialectical relationship between the montage of fragmented episodes listed on the left, and the total rhythmical and musical conception on the right. The final strength of Meyerhold's mature work lay in large measure in the tension which precisely this contradiction created.

6   Meanings

The question to be asked of Meyerhold's mature work is not so much *what* it means as *how* it means, for it is in his ways of meaning that his work is original.

'Before the director can start work', Meyerhold told Boris Zakhava in 1924, 'he must comprehend the play's key idea,'[1] and van Gyseghem records him saying ten years later, 'It is the thought contained in the play which must hold first place in our plan.'[2] The focussing on a single 'key idea' to uncover the writer's inner world led Meyerhold to distinguish between 'the representation of a style on stage', which missed the inner truth of the author's work, and 'the stylization of scenic situations', which brought it out.[3] This is what explains, for instance, his creation of a stylized 'age of powder' for the unfinished production of Hauptmann's *Schluck und Jau*[4] (1905), and his vision of the heaped-up rottenness of Nikolayan society in *The Government Inspector* (1926). In *The Mandate* (1925), the attenuation of bourgeois society in the post-revolutionary context was the key idea, and in *The Magnanimous Cuckold* (1922) bourgeois morality's reliance on property relations. In discerning the 'key idea', Meyerhold felt he, as director, was quite likely to be more successful than the author – 'I often felt like protesting his opinion', one author, Yuri Olesha, disclosed wryly, 'but in the end I invariably told myself: "Yes, he is right, and I am probably mistaken."'[5]

In this way Meyerhold fulfilled the first aim of the artist as defined by the Formalists: he did not allow everyday attitudes or habits to be taken for granted, but made us see them anew. This was precisely what Shklovsky asked of art:

The thing rushes past us, prepacked as it were; we know that it is there by the space it takes up, but we see only its surface. This kind of perception shrivels a thing up, first of all in the way we perceive it, but later this affects the way we handle it too . . . Life goes to waste as it is turned into nothingness. Automization corrodes things, clothing, furniture, one's wife and one's fear of war . . . And so that a sense of life may be restored, that things may be felt, so that stones may be made stony, there exists what we call art.[6]

Meyerhold seems never to have expressed this thought so bluntly, though he did refer in 1911 to E.T.A. Hoffmann's liking for Callot's pictures depending on 'something . . . which makes them at once *familiar yet strange*'.[7] But other artists who worked with him put it more clearly. Rodchenko, for instance, said of photography: 'We don't see what we look at. We're taught to see in a set and received way, but we must open up the world to be seen. We need to revolutionize our visual thinking.'[8]

The first way to 'revolutionize' our perceiving, to 'make a stone stony', was through the use of devices to 'defamiliarize' the material, and secondly to draw attention to the fact that it was not the material itself that was being exhibited but rather the artist's conjuration of it – to defamiliarize the medium, in other words. Meyerhold himself was aware of the interdependence of these two facets of the process and used Formalist terminology to describe it in 1921: 'in theatrical performances, the play of the actor differs from the behaviour of people in life by its special rhythm and by the special devices of playing.'[9]

Meyerhold's theatre was always one of 'devices', as previous chapters have shown. This was as true of the acting – Ilinsky as Bruno in *The Magnanimous Cuckold* (1922) standing still and slowly intoning his soliloquies at the audience one moment and leaping, tumbling or rolling acrobatically the next – as it was of the scenery – the spinning wheels in the same production were as pure examples of the 'device' as any Meyerhold ever used. It may be added that in a sense the device does not depend for its effectiveness on what it is, it depends only on the fact that it changes the focus by its unexpectedness: thereby it achieves its aim. The device gives us a new angle on what is quite probably a very old subject. Meyerhold's theatre was not so much interested in the holding of a mirror up to nature as in holding a distorting mirror up or a magnifying glass or perhaps placing the emphasis on how the mirror was being held – obliquely, above, at the side, any way which gave an unexpected viewpoint. In modern critical jargon, Meyerhold was not interested in reflecting reality but in signifying it.

And by drawing attention to the artificiality of what he was doing, to the theatricality of his theatre – the brick walls at the back of the stage, the green wig in *The Forest* (1924), the quick changing of Garin behind the flat with a hole in it in *D.E.* (1924) – in fact, 'the stylization of scenic situations' – the effect of the 'new angle' was enhanced. For an emphasis on the medium throws the onus of imagining directly onto the spectator, as Meyerhold's own description of *The Fairground Booth* (1906) makes clear:

The entire stage is hung at the sides and rear with blue drapes; this expanse of blue serves as a background as well as reflecting the colour of the settings in the little booth erected on the stage. This booth has it own stage, curtain, prompter's box, and proscenium opening. Instead of being masked by the conventional border, the flies, together with all the ropes and wires, are visible to the audience; when the entire set is hauled aloft on the booth, the audience in the actual theatre sees the whole process.

In front of the booth the stage area adjacent to the footlights is left free. It is here that the 'Author' appears to serve as an intermediary between the public and the events enacted within the booth.

The action begins at a signal on a big drum; music is heard and the audience sees the prompter crawl into his box and light a candle. The curtain of the booth rises to reveal a box set with doors stage-left and centre, and a window stage-right. Parallel to the footlights is a long table, behind which are seated the 'Mystics'; by the window is a round table with a pot of geraniums and a slender gilt chair on which Pierrot is sitting. Harlequin makes his first entry from under the Mystics' table. When the Author runs on to the proscenium his tirade is terminated by someone hidden in the wings who pulls him off by his coat tails; it turns out that he is tethered with a rope to prevent him from interrupting the solemn course of the events onstage. In Scene Two 'the dejected Pierrot sits in the middle of the stage on a bench'; behind him is a pedestal bearing a statue of Eros. When Pierrot finishes his long soliloquy, the bench, the statue and the entire set are whisked aloft, and a traditional colonnaded hall is lowered in their place. In the scene where masked figures appear with cries of 'Torches!' the hands of stage-hands appear from both wings holding flaming Bengal lights on iron rods.[10]

This is an almost perfect example of 'defamiliarization' – or even 'alienation' – before the terms were invented, though it might be added that it is only successful because the audience knows the usual conventions, and expects the play to conform to them. Then of course, something quite different happens. If all productions used the 'devices' of *The Fairground Booth* they would no longer make us see afresh. But here we have all the classic features of Formalism: the device is 'bared', the act of expression itself is 'foregrounded', the material is 'made strange', the friction between 'fable' (what happens) and 'plot' (how it is presented) is obvious.

The question arises: has the production anything more than a purely aesthetic function? In what way is it different from, say, Alexander Tairov's 'abstract–formal' type of theatre? There is, it is true, some anger – and some irony – in the content of Blok's play, but the production seems dangerously close to 'art for art's sake' for Meyerhold, who as early as 1896 was scribbling notes about '*liberté, égalité, fraternité*'[11] and who always hankered after tying his theatrical work in with his democratic and progressive views. So while it was an obvious gain to have discovered how to make drama out of the kind of devices the Formalist critics were noticing in literary works (and thereby producing drama which baffled most theatre critics, by the way), it was still true that Meyerhold's work had no obvious function beyond itself.

Yet it had perhaps a greater potential than was immediately apparent from the synthetic symbolism of 1906. To unravel where the potential lay it is necessary to return to the 'key idea' which focussed a production. *Don Juan* (1910) was, in the designer Golovin's words, a 'fantasy on the theme of the eighteenth century'.[12] But it was more than this, for it was also a kind of liberation from the conventional or the expected. As Yuri Yurev said, 'This was in truth a holiday for us!'[13] while Sayler wrote that 'joy' was 'the lot of

53. Tairov's 'abstract–formal' theatre: the balcony scene from *Romeo and Juliet*, 1921

him who submits himself to its spell'.[14] The 'key idea' in the production of *The Magnanimous Cuckold* (1922) related to bourgeois morality's reliance on property relations, which was seen quite correctly as dangerous. It led to the kind of violence shown by the women of the village to Bruno when they attacked him in Act 3. But here, too, in the violence – rather as in the violence of a Punch and Judy show – there was a liberating laughter which made the performance somehow a release. 'This is a most thrilling production to watch', van Gyseghem wrote, 'for the sheer joy of movement and rhythm',[15] and Garin, discussing 'the joy of the spectator's feelings brought forth by the joyful creativity of the actors', remembered 'the feeling of glad liberation which did not leave anyone till the end of the performance'.[16]

54. The women attack Bruno in *The Magnanimous Cuckold*, 1922

The reference to Punch and Judy is not accidental, for this kind of liberating experience is especially evoked by illegitimate forms of popular entertainment such as itinerant puppet shows. Komissarzhevskaya had of course sacked Meyerhold in 1907 because she thought his work was leading to 'puppet theatre', and Benois, in his attack on *Don Juan,* called it a 'dressed-up fairground show'.[17] Meyerhold replied that his 'new theatre of masks will learn from the Spanish and the Italians of the seventeenth century and build its repertoire according to the laws of the fairground booth'.[18] The first law seemed to be a *joie de vivre* and a carnival spirit which fairground booths of all eras and all countries have called forth. Thus, for *The Death of Tarelkin* (1922), Meyerhold 'directed his theatrical ship towards popular carnival and circus',[19] while the 'powerful attraction' of his production of *The Forest* (1924) 'lay in the deeply felt principle of carnival theatre'.[20]

The festival of Carnival in the centuries before the Reformation was the time when briefly the world was turned upside down. It was a festival of masquerading, laughter, satire and parades, and a celebration of human carnality. It marked the end of one annual cycle and the start of the next. If the passage of a year may be likened to a single swing of a pendulum, when it reaches the end of its swing, its perpetual motion has to stop for a split second before it can begin the swing down in the opposite direction. That short period when the pendulum is stopped is the equivalent of Carnival, for then the normal conventions of human society are all brought to a standstill. Time seems not to be going, as it usually does, towards death, but to be stuck in life, and this induces a state of ecstasy, or 'liminality'. It is, in a sense, simply a liberation from all the inhibitions imposed by convention and normal society. But it is more than that. 'Liminal entities are neither here nor there; they are

55. Traditional 'illegitimate' popular entertainment in Russia, including a puppet show, c. 1634

betwixt and between the positions assigned and arrayed by law, custom, convention, and ceremonial.'[21] They are, in other words, beyond the bounds of normal living.

This is a state to which ritual can bring a person, and drama, too, can sometimes achieve a comparable effect. When it does, the audience's 'liberation' may provide some sort of glimpse of the other consequences of the liminal state. Because the being is outside the placement of society, beyond any social structure, as it were, he or she is often able to perceive that social structure with completely unaccustomed eyes, can see that it is not, as it sometimes seems to be in everyday life, pre-ordained, eternal, and indestructable. On the contrary, its weaknesses – and perhaps its absurdities – are shown up for what they are. Carnival, which may provoke in its celebrants such a critical response, was thus often regarded as basically a necessary safety-valve for a constantly repressive society. But sometimes it was greatly more than that. Ladurie suggests why:

Carnival was not merely a satirical and *purely temporary* reversal of the dual social order, finally intended to justify the status quo in an 'objectively' conservative manner. It would be more accurate to say it was a satirical, lyrical, epic-learning experience for highly diversified groups. It was a way to action, perhaps modifying the society as a whole in the direction of social change and *possible progress.*[22]

56. *The Dawns*, 1920. The effect of the Greek chorus

Now it is not being claimed that Meyerhold's productions were somehow versions of medieval ritual, but we have already noticed that at its best his theatre had a liberating effect a little like that of Carnival, and its subject matter was often related to social change. The question of progress is, however, important here, for 'progress' in this context refers to the integration of people into a homogenous social fabric, one based on co-operation rather than division. It is an ideal the early Marxists and socialists often voiced.

Such a resolution seems far from the habitual boisterousness of popular theatre, which Meyerhold constantly advocated. 'We must utilize the experience of popular theatre of past ages', he said in 1924,[23] and Markov noted in *The Forest*, produced that year, the elements of 'full-blooded popular melodrama'. He saw Meyerhold's antecedents in the great popular theatres of the past – 'the Shakespearean stage, the stage of the Middle Ages, the popular melodrama played in the streets and squares'[24] – and others went even further back. Gregor, commenting on *The Dawns* (1920), thought the company's 'dancing is borrowed from the ancient Mime [and] their singing reproduces one of the long-lost effects of the Greek Chorus'.[25]

The strength of the fairground popular theatre, as Meyerhold well knew, was that it could encompass such an austere effect side by side with rough-

and-tumble slapstick of the type he created for *The Magnanimous Cuckold*.
Vulgarity could rub shoulders with the sublime in the fairground booth in a
way the 'legitimate' theatre could never emulate. A good example of this was
Earth Rampant. In this production, at one moment the Emperor, clad in helmet
and dress coat, urinated in a chamber pot to the strains of 'God Save the Tsar'
and then allowed his lackey to carry the used vessel, stamped with the
imperial crown, away through the auditorium, his fingers pinching his
nostrils the while. Very shortly afterwards, the death of the hero was
presented to create the maximum emotional impact. When his body was
lifted in solemn fashion onto the back of a purring lorry, the running of the
engine during the sequence somehow seemed to intensify the audience's
response.

The contradiction in utilizing carnival-like farce and sublime tragedy in the
same production suggests the Marxism which Meyerhold by this time
professed, and other traits in his work could be linked with then-current ideas
in Marxist thought. Georgi Plekhanov, for instance, until then the most
important exponent of dialectical materialism in Russian literary criticism,
had held that characters should be presented as types, 'historic individuality'
having a significance which mere individual psychology necessarily lacked.
Meyerhold's practice showed that he agreed. More important, Marxism had
its own answer to the question of the function of art, which went beyond the
Formalist's idea of making a stone 'stony'. In the Marxist view, the stone had
to be seen not simply as stony, but as a potential component of a barricade or
a castle, as the projectile of a striking worker or the cobble over which some
men walk to work while others ride to their leisure. Art in this view makes us
see anew not simply the object itself, but the object's potential in the concrete
world. In Bukharin's phrase of 1921, 'art is a means of socializing' the
apprehensions.[26]

And here we return to the relevance of Carnival, for the 'integration of
people into a homogenous social fabric', which was suggested as the promise
it hinted at, complements neatly this concept of Bukharin. The goal of the
October revolution was no less than the end of human alienation, and the
theatre, as the most public of the arts, inevitably had a contribution to make in
the process of integration and socialization. Where bourgeois society would
relegate theatre to the realm of private psychologies, in revolutionary Russia
it was assigned a much more public role. This was obvious in events like the
mass spectacles,[27] but beyond this Meyerhold was in the forefront of those
arguing that all theatres should be public forums and performers actor-
tribunes whose work was vital to society. On one level that was exactly what
the call for an 'October in the theatre' meant. And while all dramatic stages
may be said to be models of the real world, leftist revolutionary artists like

Mayakovsky and Brik took the view that the arts 'had to be applied to the very reconstruction and transformation of society as a result of the Bolshevik revolution'.[28] The mood was caught by Ehrenburg and El Lissitzky in the first number of *Object* when they wrote that the 'mission' of 'constructive art' was 'not after all to embellish life, but to organize it'.[29]

The method whereby art 'organized' was – for Meyerhold, Mayakovsky, Eisenstein and others – the 'montage of attractions', for not only does the montage construct the rhythm, as has been pointed out, it also (and more importantly, perhaps) produces the meaning. Eisenstein argued that the 'instrument' which would 'lead the spectator in the desired direction' was, first, the 'attraction', which he defined as 'any aggressive moment of theatre' (and which is therefore directly comparable to the Formalists' 'device' and to Meyerhold's own 'silhouettes' and 'antics appropriate to the theatre'). Then, according to Eisenstein, the single attraction should be 'experimentally adjusted' so as to become one of 'the sequence of emotional jolts which together constitute the whole'. Only when each attraction has been appropriately 'adjusted' can 'the ideological drift be followed and the final conclusion grasped'. In this, Eisenstein is actually suggesting nothing less than a new way of obtaining meaning in the theatre.

First of all, the movement of the performance as a whole may be considered. This is a 'free montage of items (attractions) arbitrarily thrown up, independent of each other . . . worked out (as attractions), but precisely arranged to affect the theme in a defined way'.[30] As has perhaps been implied in previous chapters of this study, this is how, say, *The Forest* (1924) was constructed by Meyerhold, its thirty-three episodes involving children's play equipment, mimed actions, rhythmic contrasts, popular song and so on, put together not so as to depict Ostrovsky's somewhat sentimental, certainly lyrical portrait of faded nineteenth-century rural gentlefolk, but a free montage, whose collisions created the metephysical sparks necessary for a sharp dissection of the nature of exploitation, self-indulgence and personal liberation. As Markov says, 'the theme does not unfold itself as the consecutive development of a plot, but as a succession of pictures following in accordance with principles of association and contrast'.[31]

Equally, Eisenstein directed attention to the way individual attractions – or perhaps more accurately, two individual attractions – can create meaning. He probably put it most clearly years later when discussing film, though the principle obviously applies with equal relevance to live theatre: 'the juxtaposition of two separate shots by splicing them together resembles not so much a single sum of one shot plus another shot - as it does a *creation*. It resembles a creation – rather than a sum of its parts – from the circumstance that in every such juxtaposition *the result is qualitatively* distinguishable from

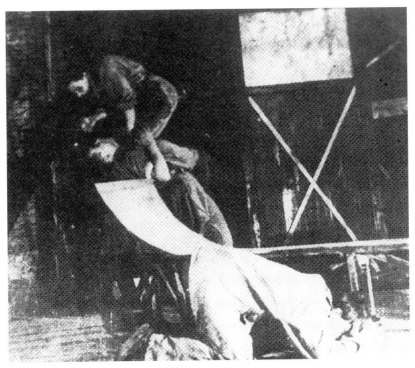

57. The Cooper leaps on Bruno's chest in *The Magnanimous Cuckold*, 1922

each component element viewed separately'.[32] Thus, in *The Magnanimous Cuckold* (1922), when we see, first, Bruno in a mask, then the village women thrashing him, we conclude Bruno is a danger to their hearthside peace. This conclusion is, of course, correct, though the women do not realize it since they have mistaken Bruno for someone else. When the Cooper comes to Bruno for a letter to send to his beloved, Bruno suspects him of dallying with Stella, and slaps him several times, provoking a growl each time from the Cooper. The Cooper then leaves by one door, re-enters by another and leaps onto Bruno's chest (performs the biomechanical exercise, in fact). Bruno almost faints several times, each time being caught as he falls, till he lies down and pretends to be dead. From such a sequence of attractions, we 'create' our own meanings – the animalism and selfishness of these people's 'love'; the violence, danger and hypocrisy of it; perhaps, too, their childishness, particularly Bruno's, for whom playing is virtually indistinguishable from serious behaviour. The spectator has to do his own work, in other words, to make the play mean.

Meyerhold himself described the process more mildly in 1936 when he

58. The end of *The Forest*, 1924

wrote of a performance consisting of 'a series of "passes", each intended to evoke some association or other in the spectator (some premeditated, others outside my control). Your imagination is activated, your fantasy stimulated, and a whole chorus of associations is set off. A multitude of accumulated associations gives birth to new worlds.'[33] Meyerhold was in fact discussing cinema here, and the whole technique has undoubtedly been more thoroughly explored in terms of film than in connection with the live drama. Nevertheless, the implications of it are also highly relevant to theatre. For the act of seeing also involves an act of interpretation, and Meyerhold, understanding this, was concerned to provide something worth interpreting – an attraction, an 'aggressive moment of theatre'. His reward lay in remarks like Belyaev's comment on *Don Juan*: 'They are showing Molière's *Don Juan* and are asking you to be surprised',[34] or Markov's on *The Mandate*: 'The production makes you think. It questions premises and proceeds by deduction.'[35]

For Meyerhold, such a response resulted from 'intensifying the fundamental relationship of performer and spectator'.[36] It explains his constant rewriting of received texts, so that they engaged with contemporary life, not in a frivolous 'updating' sense, but so that the encrustations of the old ways of interpreting them were neutralized and a new way of utilizing the play opened up. Put another way, Meyerhold's rewriting demonstrated his understanding that the written text of a play is not an eternal object, but something which functions within specific cultural contexts. Furthermore, by claiming 'authorship' of his productions, Meyerhold implicitly challenged the old notion of the author as inherently superior to the theatre practitioner. This is admitted in the art of film (*Battleship Potemkin* is thought of primarily as the achievement of Eisenstein, the director, rather than of Agadyanova, the scenarist), but not yet in the live theatre.

It is now possible to see how Meyerhold transcended Formalism, whose tenets he exemplified in so many theatrical ways. For Shklovsky, 'art is a way of experiencing the making of a thing'.[37] But Meyerhold asks his audience member not just to experience its making, but to make it for his own use. Thus, the performance of *The Forest* (1924) did not so much reinterpret the play or present it in a new critical light, as make it available for a new kind of audience. His version, which played over 1,700 times, was aimed at young people and proletarians of 1920s Russia, which Ostrovsky's original could not have been. Nineteenth-century rural Russia was of slight interest to them; but self-realization in the face of exploitation was quite another matter. By producing *The Forest* to bear on that problem, Meyerhold was not merely interpreting the world, but contributing towards changing it.

7   *Masquerade*

When still a teenager in Penza, Meyerhold had seen Alexander Lensky perform the part of Arbenin in Mikhail Lermontov's *Masquerade*, and the experience seems to have stayed with him for the rest of his life. Perhaps because of the impression this made on him, Meyerhold always included Lermontov in his list of Russian masters who would form an alternative, and for him more vital, Russian dramatic tradition to that of Ostrovsky, Chekhov and Gorky. The line of Griboyedev, Pushkin, Lermontov and Gogol was, he felt, in some respects perverted by the more recent turning to naturalism.[1]

Though he began to prepare his production of *Masquerade* in 1911, the first public presentation of a Lermontov play by Meyerhold was *The Two Brothers*, which opened at the Mariinsky Theatre on 10 January 1916, and was afterwards transferred to the Alexandrinsky Theatre. The play, widely regarded as little more than an appendage to Lermontov's poetic work, was in Meyerhold's opinion largely misunderstood which explained why his production was misjudged by the literary critics who attended it. Though the acting seems to have been uneven, L. Gurevich wrote that: 'The lovely decorations and costumes by Golovin, particularly the semicircular living room in Ligovsky's house and the romantically moonlit, abandoned hall receding into the depth of the stage from some fantastic vestibule with choirs and a spiral staircase, these dressed up and gave a stylistic beauty to the entire production.'[2] And Y. Slonimskaya, calling the fact that the production had occurred at all 'a miracle', added that:

Lermontov's 'new' play does indeed seem new, and may perhaps be used as an example for the modern theatre. The concentrated intrigue, unencumbered by a single unnecessary detail, concerns the clash of vivid passions and sharply delineated characters, with stormy and impetuous actions which completely captivated the audience . . . The theatregoing public must be grateful for something so handsome being shown on the stage, a miraculous, youthful work by Lermontov.[3]

Less friendly, but perhaps equally telling, was a third review, which admitted that the play was 'watched not without interest' but then stated: 'What seems deep penetration is of course actually a trick of the fairground booth, and instead of living people, the characters become marionettes. This was the principle of the whole production. The *mise-en-scène*, the costumes, the actors – all were adorned with fairground boothery.'[4]

Such a comment, however pejoratively intended, indicates Meyerhold's

59. *Masquerade*, 1917. Nina's death

approach. *The Two Brothers* seemed important to him for its own 'authentic theatricality',[5] equally uncontaminated by influences from the *pièce á thèse* on the one hand, and the sentimentality of much Russian romanticism on the other. Even more significant, perhaps, is Meyerhold's comment that 'the simple stage situation of the interrelationship of two brothers and one wife is elaborated like a refined musical composition according to the strict rules of theatrical orchestration',[6] for this was the angle from which he approached Lermontov's mature dramatic masterpiece, *Masquerade*.

The play tells of a gambler and rake, Arbenin, who has been reformed by the love of his innocent young wife, Nina. He thinks he has discovered that she has been unfaithful with Prince Zvezdich, and makes to kill him. When he fails, he tries to humiliate him by throwing cards in his face in a gambling den. In fact, Nina has not been unfaithful: she lost a bracelet at a masquerade, the Baroness picked it up and gave it to an admirer. He was the Prince, who is now himself uncertain whose favours he has been seeking. Arbenin refuses to believe in Nina's innocence, especially when he sees her speak to the Prince at a society ball. He poisons her ice cream there, and when they return home tells her what he has done. After her death, he is driven mad by remorse, prompted by the Stranger, who had earlier predicted the catastrophe during the masquerade.

Meyerhold's production of *Masquerade* was in rehearsal for almost six years. Despite the jokes and gossip this aroused, it was allowed by the director of the Imperial Theatres, V.A. Telyakovsky, because of Meyerhold's desire to disprove the legend of the 'unstageability' of this landmark of Russian romanticism. Rehearsing was, in fact, pursued somewhat desultorily, with a week or two of work followed by perhaps a few months away from the play. It may be suspected that such an approach helped this particular production, however, as the unfamiliarity of the idiom, and the monumental qualities Meyerhold wished to impart to the work, needed time to mature.

So absorbed did the participants become during the last few weeks of rehearsal, as the production moved finally towards performance in February 1917, that they barely noticed the gathering storm of the first revolution of that year taking place beyond the walls of the theatre. And in spite of the demonstrations and the growing anger of the people, 'the interest in *Masquerade* among the theatregoing public dwindled not at all'.[7] Not only did the elite of Moscow journey to Petrograd for the occasion, but Yuri Yurev, Arbenin in the production, was telephoned at home by 'not a few high-ranking people (including some ministers)' to ask for tickets.[8] Nevertheless, with the revolution gathering momentum, simply getting to the theatre for the premiere proved extremely hazardous. Yurev was turned back by one group of soldiers, and allowed through by another only because the commander had seen him act; Meyerhold and Golovin had to run through flying bullets in order to cross the Nevsky; and one person was shot dead in the entrance to the theatre that night.

On the whole, the first night, which was also Yurev's benefit night, seems to have been a success. The play actually remained in the theatre's repertoire in one form or another for thirty years until 1947. Meyerhold twice reworked it, in 1933 and 1938, and in 1941 the sets and costumes were destroyed during the bombing of Leningrad. When the Alexandrinsky Theatre, renamed the Pushkin State Academic Theatre, was evacuated to Novosibirsk, the production became a 'concert performance', continuing after Meyerhold himself had been executed, and even back in Leningrad again when the war was over. Yurev, by the way, whose career had begun in 1892, continued to play Arbenin to the end, when he was well into his seventies.

All this tends to suggest what is clearly the case, that *Masquerade* was one of Meyerhold's most influential productions. Early audiences found it difficult to come to terms with:

In general, they were carried away by the production, but nonetheless with one voice they all protested at the division (or if you like, the segmentation) of the episodes ... by the device of lowering the curtain in the middle of the dialogue. The actors in the particular episode were then separated by the curtain from the stage itself, and it was as if they were in 'close-up' or had crossed the proscenium line and entered the auditorium. 'It

60. *Masquerade*, 1917. Design for scene 3, Arbenin's drawing room, by Alexander Golovin

breaks the illusion . . .' – 'It distracts your attention, it stops you concentrating . . .' – 'Lermontov didn't want this . . .'[9]

It may not be without significance, however, that Eisenstein, for instance, was profoundly impressed with this work which, more than any other single factor, determined him to enter the theatre himself. And as time went by, audiences of all types came increasingly to recognize the originality and the resonance in Meyerhold's creation.

The audience at *Masquerade* was plunged immediately into an unfamiliar relationship with the performers through the arrangement of stage and auditorium, and of course by the fact that the lights in the hall never dimmed to give them a comfortable darkness to watch from. A semicircular forestage swept out into the audience, at either end of which stairs with elegant bannisters descended into the orchestra pit. Further back, and at either side, were gigantic double doors, sculpted with motifs drawn from the decorations of the auditorium and flanked by huge frosted glass mirrors which reflected audience and stage to each other and to themselves, thereby seeming to cancel the distance between them. Beyond and outside them were two sofas, permanently set.

This stage arrangement helped significantly to determine the action, which proceeded as a pattern of silhouettes and antics, each cutting across the other and working directly on the audience as almost self-contained units. Thus Meyerhold himself in 1939 described the key moment when Arbenin discovers – or thinks he discovers – that Nina has given away the bracelet in terms which emphasize its qualities as a silhouette: 'Nina falls on her knees before Arbenin. Having registered the disappearance of the bracelet, Arbenin raises her with his hand – it is as if she were being crucified.'[10] This silhouette did not simply appear within the scene, but by virtue of the thrust stage and the way the decor on stage echoed that in the auditorium, it seemed to be almost among the spectators. Yet the decor simultaneously emphasized something else: behind the oval table, with two plush upright chairs framing it on either side, was a double window giving directly onto the night sky, where a few tiny stars twinkled in infinity. The contradictions – or the different simultaneous spatial dimensions – apparent here, are central to Meyerhold's conception.

The silhouette is not necessarily motionless. Consider the carefully patterned movement from scene 8 when Nina and the Prince meet fortuitously, and Arbenin is close by. Nina enters through the portal, stage left, and stops. The Prince, seeing her, steps forward. She moves uneasily away a pace or two, halting beside an enormous vase. The Prince follows, but respectfully. They have a short conversation, during which the Prince tries to set matters to rights. Then he moves off, across the stage to the doorway from where, unknown to them, Arbenin has been watching them. As he approaches, Arbenin steps forward. Both halt. The Prince glances at Nina, innocently in fact, but a glance which is misinterpreted by the neurotic Arbenin. Nina moves upstage and away, the Prince goes on past Arbenin. When they have gone, Arbenin crosses heavily to the vase beside which his wife stood to hear the Prince's comments. Here is movement carefully patterned to create the same effect as the silhouette.

The exit of the Prince from the Baroness's airy drawing room is another sort of silhouette. In this, the overwrought Baroness is playing the piano stage right, while the Prince is at an occasional table on the other side of the stage. She stops playing, says harshly that she has some advice for Nina (whom she imagines is having an affair with the Prince) and abruptly returns to the keyboard. The Prince, with lazy swagger, stands and crosses to her. A brief pause, while she continues to play the piano and a sarcastic smile spreads slowly across his face. 'And what advice will you give me?' he asks. The Baroness plays on. 'Boldly to continue what you have begun', she says wildly, still playing. Then she stops abruptly in the middle of a musical phrase, leans back, and adds, 'And value the honour of ladies more highly.' She turns back to the piano and bangs out some noisy chords. The Prince winces momentarily, then put on his gloves very deliberately, stretching

61. *Masquerade*, 1917. Scene 8: Prince on stage, left. (1) Nina enters. (2) Prince steps forward. (3) Nina moves away. (4) Prince follows. (See illustration 63) During the action, Arbenin enters stage right

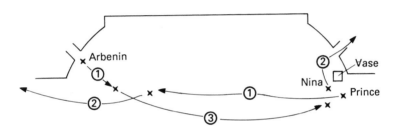

62. *Masquerade*, 1917. Scene 8 continued: (1) Prince moves away from Nina, Arbenin steps forward. (2) Prince and Nina, having exchanged a glance, exit at opposite sides. (3) Arbenin crosses to where Nina was

them over his hands with his head and his torso somewhat inclined. As he finishes, he remarks drily, 'That's two pieces of advice . . .' He leans down to take her hand which he kisses, then straightens up rapidly, clicks the spurs on his heels, and says, 'I thank you twice.' And unhurriedly, apparently bored, he leaves the Baroness alone on the stage. This tiny scene illustrates how Meyerhold solved what he called 'the problem for the actors – to follow the beautiful forms, but not to forget that they must rage with passion under this glossy facade'.[11]

Such a scene is almost a self-contained pantomime in miniature. Another came in the last scene. While the crazed Arbenin agonizes in soliloquy over his doubts about Nina's guilt, a strange sequence of mimed episodes proceeds, dislocating and undermining our expected responses to the demented hero. First a nun, a professional mourner, walks slowly past, stopping near the exit to turn and stare at Arbenin. She folds her arms in the sleeves of her habit and remains motionlessly staring. Nina's old nanny then appears, wailing too

63. *Masquerade*, 1917. Scene 8: Prince speaks briefly to Nina in front of the large vase

loudly. She crosses the stage, streaming tears, and takes the nun's arm. Both leave together. They are followed by an old lady and her niece, an old man, the doctor: each serves to break the flow of the scene. A similar interruption occurs during Arbenin's soliloquy in the ball scene, when he is determining to poison Nina: just as he realizes he cannot forgive her, an extremely young couple of guests, almost schoolchildren, dash across the stage towards the ballroom, and bump into Arbenin as they go. They bow awkwardly and hurry on, trying to laugh off their confusion.

In the masquerade itself, this approach was particularly powerful. On a gaudily decorated stage, the merry and exotic figures pranced – Harlequin and Columbine eternally chasing one another, an orange and green Polichinello flitting in and out, a blue Pierrot flaunting himself, big masks, Turkish turbans, officers' red tunics. In the midst, Arbenin the malcontent, watching contemptuously. The masked Nina is surrounded by masqueraders wanting to inveigle her into their flirtation. She confusedly breaks loose from them and flees, inadvertently dropping her bracelet as she goes. Later the Stranger appears, mysterious and threatening in his black domino and ghastly white mask. He follows the semicircle of the forestage, and behind him, like awestruck children behind a horrifying Pied Piper, a line of cowering

64. Blue Pierrot

revellers follow. The Stranger suddenly stops, turns and glowers at them, and they freeze like icicles. He warns Arbenin enigmatically, leaving him disgusted and dissatisfied. And as the gloomy hero moves wearily off, a loud and brilliant crowd of dancers clatters and gallops along the same semicircle of forestage. The effect has been evocatively described by Znosko-Borovsky:

Meyerhold transformed the small scene of the masked ball into a completely terrifying and nightmarish one. It was as if fate itself haunted the jealous husband, as he writhed in the circle of his suspicions, in the circle of the dancers. The masks became distorted, the faces were frightening, the whole fatal circle narrowed, and as they surrounded him with general jollity and light-hearted teasing, the unconstrained dancing acquired a strange and menacing appearance, the danger growing all the greater, a whirlwind and a tornado spinning round on the stage, till finally we seemed to be among improbable monsters, created by the diseased, disordered imagination of the husband, who had a guiltless wife

65. Nina at the masquerade. Note the plain bracelets

and did not believe in her innocence. With his own hand he gave her the poison in order to kill not her, but his own dark thoughts which had acquired such terrible immediacy.[12]

This kind of staging was the first means by which Meyerhold attempted to shift the perception of Arbenin from the conventional interpretation of him as a melodrama villain towards a different kind of saturnine, perhaps Gothic, hero. 'The task is to achieve a tragic tone, not a romantic one', he wrote, [13] and the device of using the crowd as a kind of fantastical antagonist was one method of doing this.

The *mise-en-scène* was another. Its fabulous richness cast a glossy patina over everything – the spectator looked, and had his breath taken away by the sheer splendour. Alexander Golovin, the designer, had already established a reputation both at the Imperial Theatres and with Diaghilev as a scenic artist with a particular mastery of colour rhythms used to draw in the spectator. With *Masquerade* he created a stage setting which itself became the subject of fine art criticism and of at least one major art book.[14]

Everything for the set of *Masquerade* was specially made, and it was all made slightly larger than life so that a faint unease or disorientation was experienced by the audience. The stage was dominated by cards, masks, candles in a profusion of mystery and opulence. Flowers proliferated – camellias under the chief boxes and in sixteen tubs or huge vases for the ball scene, bouquets in vases at the Baroness's, at the Prince's, at Arbenin's, even two small ivy bushes in pots in Arbenin's room. The mourners in the final scene carried individual bouquets, the masqueraders in scene 2 flung individual flowers. The lighting, too, expressed the glitter and the polished opulence: the brilliance of the masquerade was obtained through a multitude of wax candles, while other scenes were dimly lit and the spectator often seemed to glimpse through the windows darkened skies with a few stars or, in scene 7 when Arbenin throws the cards at the Prince, a waning moon. Within this vaguely disturbing luxuriance, some costumes provided starkly contrasting images, like Nina's black or white gowns, and the Prince's blood-red tunic, while others, such as the blue Pierrot who teased Nina at the masquerade, set up more complex reverberations.

Set, costumes, props and all were enveloped in a series of heavy curtains whose workings provided a key to Meyerhold and Golovin's conception, for they both revealed and concealed. At the start, the first curtain rose to disclose another; this rose and another was behind it; the third curtain rose and behind it, there was a gauze, filmy and transparent, through which the figures of the drama were first discerned. During the performance, curtains might be lowered or raised to section off particular stage areas where the action proceeded, a device which enabled Meyerhold to use the vast stage space in unexpected and original ways. Only the masquerade and the ball scene used the full width and depth of the space; the other scenes all took place in areas defined by the hangings.

The production was thus organized around unusual spatial rhythms. But the curtains also served to avoid unneccesary delays in the action, so that they contributed to the production's pace as well. 'The extraordinary speed of the action' was, in Meyerhold's opinion, the first and most noticeable feature of *Masquerade*,[15] even for the reader. The production had to crystallize this feature in action. Lermontov had divided the play into four conventional acts, but Meyerhold, anxious to create the right stage rhythm, split this down into ten episodes. These then grouped themselves into three movements: the first dealt with Arbenin and Nina, the second with Arbenin's attempts to come to terms with his fears and suspicions, and the third with the tragic ending of Arbenin and Nina's relationship. This three-part structure, however, worked contrapuntally with the gradual growth of the Stranger's power, a steady, accelerating climb, and with Meyerhold's insistence on treating each scene for itself. It was therefore a complicated series of cross rhythms which provided the springs for the production, and it is no wonder that when Meyerhold came to rework it in 1933 he wrote that 'above everything else, the questions of the tempo and the rhythm of the perform-ance' were what he had to 'renew'.[16]

The rhythm within individual scenes was just as carefully plotted. Scene 3, for example, after the masquerade, began with complete silence and an empty stage (this in itself a rhythmic response to the noisy and boisterous gallop with which the previous scene had ended). Arbenin enters gloomily, and sits deep in his armchair, deeper in thought. A bell rings, Nina enters vivaciously, Arbenin springs up to greet her. But his gloom returns when he sees her fresh vivacity, and discord ensues. One mood, as it were, interrupts another, building unexpected and challenging rhythmic patterns. In scene 5, the sparring, quick-fire repartee between Shprikh and Kazarin is interrupted by the heavy tread of Arbenin entering, reading a letter. As Nina and Prince Zvezdich discuss the lost bracelet apparently lightly, the mood is suddenly cracked by the Prince's loud and 'harsh laugh, bordering on rudeness'.[17] The scene between Nina and her maid after the ball, on the other hand, was built almost entirely on pauses, during which one mood gave way to another with discernible slowness.

One is left with an impression of a montage effect, a series of moments which exists primarily for themselves but which, just as they are taking hold, are interrupted by other, often contradictory, moments. The effect, 'gro-tesque' in Walzogen's sense,[18] can also be seen in the interaction between text and music. Thus, in the scene of the masquerade, the Stranger confronts Arbenin while the first figure of the quadrille is in progress. As the quadrille ends, the Stranger 'disappears into the crowd'.

ARBENIN: Stay! He's gone. Who was he? God has played a trick on me . . . It was probably some cowardly mischief-maker. There are endless numbers of them. Ha ha ha. Farewell, friend, bon voyage![19]

As Arbenin begins to laugh, heavy and ominous music is heard. This lasts for perhaps twenty seconds, then gives way to 'Pantomime 4', the music which accompanies Lermontov's stage direction: 'Two female masks are sitting on the *settle. A man approaches and makes a pass at one of them, taking her hand. She withdraws it and departs. A bracelet falls from her wrist onto the floor.'* In Meyerhold's production, 'a man' became the dancing blue Pierrot. At the end of this sequence, the second figure of the quadrille began, apparently just off stage, while Shprikh and Arbenin argued, at the end of which Arbenin departed, leaving Shprikh impotently vengeful ('as if wanting to recruit his own devilish army of intriguers', Meyerhold noted for Glazunov[20]). 'Pantomime 5' begins: Shprikh curses Arbenin and stalks off, as the Baroness in her mask rushes onto the stage, entering across the forestage. The music changes tone to keep pace with her. As she sinks down anxiously on the settle, that music dies, and the third figure of the quadrille is heard. Breathlessly she speaks her soliloquy, trying helplessly to think what to do, until she sees the bracelet. By now, the quadrille has ended and 'Pantomime 6' begins. And so the scene proceeds.

The music emphasizes and intensifies the moment as a moment, then rapidly and unexpectedly gives way to something quite different as the mood or the action changes. It should be noted that there were two orchestras playing, the larger for the main pieces, such as the quadrille, and the smaller for the more specific effects. The music, in a sense, tries to reveal what the characters want to conceal, ten years before Brecht employed music in his most famous musical work, *The Threepenny Opera*, as 'a muck-raker, an informer, a nark'.[21] Alpers suggested that Meyerhold was probably the first director to be equally at home in opera and drama, and described how 'the complicated score of Glazunov (for *Masquerade*) gave an almost constant musical accompaniment to the action of the play, and unfolded a unique musical commentary to the basic moments of the show'.[22] Lev Arnshtam, the pianist, wrote: 'Neither before nor since have I seen the equal as a dramatic presentation of *Masquerade* by Lermontov − and by Meyerhold, who resolved the plasticity by tying it in completely to the music. I confess it struck me as an operatic presentation which revealed the true depths of the musical poetry of opera.'[23]

It was precisely in the interplay of movement and music, the spatial and aural rhythms, that Meyerhold's particular mastery revealed itself most originally. For Nina's song, the fact that Katerina Roshchina-Insarova, who played Nina, could not sing, led Meyerhold to stage it so that she had her back to the audience while the operatic soprano M. Kovalenko actually sang the verses offstage. The resultant disorientation was clearly alarming, as the artistically grouped 'listeners' round the piano kept their eyes fixed on Nina, and at the end, clapped their kid-gloved hands quickly and softly, like leaves rustling.

Such a moment suggests a reason why the collaboration between

66. The Stranger

Meyerhold and Golovin was coming to an end (apart from the fact that Golovin emigrated after the revolution and even though Meyerhold expressed interest in working again with him in the 1920s). Golovin was essentially a painter, and though he was able to create the impression here for instance that the luxury was, for the tsarist aristocracy, a substitute for life, Meyerhold now required something more functional from his settings. As Yakovlev noted in a publication some years later when the production was on tour in Leningrad, Meyerhold saw the director as the 'prism' through whom the author's work reached first the actor and the designer, and then the audience.[24] *Masquerade* was on one level the creation equally of Golovin and

Meyerhold. Later, after a period of work with constructivist sculptor–artist–designers, Meyerhold took to designing his own sets.

The problems inherent in collaboration become clear when the meanings achieved are considered. For Meyerhold, the protagonist in the play was Arbenin, and his antagonist was primarily embodied in the Stranger. But who or what was the Stranger (a question not simplified by the fact that Lermontov reconceived and rewrote the part more than once)? For Meyerhold he seems to have been at bottom the representative of Society, 'a hired killer, Society hires the Stranger to take vengeance on Arbenin for "that infernal contempt of everyone, which" he "celebrates everywhere".'[25] But Golovin's creation of the figure, compelling as it was in itself, nevertheless suggested too strongly a kind of demonic Fate, thereby obfuscating the more concrete concept of Society. This may have reflected some lack of clarity in Meyerhold's mind as well, or perhaps the fact that the two artists worked on the production for so long. But it undoubtedly left a certain confusion at the heart of the production, enabling audiences to draw conclusions they were predisposed to, rather than forcing them to think again.

Any discussion of the meaning of this extraordinary production tends to devolve into a discussion of the Stranger. Yet this really misses the point of the work. It is true that the Stranger is on one level a symbol for tsarism, and the spectator who 're-makes' (in the Formalist sense) this character has to consider the implications for him or herself. But that is different from the old idea of 'character analysis', for it actually demands an attitude to tsarism. The production presented an 'image of palatial, majestic and monumental Russia'[26] which fascinated and repelled simultaneously. It concerned the fate of Russia at Russia's most fateful hour – February 1917. Consequently, it did not yield up a 'meaning' in the conventional sense, any more than, say, a symphony can yield a 'meaning', but it clearly was complex and resonant and it did enable its audiences over the years to 'take possession of' tsarist Russia. That is why spectators in 1917 found it both annoying and attractive, and why it continued to draw audiences for decades after the revolution.

8   Meyerhold and Mayakovsky

Meyerhold was throughout his career interested in the work of new play-wrights, but he was also extremely particular and not a litle demanding. His admiration for Blok has been noted, and he worked productively with Sologub, too, though the latter was over forty when they met. It was, however, Mayakovsky, twenty years Meyerhold's junior, with whom the director had the most fruitful relationship, and their partnership, though it encompassed only three plays over twelve years, may properly be considered one of those which raise the practice of theatre to special heights.

In December 1913, Meyerhold attended the performance in Petersburg of Mayakovsky's first play, and no doubt noted its affinities with his own much more accomplished work. In 1915 or 1916 the two met, and Mayakovsky visited Dr Dapertutto's Studio where he read his poems to the students.[1] In 1917, their friendship ripened – 'we agreed immediately on "politics"', Meyerhold declared later, which at that time was 'the main thing'.[2] They collaborated on the highly original and extremely successful *Mystery Bouffe*, presented in two versions in 1918 and 1921, but then not again until 1929. By then, according to one hostile critic, N. Osinsky, in *Izvestia*, Meyerhold's theatre was beginning to 'freeze'.[3] Meyerhold's publicly stated view was different: he said the work on classical Russian plays in the preceeding years had been – among other things – 'clearing the way' to Mayakovsky.[4] In private he had badgered Mayakovsky for a new play for years,[5] and as soon as he received *The Bedbug* put it into rehearsal with extraordinary haste.

Mayakovsky attended these rehearsals, as he did those of his other plays which Meyerhold directed. In this, Meyerhold was paying him a unique compliment, for usually the presence of the author was anathema to him. With Mayakovsky's plays, however, 'I simply could not begin work without him.'[6] Later, Meyerhold recalled that 'Meetings with Mayakovsky always excited me. I regarded him as a very great man, not only a great poet, but a great man in general, a man who overwhelmed one with his greatness. He was so out of the ordinary, so witty, so wise that even a man of the world, like myself, felt a bit ill at ease in his presence.'[7] Meanwhile, according to Fevralsky who worked at the Meyerhold State Theatre when the two men were collaborating, 'Vladimir Vladimirovich [Mayakovsky] thoughtfully deferred to Meyerhold's remarks, gladly inserting in the play additions and emendations, following his advice', while Pavel Tsetnerovich, a production assistant, described how 'Mayakovsky's deep respect for Meyerhold's enormous talent was obvious.'[8]

Maria Sukhanova stated simply that 'To work with Meyerhold and Mayakovsky was happiness.'[9] When news of Mayakovsky's suicide reached Meyerhold he was on tour in Germany. The press demanded to know his reaction, and he came to a press conference to answer their insistence. Yet when the moment came to say what Mayakovsky meant to him, this usually self-controlled man turned away, pulled out his handkerchief, passed the question to one of the actors and made a rapid exit from the room.

Mayakovsky's work was, as even the unenthusiastic Trotsky had to admit, 'organically connected to October'.[10] He summed up his theatrical aesthetic in a series of quatrains. One reads:

> Theatres
>   are not
>   stony piles
> for unravelling
>   of miniature souls.
> Let's strip such individuation
>   of its robes.
> Make art
>   from all
>   for all![11]

Contrasting his own theatre work with that of the naturalist school, he proclaimed in the Prologue to *Mystery Bouffe*:

> We, too, will show you life that's real —
> very!
> But life transformed by the theatre into a spectacle most extraordinary![12]

These three lines sum up his aims, and those of Meyerhold, with extreme accuracy. Real life is their subject matter, 'transformation' is the action the medium performs on that reality, and 'spectacle', something 'most extraordinary', is the product. The spectacle's relation to life is through the theatre, which, since it is an art form, challenges us to see its subject matter afresh. In another quatrain, Mayakovsky wrote:

> Set up a searchlight,
>   so the footlights will fade,
> Bright,
>   so the action
>   crackles, doesn't bask.
> The theatre
>   is not a reflecting mirror
> But —
>   a magnifying glass.[13]

Mystery Bouffe, Mayakovsky's 'heroic, epic and satiric' drama of the revolution, was the first of his plays to demonstrate this. It concerns a group of the 'Unclean' (i.e. proletarians), who reach the North Pole, the last dry place on the earth, everywhere else having been drowned in the revolutionary flood. Unfortunately, some 'Clean' people have also arrived, and they make the Unclean build an Ark to save them. Their attempts to dominate eventually so infuriate the Unclean that they throw them overboard, and just when they think they are adrift, the Person of the Future approaches, walking on the water. They are encouraged to sail on, harrowing hell, purging heaven, smashing through the Land of Chaos, till they finally reach the Promised Land – their home town, now revolutionized, cleansed of exploitation, rich with promise and potential.

It was read to Meyerhold's company at the Alexandrinsky Theatre in August 1918. The actors were aghast, made a series of feeble excuses, and more or less refused to perform it. Meyerhold, Mayakovsky and others involved then obtained the Music Drama Theatre for three nights over the anniversary of the revolution, advertised in the press for actors, and the whole project was put together in a few hair-raising weeks. When the play was put on again in a heavily rewritten version in 1921, it had lost none of its original 'hooligan communism' attributes, but had gained in both resonance and humour. It had become in fact not simply the first Soviet play (though it was proudly proclaimed as that), but the first piece of epic theatre as we understand the term today. How far this was recognized at the time is hard to estimate. Ilinsky called the 1921 production of *Mystery Bouffe* 'a major cultural event . . . the whole of theatrical Moscow's attention was glued absolutely to it'.[14] Yet few reviews of it seem to have been published. The ever-optimistic Boris Malkin almost promised Meyerhold that Lenin would attend a performance. The revolutionary leader, however, remained at home.

Meyerhold, however, was sure enough of the dramatic gifts of *Mystery Bouffe*'s author to yearn for another play from his pen. In 1926, Mayakovsky was reportedly writing a 'comedy with murder' for Meyerhold; the following year this had become a film script; but by 1928 it was *The Bedbug*, a stage play telling of a worker, Prysipkin, who wishes to better himself by marrying a hairdresser. She – or her family – has done well out of NEP, and he has 'an immaculate proletarian origin and a union card'.[15] At the drunken wedding feast, the restaurant burns down, despite the efforts of the firemen who douse it with water in the freezing night. Fifty years later, a frozen block is found, and in it the former worker, and a bedbug. These are revived, but unable to adjust to the desicated society of 1979, they become exhibits in a zoo. The worker appeals to the audience to join him in his cage.

'With this play', Meyerhold wrote, 'Mayakovsky gives a new utterance in the field of playwriting, and at the same time the work dazzles with its virtuosity of language.'[16] Moreover, the play seemed to fit Trotsky's prescription exactly, even to the extent of following *The Government Inspector* and *Woe to Wit* in the Meyerhold Theatre's repertory. Trotsky wrote:

> Our theatre is terribly in need of a new realistic revolutionary repertory and above all, of a *Soviet comedy*. We ought to have our own 'The Minors', our own 'Woes from Being Too Wise', our own 'Inspector General'. Not a new staging of these three old comedies, not a retouching of them in a Soviet style, as for a carnival parody, though this would be more vital than ninety-nine per cent of our repertory – no; we need simply a Soviet comedy of manners, one of laughter and of indignation... A new class, a new life, new vices and new stupidity, demand that they shall be released from silence, and when this will happen we will have a new dramatic art, for it is impossible to reproduce the new stupidity without new methods.[17]

By the time *The Bedbug* was written, however, Trotsky had fallen, so that any similarity passed wholly unmentioned.

And if *The Bedbug* seemed to fulfil Trotsky's prescription, *The Bathhouse* was even more pertinent. Mayakovsky had had his only small piece of praise from Lenin for a poem satirizing bureaucracy; here he made his masterpiece out of the subject. Chudakov, a scientist, has invented a time machine by which a person of the future is going to arrive in the Soviet Union very shortly. When he tries to make the authorities aware of what is happening, he is fobbed off by the bureaucrat Pobedonosikov, who, it transpires, is in the theatre watching – and disapproving of – the play. The Phosphorescent Woman arrives, and decides to take into the future those who are helping it (i.e. the future). Pobedonosikov takes charge of the arrangements, but at the moment of departure the space ship spits him and his colleagues out, roaring away with the workers and scientists, those who are genuinely building the future.

Meyerhold considered it Mayakovsky's best play,[18] and compared it with Molière – the only other playwright 'who had access to the lightness with which this play was written'.[19] Mayakovsky, too, felt it was his best work, protesting vigorously against any dissenters from this view.[20] The title itself affords some insight into its multi-facetedness, for a bathhouse is, of course, a place where one is cleansed, but it is also common cant for a brothel as well as being a place where one receives just reprimands ('to give someone a bath' in Russian is equivalent to 'giving them a roasting'). Elizabeth Warner has described how in the folk play *The Fool, the French Doctor and the Young Woman*, 'the fool, who complains of every conceivable ache and pain, is led to the communal bath-house (places noted for immoral behaviour in the 17th and 18th century) where a beautiful young woman soon cures him of all his ills'.[21] The richness of the connotations of Mayakovsky's title are obvious.

67. *The Bathhouse*, 1930. Pobedonosikov (*right*) with his aptly-named 'adminis-
trative secretary', Optimistenko

How much of this was brought over in performance is difficult to tell. After
the first night, Mayakovsky wrote: 'I liked it, except for certain details. In my
opinion, it is the first piece of mine well produced. Straukh (who played
Pobedonosikov, the main part) excellent.'[22] But the production was so
rapidly engulfed in a controversy at once fatuous and almost inconceivably
vicious, that genuine responses are hard to be sure of. Mayakovsy added:
'The audience is riduculously divided. Some say they have never been so
bored, others – they have never enjoyed themselves so.'[23] The actress Maria
Sukhanova, usually a sane voice amid the screams, confirms this: 'The
audience received it most oddly: some spectators sat as if made of stone,
others reacted well.'[24] Actually of course, this was precisely the kind of
response Meyerhold usually strove for, and though he took exception to
some of the more bilious attacks – 'to pass judgment, on the basis of a
[published] fragment, on a play composed for the theatre is tantamount to a
total lack of understanding as to what happens with a play when it receives a
theatrical form (that is, when it is produced)'[25] – it is probable that the
contradictory audience responses did not disconcert him.

The similarly mixed reaction to *Mystery Bouffe* has already been noted. In
this, the strength of audience feeling was encouraged not only by typical

incidents such as that remembered by Bogolyubov – 'Mayakovsky in the foyer in animated conversation with a group of Red Army soldiers'[26] – but also by such directorial devices as bringing pieces of action into the auditorium. Maria Sukhanova again describes this well:

The stage box was broken. The action was brought out into the auditorium, for which purpose several rows of seats were removed from the stalls. In front, in the foreground, a globe of the Earth was constructed or, rather, a portion of the globe. The wings were all removed . . . Objects and machines were placed in the loge boxes. 'The Person of the Future' appeared in the right portal of the stage (looking from the audience) at the very top by the ceiling on a specially built platform.[27]

A similar technique was used in *The Bedbug*, when in the first scene, for instance, some of the street vendors entered through the audience shouting their wares and made their exits the same way when the policeman appeared. And something of the same mixed but powerful reaction was provoked: the textile workers of the Krasnaya Zarya factory 'unanimously stated that the play made a great impression on them. At the same time the audience points out to the theatre certain faults which in future can certainly be corrected.'[28] The power of the impression can be further gauged from the fact that the bedbug entered contemporary folklore: sitting on a trolley bus, Mayakovsky 'overheard one comrade annihilate another with the invective, "You scum, you bedbug out of Mayakovsky!"'[29]

The 'magnifying glass' rather than 'reflecting mirror' style of the presentation was partly responsible for the unforgettability of the plays. As far as the acting was concerned, the characters must have 'no biographies', Mayakovsky insisted. 'Everything must be understandable. No psychologizing.'[30] The style derived from 'the little genres – circus, variety stage, music hall',[31] as Vladimir Lyutse noted. 'The actor's performance is created through the solving of a series of physical problems', he added, and asked of the actor the ability while on stage constantly to change genres: at one moment he had to be a singer, then a dancer, an acrobat, a dramatic actor, and so on. And not only must the actor be able to effect these transformations, but often he is required not to *be* what he is showing, but to create an exaggerated parody of it. These demands fully reveal the purpose of the biomechanical training.

Meyerhold's own keen fascination with the 'little genres' was at last matched by a similar fascination on the part of his author. Mayakovsky had actually worked with the famous clown, Vitaly Lazarenko, before the revolution, and Lazarenko had agreed to play a small part in *Mystery Bouffe*. Mayakovsky's last dramatic work, *Moscow is Burning*, was directed by Sergei Radlov for the Moscow State Circus. The result was the kind of performance with which Igor Ilinsky made his name.

Ilinsky's initial success was as the Menshevik in *Mystery Bouffe*, a part he

68. *Mystery Bouffe*, 1921. The Menshevik, designed by Viktor Kiselev

was given only twelve days before the show opened on May Day, 1921. He played it as the red-haired clown of the circus, the fall guy, the buffoon who gets slapped. Rushing hither and thither, always intervening to preach compromise where no compromise was possible, he was whacked, knocked down, browbeaten and made a jackass of in almost every scene, yet always he came back for more. This was the period when Mayakovsky was creating the propaganda window posters for ROSTA, and Ilinsky's performance was like

69. *The Bedbug*, 1929. Prysipkin is about to be awakened into the future

one of those – clean, dynamic, hilarious, a one-dimensional howl of laughter, which however was not without its own subtler reverberations.

And as Prysipkin in *The Bedbug*, he took his style a step further. He began by modelling himself on the author:

I began to build Prysipkin's part as a 'monumental' flunkey and boor. This monumentalism made for a larger scale of that character. Though it may seem paradoxical, I adopted for Prysipkin, even externally ... Mayakovsky's manner. But to his manner, in itself impeccable, and even perfect, I added certain compromising shades: I enlarged the briskness of his movements, I imbued the majestically fixed expression on his face with dull cretinism, I stood pigeon-toed. The characteristic contours, for the moment external, of a pathetically triumphant philistine began to take shape. External characteristics then had to be enriched by more and more living traits. Decisive convictions turned into self-complacency; self-confidence and glibness, into hopeless insolence . . .[32]

The result was something certainly comical, highly unpleasant, but also uncomfortably close to home. *Pravda*'s reviewer stated that 'the image he creates is original and unforgettable. He disturbs the spectators and makes them laugh, and holds their intense attention on himself absolutely all the time till the end.'[33]

Specific moments were treated as 'turns' in their own right – his lascivious dance with the bride at his wedding, his black-gloved hand slipping down and around her white wedding-dress in an individual dance of its own; the unfreezing of Prysipkin, when the depersonalized professor's long series of quasi-scientific orders called forth whirrs, buzzes, flashing lights and so on till Prysipkin woke lazily, stretched, peered round and said in a most matter-of-fact way, 'Where am I?'; and the chase of the bedbug, and then the attempt to befriend it. But others, too, had such 'turns' — like Alexander Kostomolotsky as the incredibly aged waiter who served the ham at the wedding breakfast, bent double and groaning grumpily.

Clearly such 'unpsychological' acting required a particular kind of set, and Meyerhold's productions of these plays reveal the kind of contribution he wanted the *mise-en-scène* to make. The brilliant but erratic Kasimir Malevich was invited to design the first production of *Mystery Bouffe*. The result was weird and unsettling. He had designed *Victory Over the Sun*, a pre-revolutionary futurist opera which Mayakovsky had apparently liked (the Promised Land in *Mystery Bouffe* owed a clear debt to this opera), but it seems his designs for *Mystery Bouffe* were too much the work of a painter for Meyerhold's liking. Heaven was the pink of raspberries and cream, the Promised Land steel blue and grey like a battleship. The problem was that the *mise-en-scènes* were conceived as a series of interrelated kinetic cubist paintings, and though provocative as art works, they were evidently not particularly successful as a stage setting.

Malevich's geometrical and angular conception did not wholly disappear from the second production, created by a collective under Meyerhold's own direction. But now there was a conscious attempt to mediate with some admixture from the ancient popular theatre, as Mayakovsky had done in the writing. Filtered through the sensibilities of a twentieth-century artist, the mystery-play Heaven was thus poised above Hell in a manner strongly reminiscent of Bilibin's design for *The Act of Theophilus* at Evreinov's 'Ancient Theatre' in 1907, but tempered with cubistic modernism. The costumes, took on a cruder, more popular quality, somewhat akin to Mayakovsky's ROSTA window designs. In fact, the 'Unclean' wore the first of several attempts by Meyerhold's theatre to create stage-work clothes (*Prozodezhdy*), and this particular example influenced the typical costumes of the Blue Blouse agitprop troupes who were just coming into existence.

Despite the fact that the second design for *Mystery Bouffe*, which was the more successful, was not the work of a professional artist as such, when *The Bedbug* came to be prepared, Meyerhold and Mayakovsky decided to invite artists rather than stage designers to create the settings. This time, however, they had the clever idea of asking one artist (or rather three — the Kukriniksy team) to design the first half set in the present day, and another, Rodchenko, the second half, set in the future. They thus ensured a complete contrast between the two parts of the play. The first half, a series of fairly conventional stage settings, were dressed with artefacts bought over the counter in Moscow shops and deployed to create what Gorchakov described as a 'nightmare' effect.[34] The second half was completely different, all severe

70. *The Bathhouse, 1930.* The workers climb up to the time machine which is to take them into the future

shapes and symmetrical lines. The contrast was heightened by the use of lighting; in the first half, warm lights, mostly reds and yellows, were used; in the second half, white and blue, with Ilinsky often in a harsh spotlight. At the moment when he recognized the audience the house lights came full on. There was no escape.

Interesting though this set was, *The Bathhouse* was considerably more inventive and challenging, and it was the work not of any artist but of Meyerhold himself and Sergei Vakhtangov, his permanent designer. What they achieved was the artist's overall conception modified by a theatricality which made it perhaps Meyerhold's most successful set. At least, it might have been, if the budget had been able to stretch to what was planned. As it was, the time capsule had to be presented as invisible, and when it vomitted out the bureaucrats at the end, this had to be done offstage. Nevertheless, the set as presented was an exciting 'machine for acting', consisting of a series of staircases and platforms, always stretching out in a dynamic appearance of upward thrust. Juxtaposed to this were, at one time, the light-coloured walls of the scientist's laboratory, with the slender lines of the diagrams, and at other times the slogans on what look like fragile Venetian blinds. They in turn were contradicted by the heavy leather armchair, the solid, even sinking,

71. *The Bathhouse*, 1930. The scientist's laboratory

72. *The Bathhouse*, 1930. Pobedenosikov in his heavy armchair

comfort of the official's office, and the chunky figure of the chief bureaucrat himself. The clothes, the lighting, the props all contained this three-way interplay so that Meyerhold was able to devise some of his most striking groupings.

There were complaints that the music by Vissarion Shebalin in this production was too loud – the same complaints had been made about the music for *Mystery Bouffe*. That had been accused of 'desperate harmonic and melodic vulgarity', 'an unendurably trite march in the second act' and 'a perversion of "The Internationale" and "The Marseillaise".'[35] (Yet the effectiveness of, for instance, the use of 'The Internationale' can be gauged from the fact that after this, many other productions and plays, such as Vassily Kamensky's *Stenka Razin*, not to mention foreign productions, several by Erwin Piscator in Germany, for instance, used it as a finale.) Shebalin, a former pupil of Meyerhold's longstanding partner, Mikhail Gnesin, and a composer of sensitive yet trenchant scores, became Meyerhold's favourite musical collaborator, and particularly pleased him with this score and that for *The Lady of the Camellias*. As one Soviet commentator recorded, his work has 'points of contact with folksong, and his creative work is enriched by the harmonies and polyphonies of popular music'. But he fell under a shadow, perhaps inevitably, because, as the same writer adds, in some of his compositions of this period 'it is possible to detect features of West European expressionism'.[36]

Probably the most interesting score for a Mayakovsky play from a musical point of view was Dmitry Shostakovich's for *The Bedbug*, a score he almost did not write, since Prokofiev was invited to compose the music for the production first, and only declined because of the pressure of time. Shostakovich was the theatre's resident pianist at the time, and particularly close to Meyerhold. He has recorded that he had

several conversations with Mayakovsky about my music for *The Bedbug*. 'Do you like firemen's bands?' asked Mayakovsky. I said that sometimes I did, and sometimes I didn't, and Mayakovsky replied that that . . . was the sort of music that should be written for *The Bedbug* . . . Speaking about the music for the second part of the play, he asked me to make it simple, 'simple like mooing', so that it wouldn't evoke any particular emotion, as he put it. We didn't talk about the music of the future in general, but about the music for a definite part of the play – for example, for the zoological gardens scene, the band plays a festive march. I don't take it upon myself to judge whether Mayakovsky liked my music or not, but he listened to it and said briefly: 'Suitable, on the whole!'[37]

Shostakovich's music turned out to be dynamic, salty and at times cacophonous, and it played a crucial part in the creation of the dramatic rhythm the author and director were attempting to achieve. Meyerhold himself described how 'in *The Bedbug* there are a number of extraordinary shifts from one episode to another in which we feel the best rhythmic modulations of Shakespeare'.[38] These were often achieved with the aid of Shostakovich's music. For instance, Bayan plays a smoochy foxtrot during the wedding scene, and this is then picked up by the offstage band and put into the relative major key to become, in Rudnitsky's words, 'stormy' and 'grotesque'. Quite quickly the theme was 'devoured by wild, unthinkable collisions between ever-stronger sounds'.[39] It effected the transition to the future.

The music thus became not simply a means of moving from one attraction to another, but an attraction in its own right. Lyutse noticed that 'a production which is properly faithful' to the author's intentions 'will be built as a montage of attractions',[40] and, according to *Pravda*'s reviewer, Meyerhold's production achieved this: '"Psychology" is completely absent. The action proceeds by shocks and merrily. The laughter is by no means Chekhovian, but is the harsh, rather coarse, uncompromising laughter of a social activist, political laughter which has its own form.'[41] Rudnitsky has suggested that *Mystery Bouffe* proceeded in precisely this way, and indeed that 'five years before the publication of Sergei Eisenstein's famous article "A Montage of Attractions", Mayakovsky already had created such a montage'.[42] Just as Eisenstein listed attractions from his production of *The Wiseman*, so Rudnitsky does the same for the first act of *Mystery Bouffe*:

1. The clownlike entrance of the fisherman and the Eskimo who has plugged the hole in the globe with his finger. 2. The Frenchman's expository monologue. 3. Two paired clownlike entrances (the pair of Australians; the Italian and the German). 4. The fencing duel between the Italian and the German. 5. An acrobatic trick: the merchant falling onto the head of the Eskimo. 6. The parade of the clean and the unclean. 7. The rally scene. 8. Farce: commencement of the construction of the Ark.[43]

This method of play construction, invented virtually single-handed from a playwriting point of view by Mayakovsky, was a remarkable feat. Certainly it owed a good deal to what Mayakovsky had learned from his close relationship with Meyerhold's theatre (even when he was not writing plays for it, he was heavily involved in the polemics surrounding it, and defended it in many a public dispute). But it is also a development from Mayakovsky's poetry, in which the most striking and subtlest effects often arise from his fascination with the interplay between sound and rhythm, in what seems remarkably like a poetic montage. And in addition it is worth remembering that he was a trained and practising artist, which certainly encouraged him to seek arresting and original visual effects.

The creation of a series of vivid moments, each stimulating it its own right, but gaining richness from being set beside others, may be described as a

73. An 'attraction' from Act 6 of *The Bathhouse*

dialectical procedure. Mayakovsky himself hinted at this in his own description of *Mystery Bouffe* as

our great revolution, condensed in poetry and theatrical action. The mystery is the greatness of the action, the bouffe, the laughter in it. The verse of *Mystery Bouffe* is found in the slogans of meetings, the cries of street vendors, the language of the newspapers. The action of *Mystery Bouffe* is the action of the crowd, the conflict between classes, the struggle of ideas – the world in miniature within the walls of a circus.[44]

But if dialectics is the dynamo powering *Mystery Bouffe*, a 'heroic, epic and satiric' cross between a mass meeting and a clown show, so it is with equal if not greater vibrancy in *The Bathhouse*, particularly in Act 3. This richly comic scene enabled Meyerhold to set up an almost infinite series of cross references and paradoxes. The characters from the play entered through the auditorium, as if they were members of the audience, and began to discuss the drama, and their own reality – or even probability – in it. The whole sequence out-Pirandellos Pirandello, and in it Meyerhold displayed with dazzling dexterity the whole gamut of styles of theatre, from naturalism through dance to agitprop. Each served as an attraction in itself, but as a sequence it became a stinging challenge to critical and therefore ideological and therefore political complacency. It was defamiliarization of the most startling kind.

The final element in this extraordinary mixture which was Mayakovsky and Meyerhold's dramatic form, and what gave it perhaps its most distinctive edge, was Mayakovsky's introduction of the future into each of the plays. Meyerhold's staging ensured that the future would be an unmistakable part of the dramatic strategy. In the first version of *Mystery Bouffe*, Mayakovsky himself played the part of the Person of the Future: 'Concealed from the audience's view, he climbed four or five metres up a metal wall-ladder behind the left side of the proscenium. Then he was attached at the waist to a length of broad leather and when the cue came he appeared to be impelled headlong into the action, skimming above the crowd of the Unclean on the ark.'[45] The awakening of Prysipkin into the future in *The Bedbug* has already been noted as one of Ilinsky's most memorable 'turns', and Zinaida Raikh's entry as the Phosphorescent Woman in *The Bathhouse*, complete with glittering black helmet and glossy white space suit, was another Meyerholdian *coup de théâtre*.

But these were not just effects for their own sake. They provided a perspective which allowed the audience to see 'today' as historically specific, rather than universal and inevitable. Mayakovsky's futurism was a way of comprehending the present in relation to the future, as opposed to the more usual attempt to understand the present in relation to the past. Futurism views the here and now not as the culmination of what has gone before, but as the springboard for what is to come. That is why it seemed to Mayakovsky to make such a natural bedfellow for communism, whose eyes are similarly fixed on the future. The precise form which 'the future' should take in any play is therefore not important, and those ideologically-motivated critics who gleefully proclaim that the future as depicted in *The Bedbug* shows Mayakovsky's disillusionment with communism are not understanding the most fundamental point about Mayakovsky's drama. The play is a 'fairy comedy': to read it literally in this way is to court silliness. The only point is that Mayakovsky needed the perspective of the future on the present. It may be, as Shostakovich and Tairov both suggested, that Mayakovsky is here depicting Prysipkin's terrified vision of the future, a petty bourgeois parody of communism. Actually, as R. Shapiro pointed out, the problem is wholly one for the designer and the director, not the armchair ideologue. It is they who must 'present the future as a background, necessary to set off more sharply all the "charms" of Prysipkin's philistinism'.[46] The fact that Mayakovsky's use of the future has caused such squirming is proof only of its power. It may be worth noting in passing, by the way, that Bertolt Brecht developed a somewhat similar 'futurist' perspective in some of his later plays, but never with the same imagination or urgency.

Apart perhaps from Blok in Meyerhold's early days, therefore, Mayakovsky was probably the only writer whose work not only complemented Meyerhold's own, but even challenged it to develop further. And as with all the most fascinating creative partnerships, the process worked both ways. Meyerhold himself remarked: 'Mayakovsky told me that while working on *The Bedbug* and *The Bathhouse*, he learned much from our productions of *The Government Inspector*, *Woe to Wit*, and *The Mandate*. This is how the collaboration between the theatre and the poet should be: both learn from each other.' Significantly, he added: 'And in some ways Mayakovsky went further and gave us new challenges.'[47] It is because of that, and because of their joint concern for the future, that the description by Igor Ilinsky, Meyerhold and Mayakovsky's greatest actor, of the beginning of their work together, is so apt:

Rehearsals for *Mystery Bouffe* began on the first warm spring day of 1921. Snow still lay in the flowerbeds of the 'Aquarium', having only just melted on the paths. The spring sun shone gaily. It was a singular beginning. The first rehearsals took place in the 'Aquarium'. We went without hats, without coats. The spring breeze invigorated us, infused us with joy and energy.[48]

9   The legacy

Vsevolod Meyerhold was perhaps the theatre's greatest representative of that wider artistic movement known as 'modernism' which began possibly thirty years before the end of the last century and continued for about thirty years into this. Certainly his influence was pervasive in the startling and arresting world of Russian theatre in its most brilliant phase between about 1910 and 1930. Yet when Peter Brook, in a programme note to his production of *A Midsummer Night's Dream* at the Royal Shakespeare Theatre, Stratford-upon-Avon, in 1970, acknowledged a debt to Meyerhold, few but the keenest theatre enthusiasts even recognized his name. To clarify his legacy, therefore, is a task of some relevance.

The obliteration of Meyerhold's memory was perhaps the more surprising since those who worked with him spread out through the theatre like ink across blotting paper. In the years after the revolution, when Meyerhold himself had gone to Moscow, the Petrograd theatre was dominated by former associates and ex-students of Dr Dapertutto. Nikolai Petrov worked on mass spectacles in the 'War Communism' period and became a leading director at the Academic (formerly Imperial) Theatres. He and Sergei Radlov were probably the most prominent theatre workers in the second Soviet city in the 1920s. Soloviev continued working there, as did Derzhavin. Kuzmin Tverskoi became a director at the new Theatre of Tragedy, Romantic Drama and High Comedy, a direct offshoot of Narkompros in 1918 and founded initially by three writers with strong government influence – Blok, Gorky and Lunacharsky – and three actors – Maria Andreevna, Yuri Yurev and Nikolai Monakhov. Dmitriev designed at the Academic Theatres, Mgebrov and others acted there. From the days of the Comrades of the New Drama, Rudolf Ungern was a respected director, and Yuri Rakitin and André Lavrentev among others, successful actors. And so on. Further afield, Alexei Gripich became artistic director of the Theatre of Revolution in Moscow after Meyerhold left in 1923, with Alpers his dramaturg. Alpers was also editor of Moscow's respected *Novyi Zritel'* (The New Spectator) magazine. Abroad, the Meyerhold influence was best seen in the theatricality of the work of emigrés like Pitoëff and Komissarzhevsky, both of whom had graduated through Komissarzhevskaya's theatre, while the interest in *commedia dell' arte* of virtually all the major Russian directors outside the Moscow Art Theatre – Evreinov, Tairov, Vakhtangov, and others – sprang from Meyerhold's

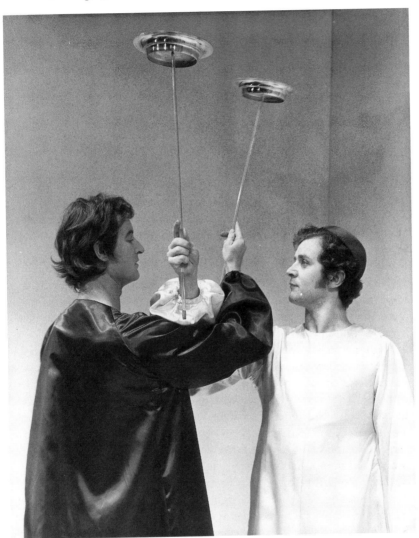

74. A scene from *A Midsummer Night's Dream*, directed by Peter Brook, Royal Shakespeare Company, 1970

pioneering experiments. The Blue Blouse movement, the agitprop developments, the living newspapers and so on, were all incalculably indebted to Meyerhold's energy, enthusiasm and above all his ideas, and from the Meyerhold Workshops after the revolution emerged not only theatre directors – Okhlopkov, Pluchek, Garin and others – but many major film directors – Eisenstein, Yutkevich, Ekk, and more. It is worth noting also that Kuleshov's

Workshop, where Pudovkin, Barnet and others trained, was housed in the same building as Meyerhold's in 1922, and there was inevitably much cross-fertilization and indeed some shared students. In 1936, the cinema director Grigory Kozintsev said: 'It seems to me that the Soviet cinema has learned more from the brilliance of Meyerhold's work that the Soviet theatre.'[1] Indeed those 1920s films preserve a certain measure of the Meyerhold style – more, probably, than we can acquire from any other source. So Soviet performing arts were imbued with Meyerhold's ideas at every level.

Equally significantly, by the early 1920s Meyerhold had discovered and utilized virtually every device of the theatre we now associate with Weimar Germany, especially with Piscator and Brecht. The half-curtain, the use of projections, the refusal to hide the artefacts of the theatre – brick walls, electric lights, and so on – the snapping on and off of the house lights, the bright stage lighting, the use of music and song, the striving for few but telling properties, the refusal to 'identify' the actor with the part, the formal groupings of actors on the stage, the breaking down of the drama into episodes, the willingness to adapt a given text, 'montage' not 'growth', 'each scene for itself' in a 'narrative', not 'one scene making another' in a 'plot',[2] all these and more were employed equally by Meyerhold and Brecht, but in every case the Russian preceded the German by years.

Furthermore, we know that by the early 1920s Brecht was interested in Soviet art generally and Soviet theatre in particular. His first sources were Bernhard Reich, who had been attached to Kuleshov's Workshop, and his wife Asja Lacis, who had studied with Komissarzhevsky, both of whom travelled between Germany and the Soviet Union throughout the 1920s and 1930s. His second source was Sergei Tretyakov, whom he had met by 1930, and whose plays influenced his own, notably *Roar, China!* which the Meyerhold State Theatre performed in Berlin in 1930 and which Brecht made a rough translation of. In 1934, typically laconically, Brecht described Tretyakov as 'working along the right lines' and said he had 'found quite new means of expression'[3] in the theatre. After Tretyakov's death, he was to call him, rather more simply, 'My teacher, tall and kindly.'[4] Before then, *I Want a Child* having failed to pass the censor, Tretyakov had turned to 'factography' and translation, and his Russian versions of *St Joan of the Stockyards*, *The Measures Taken* and *The Mother* were highly valued by Brecht.

In Moscow Brecht stayed at Tretyakov's flat, and in April 1935 was taken by him to the Central Art Workers' Club to see a performance by Mei Lan-fang. At this performance, Meyerhold sat with Eisenstein and perhaps Tairov and Moskvin. Whether he – and they – discussed it with Brecht and Tretyakov is not known, but a photograph taken that evening shows Mei Lan-fang between Tairov and Eisenstein, with Tretyakov behind. At any rate,

75. At the Central Art Workers' Club in Moscow, April 1935: (*left to right*) Alexander Tairov, Sergei Tretyakov, Mei Lan-fang, Pavel Tsetnerovich, Sergei Eisenstein

next day Meyerhold delivered some typically elliptical thoughts on the evening, particularly concerning the Chinese actor's physical and rhythmical expressiveness.[5] For Brecht, it had been the Chinese actor's way of watching himself at work ('self-admiration' Meyerhold called it) which was important: 'The artist's object is to appear strange and even surprising to the audience. He achieves this by looking strangely at himself and his work . . . Everyday things are thereby raised above the level of the obvious.'[6] The language is easily recognizable: it derives from Formalist critical terminology. And according to Willett, this was when Brecht coined the term 'Verfrem-dungseffekt' (usually translated 'alienation effect') which is itself a Germaniza-tion of Shklovsky's concept of 'making strange'. It was Tretyakov, a close associate of Shklovsky and Meyerhold, who explained the concept to Brecht.

This is not to say, of course, that Brecht merely took over and regurgitated ideas from Shklovsky or Meyerhold or Tretyakov. All four shared the same aim to create a non-illusionist drama which would serve a progressive social purpose, and Brecht absorbed these Russian notions among others to produce his own unique mix. But these facts do help to explain how the legacy of Meyerhold got lost.

For by this date, with Hitler in power in Germany, Brecht was an exile with no theatre and hardly any outlet for his writings. He was a danger to the state, his books burned, his person wanted, but as an exile he could survive. In the Soviet Union, the situation for the artist was not quite so clearcut. Here the heavy blanket of conformity came down more slowly, over years, and major artists whose work had been honoured by the state, like Meyerhold, probably never quite believed that a death sentence was a reality for them. After all, the arguments over Marxist art still proceeded. Essentially, for the socialist realists, a work of art aims to fuse conflicting strands of reality into a complex whole, thus integrating the spectator into the socialist reality, whereas for Meyerhold and those dubbed 'Formalists' in the 1930s and 1940s, 'realism' meant exposing the 'conflicting strands' in all their contradictoriness: for the spectator's power to criticize, to seek new paths towards a genuine social harmony, derives precisely from an awareness of contradictions. Since this is a dialectical process, it makes demands on those who attempt it, energizing them rather than pacifying them. However 'socialist' or Marxist such a proceeding might seem, it could not be tolerated in Stalin's USSR, where national unity and uncritical self-sacrifice were the watchwords in the face of threats from the west: after all, the country had been invaded by − among others − Britain, France, the USA, Poland and Germany in the previous twenty or so years. A little paranoia was understandable. To execute a major artist, however, and totally to surpress his ideas, is more than 'a little' paranoid.

In this, Meyerhold's work was unlike, say, Formalism, which was also annihilated in the USSR but which spread and gradually gained acceptance in the west through the 1930s and 1940s. The difference is important, and throws a crucial light on the nature of Meyerhold's work. For Formalism was socially and politically neutral. 'Meyerholdism' (to coin a phrase) was not. And so while it was too dangerous in the east, and too dangerous for Soviet sympathizers in Communist Parties in the west, it was also too dangerous for mainstream western culture, where entertainers who were now or had ever been sympathetic to socialism were being persecuted with the utmost ferocity and vigour. In a climate where artists of the stature of Charlie Chaplin and Paul Robeson were hounded into private purgatories, what chance of being heard, let alone appraised open-mindedly, had someone like

Meyerhold, a complex Russian Marxist theatre director, who had never simplified and published his 'system'? So there was no hiding-place or refuge for Meyerhold's thought (his papers were hidden in Eisenstein's *dacha*), only a total blackout about him for at least fifteen years after his execution.

Meanwhile, Brecht, who had been living in the USA, was now forced to flee the persecutions of the House Committee on Un-American Activities. He returned to Europe in 1947, founded the Berliner Ensemble and, with his own methods, staggered the world, particularly the progressive sections of it. His techniques — too well known to need rehearsing here — became by about 1960 the acceptable face of left-wing or Marxist theatre. For years then the aesthetic of the neutral colour, the rough-textured cloth, the gestic grouping (all features of Meyerhold's production of *The Second Commander* (1929), which Brecht had seen, of course) dominated: not that it was a bad aesthetic, merely that it became numbingly predictable and thus the opposite of the Marxist — and Brechtian — ideal. But it desperately needed broadening and diversifying. It was then that the rediscovery of Meyerhold began to gather pace and direction.

For already, by 1960, in the Soviet Union, a few chinks of light had been shed on the 'illegally suppressed' Master. Pluchek and Yutkevich had restaged some of Mayakovsky's work at the Theatre of Satire, and Garin had begun to re-explore Meyerhold's 1920s repertoire at the Theatre of Film Actors. Articles by former colleagues of Meyerhold like Fevralsky and Gladkov were published, reminiscences started to appear and in 1967 *Vstrechi s Meierkhol'dom* (*Meetings with Meyerhold*), a large book of over 600 pages, was published. It was followed the next year by a two-volume collection of Meyerhold's own writings, and in 1969 by Rudnitsky's monumental study.[7] In all this there was a note of caution. It was difficult for Soviet scholars to come to terms with a towering genius whom the government you support did to death and whose memory was blotted out for nearly twenty years.

For the new generation of Soviet theatre directors, however, there were fewer inhibitions: in Leningrad, Georgi Tovstonogov and in Moscow Anatoly Efros and Yuri Lyubimov began to create a series of startling new productions, proclaiming their inheritance to be from Meyerhold. Lyubimov, who knew Meyerhold ('a miniature bust of the famous director occupies a prominent spot on Lyubimov's desk'[8]), achieved genuine and stimulating 'montages of attractions' in for example his production of *Ten Days that Shook the World* at the Taganka Theatre. Here the attitude to the spectator is stated from the moment he or she enters Taganka Square, for revolutionary music blares out from the lighted theatre, then tickets are torn by a 'Red Guard' who spikes the stubs on his bayonet, and in the foyer an apparently impromptu group of performers sing revolutionary songs, dance and make fun of the audience. Inside, the acting has a corresponding directness which is coupled with a wide variety of highly developed skills – acrobatics, clowning, dance, declamation and tableaux, all superbly distilled into a disciplined, fast-moving ensemble effect. The *mise-en-scène* we are presented with is an open stage, bare to the brick walls at the back, modified from time to time by the use of projections, single props or pieces of furniture, and brilliant lighting effects. The piece is governed by a sharp, jagged rhythm, and saturated with music – hardly any scene proceeds without musical accompaniment. And the whole produces a montage of attractions which forces the spectator to assess his or her attitude first to the revolution itself by defying preformed prejudices and stock sentimentalities, and second – equally important – to the theatre itself. The production does not show characters or a conventional story line, in which we can and should believe, it presents an essential theatricality (despite the 'realness' of its subject), which grabs us by the lapels, teases us to know more, allures us, startles us, but above all shares with us a delight in the theatricality of theatre. This ability simultaneously to make the medium illuminate the message and the message illuminate the medium is truly dialectical and dynamic.

It is Meyerhold's hallmark. For unlike, say, Stanislavsky, who created a prose theatre of realism to match the best nineteenth-century novels, Meyerhold forged a poetic theatre, popular and engaging, which had infinite potential and reverberations. For this reason, Meyerhold has seized the interest of those who have become aware of naturalism's limitations and Brecht's single-mindedness. Meyerhold's lyricism ranges from the grotesque to the pathetic; it can be astringent, even bitter and venomous, though more often it wears an ironic smile; it can be broad, exultant, pregnant with 'life's juices'; always it is quintessentially of the theatre. This finally is the justifica-tion of the work of Meyerhold, the 'Picasso of the theatre':[9] just as Picasso's career reasserted the validity of painting in an age when photography seemed to make it obsolete, so Meyerhold's made – and still makes – live theatre valid at a time when film and television threaten to obliterate it as a distinctive art form. That is his true legacy.

Appendix 1
Chronology

Year	Meyerhold	Theatre	Art and culture	Politics and society
1874	28 Jan: Meyerhold born.			
1875				
1876		Wagner, *The Ring*.	Nov: birth of Lunacharsky.	Telephone invented.
1877				
1878				
1879		Ibsen, *A Doll's House*.		
1880		Zola, *Naturalism in the Theatre*, published.		
1881		Ibsen, *Ghosts*	Feb: death of Dostoievsky.	March: Tsar Alexander II assassinated; Alexander III becomes tsar.
1882		Korsch Theatre, Moscow, founded.	May: birth of F. Komissarzhevsky.	
1883		Deutsches Theater, Berlin, founded.	Jan: birth of Gnesin. Feb: death of Wagner.	'Emancipation of Labour' (Marxist) group formed in Russia.
1884	Enters Penza Gymnasium			
1885			Dec: birth of Tatlin.	First major strike in Russia.
1886				
1887		Théâtre Libre, Paris, founded; Strindberg, *The Father*.		
1888		Tolstoy, *The Power of Darkness*; Strindberg, *Miss Julie*.		

1889		Freie Bühne, Berlin, founded.	April: birth of Popova.	Zemstvo reforms reduce peasant involvement in local government.
1890				March: Germany: fall of Bismarck.
1891		Independent Theatre Society, London, founded; Wedekind, *Spring Awakening*.	April: birth of Prokofiev. Nov: birth of Rodchenko.	Work on trans-Siberian railway begins. Winter: Russian famine.
1892	Feb: stage debut in amateur production of *Woe from Wit*; death of father.	Maeterlinck, *Pelleas and Melisande*; Hauptmann, *The Weavers*. Feb: professional debut of Yuri Yurev, Alexandrinsky Theatre.		Strikes; massacres of workers. Aug: Witte appointed Finance Minister.
1893		Shaw, *Mrs Warren's Profession*.	July: birth of Mayakovsky. Oct: death of Tchaikovsky.	
1894		Coquelin, *L'Art du comédien*, published.	June: birth of Zinaida Raikh. Nov: birth of Stepanova.	Jan: Franco-Russian entente. Nov: death of Alexander III; Nicholas II becomes tsar.
1895	25 June: changes name to Vsevolod Emilevich, takes Russian citizenship. Autumn: enters Moscow University Law Faculty.	Appia, *Mise-en-scène in Wagnerian Drama*, published.	First film made.	Strikers at Yaroslavl mill.
1896	April: marries Olga Munt. June: founds Penza People's Theatre. Sept: enrols in acting course at Moscow Philharmonic Society.	Oct: Chekhov: *The Seagull*, Alexandrinsky Theatre, Petersburg. Dec: Jarry, *Ubu Roi*, dir. Lugné-Poe, Paris.	May: first film seen in Russia – coronation of Tsar Nicholas II.	Wave of industrial unrest.

	Meyerhold	Theatre	Art and culture	Politics and society
1897				Russia gains Port Arthur from China. Winter: Russian famine.
1898	March: wins prize as best student actor at Philharmonic. June: founder member of Moscow Art Theatre.	Oct: Moscow Art Theatre's first production: A. Tolstoy, *Tsar Fyodor Ivanovich*. Dec: Chekhov, *The Seagull*, Moscow Art Theatre.	Jan: birth of Eisenstein. Feb: birth of Brecht. March: Tolstoy, *What Is Art?*, published. Nov: first number of Diaghilev's *World of Art*.	March: first conference of Russian Social Democratic Party.
1899		Appia, *Music and Staging*, published. Oct: Chekhov, *Uncle Vanya*, Moscow Art Theatre.	Jan: first World of Art exhibition, Petersburg. S. Freud, *The Interpretation of Dreams*, published.	Oct: beginning of Boer War. Winter: Russian famine.
1900			Feb: birth of M. Straukh. May: birth of Okhlopkov. Oct: birth of Babanova and Zharov. Nov: death of O. Wilde.	Formation of SR Party. May: Boxer rebellion in China; Russia occupies northern Manchuria.
1901		Jan: Chekhov, *The Three Sisters*, Moscow Art Theatre. Reinhardt's *Schall und Rauch* cabaret, Berlin, opens.	July: birth of Ilinsky.	Aug: death of Queen Victoria. Quantum theory propounded.
1902	Jan: quarrel with Stanislavsky. Feb: leaves Art Theatre. Summer: travels abroad. Autumn: founds Company of Russian Dramatic Artists.	Strindberg, *A Dream Play*. Kleines Theater, Berlin, founded by Reinhardt. Bryusov, *Unnecessary Truth*, published.	Sept: death of Zola. Oct: birth of Garin.	April: Spiagin (Minister of Interior) assassinated.

	Nov: Chekhov, *The Three Sisters*, Kherson.	Summer: Otodziro Kawakami's Japanese theatre company in Moscow. Dec: Gorky, *The Lower Depths*, Moscow Art Theatre.		SDP splits into Bolsheviks and Mensheviks. Dec: Wright brothers' first flight.
1903	Sept: founds Comrades of the New Drama.	Jan: Russian premiere of Wagner, *Götterdämmerung*, Petersburg.	Dec: Union of Russian Artists first exhibition, Moscow.	Jan: Port Arthur attack begins Russo-Japanese war. July: Plehve (Minister of Interior) assassinated. Aug: Alexei, heir to tsar, born. Nov: Zemstvo Congress demands representative assembly and civil liberties. Completion of trans-Siberian railway.
1904		Jan: Chekhov, *The Cherry Orchard*, Moscow Art Theatre. Fuchs, *The Stage of the Future*, published. Abbey Theatre, Dublin, founded. V. Komissarzhevskaya's Dramatic Theatre, Petersburg, founded.	July: death of Chekhov. *World of Art* ceases publication. Dec: birth of Yutkevich.	First Russian revolution – riots and civil disorder throughout the year. Jan 9: 'Bloody Sunday'. Feb: Grand Duke Sergei, Governor of Moscow, assassinated. March: Russian Army defeated at Mukden; tsar promises 'consultative assembly'; foundation of the Union of Unions.
1905	Summer: Moscow Art Studio Theatre.	Jan: *A Midsummer Night's Dream*, dir. Reinhardt, Berlin. Maeterlinck, *The Blue Bird*. Craig, *The Art of Theatre*, published.	June: first of many satirical magazines appears. Autumn: Vyacheslav Ivanov's 'Wednesdays' begin.	

	Meyerhold	Theatre	Art and culture	Politics and society
				May: Russian fleet destroyed at Tsushima. June: crew of Battleship Potemkin mutinies. June–Aug: widespread strikes and disorders. Oct: Bolshevik journal *New Life* begins publication; first session of Petersburg Soviet of Workers Deputies; Duma summoned; Cadet Party formed; Witte appointed Prime Minister. Nov: Moscow Soviet set up. Dec: General strike.
1906	Feb–Aug: with Comrades of the New Drama. Autumn: joins V. Komissarzhevskaya's Theatre. Nov: *Hedda Gabler*, *Sister Beatrice*. Dec: *The Fairground Booth*.	Sept: Kammerspielhaus, Berlin, founded by Reinhardt.	Jan: *Golden Fleece*, Symbolist journal, appears. May: death of Ibsen. Sept: birth of Shostakovich. Oct: Diaghilev's first Russian exhibition, Paris; death of Cézanne.	April: Witte replaced by Goremykin as Prime Minister; first Duma convened. June: Stolypin appointed Prime Minister. July: Duma dissolved.
1907	Nov: leaves V. Komissarzhevskaya's theatre.	Intimate Theatre, Stockholm, founded by Strindberg. Evreinov's 'Antique Theatre' season, Petersburg. Kokoshka, *Murderer, Hope of Women*; Synge, *The Playboy of the Western World*.	Jan: first Symbolist exhibition, *Blue Rose*, Moscow. April: Gorky, *Mother*, published. May: Diaghilev's first Russian concert in Paris.	Feb: second Duma convened. June: Duma dissolved. Aug: Triple Entente: Britain, France, Russia. Nov: third Duma convened.

1908	Feb–May: with own company in provinces. Summer: appointed to Imperial Theatres staff. Sept: Hamsun, *At the Gates of the Kingdom*, Alexandrinsky, Petersburg.	Feb: Balyev's Bat cabaret, Moscow, opens. Sologub, *The Theatre of One Will*; various, *Book on the New Theatre*, published. First number of Craig's *The Mask* appears. I. Duncan performs in Russia.	May: Diaghilev's 'Russian week' in Paris.	
1909	Feb: *The Lady from the Box*, Foundry Theatre. Oct: *Tristan and Isolde*, Mariinsky Theatre.	Jan: Sologub, *Vanka the Butler*, dir. Evreinov, Komissarzhevskaya Theatre. Summer: Evreinov and Komissarzhevsky's 'Merry Theatre for Grown-Ups' season, Petersburg. Fuchs, *The Revolution in the Theatre*, published.	Summer: Diaghilev's first season of Ballet Russe, Paris. Oct: first number of *Apollon* appears.	
1910	Oct: *Columbine's Scarf*, House of Interludes, Petersburg. Nov: *Don Juan*, Alexandrinsky.	Jan: *Parade*, dir. Fokine, House of Interludes, Petersburg. June: Stravinsky, *The Firebird*, Ballet Russe, Paris. Oct: Sophocles, *Oedipus the King*, dir. Reinhardt, Vienna.	Feb: death of V. Komissarzhevskaya. March: Khlebnikov, *Incantation by Laughter*, published. May: *Trap for Judges*, first Futurist anthology, published. July: death of Petipa. Nov: death of L. Tolstoy. Dec: first Jack of Diamonds exhibition.	
1911	Jan: directs Chaliapin in *Boris Godunov*, Mariinsky. Nov: Soloviev, *Harlequin, the Marriage Broker*, Assembly	March: Scriabin, *Prometheus*, Moscow. June: Stravinsky, *Petrushka*, dir. Fokine, Paris.	Dec: Kandinsky and Marc found 'Blue Rider', Munich.	Sept: Stolypin assassinated in Kiev Theatre.

	Meyerhold	Theatre	Art and culture	Politics and society
	Rooms, Petersburg.	Oct: folk play, *Tsar Maximillian* des. Tatlin, Literary Circle, Moscow. Dec: Hofmannsthal, *Everyman*, dir. Reinhardt, Berlin; *Hamlet*, des. Craig, dir. Stanislavsky, Moscow Art Theatre. Dec: Stray Dog cabaret opens, Petersburg.		
1912	Summer: presents season of plays with friends in Terioki, Finland. Dec: *On Theatre* published.	May: Debussy, *L'Après-midi d'un faune*, dir. Nijinsky, Paris. Evreinov, *The Theatre of the Soul*, published.	May: death of Strindberg. Schoenberg, *Pierrot Lunaire*.	April: first issue of *Pravda*, Bolshevik paper; striking miners shot at Lena, sinking of the *Titanic*. June: third Duma dissolved. Oct: Balkan War breaks out. Nov: fourth Duma convened.
1913	June: D'Annunzio, *La Pisanelle*, Paris. Sept: Dr Dapertutto's Studio opens, Petersburg.	May: Stravinsky, *Rite of Spring*; Debussy, *Jeux*, both dir. Nijinsky. Paris. Dec: Mayakovsky, *Vladimir Mayakovsky, a Tragedy*; Kruchenykh, *Victory Over the Sun*, both Luna Park, Petersburg.	Exhibition of Russian ikons, Moscow.	Romanov dynasty celebrates 300 years on the throne. May: end of Balkan War. June: second Balkan War breaks out. Sept: anti-semitism in Russian government exposed. Einstein publishes general theory of relativity.
1914	Jan: first issue of Dr Dapertutto's journal, *The Love of*	Summer: Kamerny Theatre, Moscow, founded by Tairov;	Jan: Marinetti in Russia; Russian Futurists begin tour of country.	June: Franz Ferdinand assassinated at Sarajevo.

	Three Oranges April: Blok, *The Fairground Booth* and *The Unknown Woman*, Tenishevsky Hall.	Third Studio of Moscow Art Theatre founded by Vakhtangov. Dec: Kalidasa, *Sakuntala*, dir. Tairov, Kamerny, Moscow.	Feb: film, *Drama in the Futurists' Cabaret*. Shklovsky, *Resurrection of the Word*, published.	July: French President Poincaré visits Russia. Aug: opening of Panama Canal; Germany at war with Russia, then France, then Britain. 19 Aug: Russia wins battle of Gumbinen. 29 Aug: Russia defeated at Tannenberg. Sept: Russian offensive against Austria-Hungary.
1915	Jan: Lermontov, *The Two Brothers*, Alexandrinsky. Feb: 'An Evening at the Studio of Vs. Meyerhold'. April: Calderón, *The Constant Prince*, Alexandrinsky. Dec: premiere of *The Picture of Dorian Grey*, film dir. Meyerhold.	Jan: Goldoni, *The Fan*, Kamerny, Moscow. Feb: Stray Dog cabaret closes. Nov: first part of Evreinov, *Theatre for Itself*, published (parts 2 and 3 published 1916).	Roslavets, *Piano Compositions*. March: Tramway V – first Futurist exhibition. April: death of Scriabin. Dec: 0:10, 'the last Futurist exhibition of paintings', includes Suprematist works by Malevich.	Feb: Gallipoli campaign to relieve Russia begins. May: Austro-German offensive against Russia. Sept: tsar becomes commander-in-chief.
1916	Jan: Ostrovsky, *The Storm*, Alexandrinsky. Spring: helps found Comedians' Rest cabaret. Dec: last issue of *The Love of Three Oranges*.	Feb: Cabaret Voltaire, Zurich, opens. Pirandello, *Right You Are*; Kaiser, *From Morning Till Midnight*	Bely, *Petersburg*, published.	Feb: Germany attacks Verdun. April: Dublin rising. June: Brusilov offensive against Germany. July: battle of the Somme begins. Dec: Rasputin assassinated.
1917	Feb: Lermontov, *Masquerade*, Alexandrinsky. March: joins Freedom for Art	May: Satie, *Parade*, Paris. July: Comedians' Rest cabaret closes.	Jan: first Dada exhibition, Zurich. March: Petrograd Artists' Union	Jan: USA enters the war. Feb: general strike in Russia; tsar abdicates.

	Meyerhold	Theatre	Art and culture	Politics and society
	group. Nov: with other artists, meets representative of new Bolshevik government.	Nov: all Russian theatres placed under state supervision.	formed; first 'Republican Evening of Art' organized by Mayakovsky and Burlyuk. Oct: Proletkult founded. Nov: Narkompros established, Lunacharsky commissar.	March: provisional government formed by Prince Lvov. April: Lenin returns to Russia. June: first All-Russian Congress of Soviets. July: Russian offensive on eastern front; second provisional government formed by Kerensky. Sept: Bolshevik majorities on Petrograd and Moscow Soviets. Oct: second All-Russian Congress of Soviets; revolution establishes Bolshevik and Soviet power. Nov: Russia withdraws from war.
1918	Jan: appointed head of Petrograd Theatre Section of Narkompros. May: Stravinsky, *The Nightingale*, Mariinsky. Aug: joins Bolshevik Party. Nov: Mayakovsky, *Mystery Bouffe*, Theatre of Music Drama, Petrograd.	Brecht, *Baal*. Kerzhentsev, *The Creative Theatre*, published.	Vishnegradsky, *Quarter Tone Pieces*. Jan: Blok, *The Twelve*, published. Feb: Proletkult conference, Moscow; Berlin Dada movement begins. March: death of Wedekind. April: Prokofiev, *First Symphony*, Petrograd. May: May Day celebrations in Russia include street decorations, theatre, etc: the	Jan: old-style calendar replaced by modern; Constituent Assembly meets, dissolves. March: Moscow becomes capital of RSFSR; German offensive on western front; Treaty of Brest-Litovsk. June: British forces land in Murmansk. July: tsar and family executed; German offensive halted. Aug: British and French forces

1919	May: Meyerhold with TB goes to Yalta. Aug: arrested by Whites, sentenced to death; escapes. Sept: joins Red Army.	April: decree mobilizing entertainers to travel to battle lines. July: Falla, *The Three-cornered Hat*, London. Aug: all Russian theatres nationalized. Sept: Tolstoy, *The First Distiller*, dir. Annenkov, Hermitage, Petrograd. Oct: Prokofiev, *The Love of Three Oranges*. Nov: Congress of Workers and Peasants' theatre workers, Moscow; TEREVSAT founded in Vitebsk; Grosses Schauspielhaus, Berlin, founded by Reinhardt.	beginning of agitprop. Oct: film, *Shoulder Arms*, Chaplin. Nov: first agit train inaugurated by Lenin. Dec: journal, *Art of the Commune*, appears.	land in Archangel; Entente offensive against Germany launched. Oct: German fleet mutinies. Nov: German revolution begins; Kaiser abdicates; Armistice; emperor of Austro-Hungary abdicates. Dec: Congress of Soviets, Berlin.
			Reed, *Ten Days That Shook the World*, published. Film, *The Cabinet of Dr Caligari*, dir. Weiner. Jan: 'KomFut' group formed round *Art of the Commune*. Feb: first State Exhibition of paintings, Moscow. March: first mass festival in Petrograd; Bauhaus opened in Weimar. Autumn: first ROSTA windows. Oct: Opoyaz group (Formalist) founded.	Civil war throughout former Russian Empire, with interventions by western powers; disease, famine. Jan: murder of Luxemburg and Liebknecht, Germany. March: third Communist International (Comintern), Moscow; Soviet government established in Hungary (ousted, August). July: Weimar Constitution, Germany. Oct: British and French troops evacuate Archangel.
1920	Sept: appointed head of Theatre Section, Narkompros. Nov: Verhaeren, *The Dawns*, First Theatre of RSFSR.	Jan: Radlov, *The Corpse's Bride*, Popular Comedy, Petrograd. April: TEREVSAT moves from Vitebsk to Moscow.	Paul Whiteman's jazz band tours Europe. Aug: Gabo and Pevsner, *Realistic Manifesto*, published.	League of Nations founded; Lenin, *Left-wing Communism*, published. Jan: western powers end

Meyerhold	Theatre	Art and culture	Politics and society
Dec: calls for 'theatrical October'.	May: *Mystery of Freed Labour*, first mass spectacle, Petrograd; Stravinsky, *Pulcinella*, Paris; Lunacharsky, *Faust and the City*, Alexandrinsky, Petrograd; Foregger's Theatre of Four Masks, Moscow, founded. Aug: first Salzburg Festival: Reinhardt, Strauss, Walter, Hofmannsthal. Oct: Proletarian Theatre, Berlin, founded by Piscator. Nov: *Storming of the Winter Palace*, mass spectacle, Petrograd; Stravinsky, *Petrushka*, Mariinsky Theatre, Petrograd; Mayakovsky, *Championship of the Universal Class Struggle*, State Circus, Moscow.	Oct: first All-Russian Congress of Proletkult; Narkompros takes over Proletkult. Nov: Tatlin exhibits model of *Monument to Third International*.	blockade of Russia: Kolchak's White Army defeated. April: Vrangel takes command of White Army. May: Poland invades Russia. Aug: Red Army at Warsaw, driven back.
1921 Marriage with Olga Munt ended. April: resigns as head of Theatre Section, Narkompros. May: Mayakovsky, *Mystery Bouffe*, First Theatre of RSFSR. Sept: First Theatre of RSFSR dissolved.	Jewish Theatre, Moscow, founded by Granovsky; Mastfor, Moscow, founded by Foregger. Jan: Mayakovsky, *Small Play for Priests*, TEREVSAT. Feb: Tairov, *Notes of a Director* published; Evreinov, *The Main Thing*, Free Comedy, Petrograd.	Jan: first Constructivist exhibition, Moscow. Aug: death of Blok. Sept: $5 \times 5 = 25$ exhibition, Moscow. Oct: Gorky emigrates. Dec: Kandinsky emigrates.	March: Treaty of Riga cedes Russian land to Poland. New Economic Policy (NEP) inaugurated. Summer: drought and famine in central Russia. Nov: Kronstadt mutiny; fall of deutschmark begins.

	Oct: appointed director of GVYRM. Dec: founds Meyerhold Free Workshop.	July: Petrograd Theatre Section begins charging for admission. Nov: I. Duncan at Bolshoi Theatre, Moscow; Mayakovsky, *Yesterday's Exploit*, dir. Foregger, Riazan. Dec: Crommelynck, *The Magnificent Cuckold*, dir. Lugné-Poe, Paris; FEKS, *Eccentric Manifesto*, published.		
1922	Jan: Actors' Theatre formed. Feb: marries Zinaida Raikh; GVYRM becomes GVYTM. April: Crommelynck, *The Magnanimous Cuckold*, Actors' Theatre, Moscow. Summer: coins term 'biomechanics'; publishes *Amplua Aktera* with Bebutov and Aksenov. Sept: appointed to GITIS. Nov: Sukhovo-Kobylin, *The Death of Tarelkin*, GITIS. Dec: appointed to Theatre of the Revolution.	Jan: Ansky, *The Dybbuk*, dir. Vakhtangov, Habima Theatre, Moscow. Feb: Racine, *Phèdre*, dir. Tairov, Kamerny, Moscow; Gozzi, *Princess Turandot*, Third Studio, Moscow Art Theatre. Sept: Brecht, *Drums in the Night*, Munich; Schlemmer, *Triadic Ballet*, Bauhaus. Autumn–winter: Moscow Art Theatre in Paris and Berlin. Nov: Kaiser, *Gas*, dir. Khokhlov, Dramatic Theatre, Moscow. Dec: Cocteau, *Antigone*, Paris; Mass, *Kindness to Horses*, dir. Foregger, Eisenstein, Mastfor.	Lewis, *Babbit*; Joyce, *Ulysses*; Eliot, *The Waste Land*, published. Feb: Persymfans concert (without conductor), Moscow. May: film, *Kino-Pravda*, dir. Vertov; first 'heroic realism' exhibition, Moscow; death of Vakhtangov; Esenin and I. Duncan married. June: death of Khlebnikov. Sept: Kandinsky joins Bauhaus. Oct: BBC founded. Nov: factory sirens concert, Baku. Dec: Gan, *Constructivism* manifesto published.	April: Treaty of Rapallo between Germany and Soviet Russia; Stalin becomes general secretary of Communist Party. Nov: Mussolini takes power in Italy.
1923	Spring: theatre named after Meyerhold. March: Tretyakov, *Earth Rampant*, Meyerhold Theatre.	Blue Blouse groups formed; Glavrepkom (organ of censorship) created. Jan: Moscow Art Theatre in	March: first number of Mayakovsky's *LEF* appears. April: Italian Futurists declare support for Mussolini.	Jan: France occupies Ruhr. March: Lenin suffers third stroke. Nov: stabilization of

	Meyerhold	Theatre	Art and culture	Politics and society
	April: becomes People's Artist of RSFSR. Nov: leaves Theatre of Revolution.	USA. Spring: Kamerny Theatre in Paris and Berlin. Feb: *Machine Dances*, dir. Foregger, Mastfor. April: Ostrovsky/Tretyakov, *The Wiseman*, dir. Eisenstein, Proletkult Theatre, Moscow. May: Khlebnikov, *Zangesi*, dir. Tatlin, Petrograd. Oct: Moscow Art Theatre in Paris. Nov: Tretyakov, *Listen, Moscow*, dir. Eisenstein, Proletkult, Moscow. Dec: Chesterton, *The Man Who Was Thursday*, dir. Tairov, Kamerny, Moscow.	June: Eisenstein, 'The Montage of Attractions', published in *LEF*. July: Bauhaus exhibition: 'Art and Technology: a new unity'. Sept: first 'Agricultural Handicraft Industrial' exhibition, Moscow. Dec: Trotsky, *Literature and Revolution*, published.	deutschmark.
1924	Jan: Ostrovsky, *The Forest*, Meyerhold Theatre. June: *D.E.*, Meyerhold Theatre.	Stanislavsky, *My Life in Art*, published. March: Tretyakov, *Gas Masks*, dir. Eisenstein, Proletkult, Moscow; Capek, *R.U.R.*, dir. Komissarzhevsky, Paris. May: Paquet, *Fahnen*, dir. Piscator, Berlin. June: Moscow Art Theatre in USA.	April: film, *The Extraordinary Adventures of Mr West in the Land of the Bolsheviks*, dir. Kuleshov. May: death of Popova. Sept: film, *Aelita*, dir. Protozanov. Oct: film, *Kino-Eye*, dir. Vertov; 'Universal German Art' exhibition, Moscow.	Jan: Constitution of USSR ratified; death of Lenin. Feb: British Labour government; Britain, then Italy and France, recognize USSR. May: French Socialist government.

1925	April: Erdman, *The Mandate*, Meyerhold Theatre.	Dec: Kabarett der Komiker, Berlin, founded.	March: Evreinov emigrates. Teatro d'Art, Rome, founded by Pirandello. Dec: Berg, *Wozzeck*, Berlin.	Dec. film, *The Adventures of Oktyabriana*, FEKS, dir. Kozintsev and Traubert.	Jan: first number of *Novy Mir* appears; *LEF* ceases publication. April: film, *Strike*, dir. Eisenstein; International Exhibition in Paris includes large Russian avant-garde representation. June: New Sobriety exhibition, Mannheim; death of V.N. Davydov. Dec: death of Esenin; film, *Battleship Potemkin*, dir. Eisenstein.	Jan: Trotsky ill, resigns as Commissar for War. April: Hindenburg elected president of Germany. Oct: German–Soviet trade agreement.
1926	Dec: Gogol, *The Government Inspector*, Meyerhold State Theatre.	Foregger, *Experiments in The Art of Dance*, published. Feb: Prokofiev, *Love of Three Oranges*, dir. Radlov, Leningrad. June: Prokofiev, *Pas d'acier*, Paris. Sept: Brecht, *Man Equals Man*, Darmstadt. Nov: Bartók, *Miraculous Mandarin*, Cologne.			Jan: Shostakovich, *Symphony No. 1*. Feb: death of L. Reisner. March: *Battleship Potemkin* banned in Berlin; ban lifted in April. March–May: Toller in USSR. Oct: film, *Mother*, dir. Pudovkin. Dec: films, *By the Law*, dir. Kuleshov; *A Sixth of the World*, dir. Vertov.	April: German–Soviet treaty of friendship. May: Pilsudski seizes power in Poland. Sept: Germany admitted to League of Nations.
1927	Work on Tretyakov, *I Want a Child*, which continues till 1930.	Artaud, *The Spurt of Blood*, published. Feb: Krenek, *Johnny Spielt Auf*, Leipzig.			Proust, *Le Temps retrouvé*, published. Jan: first number of *Novy Lef* appears; Prokofiev plays 3rd	May: Lindberg flies across Atlantic Ocean. Oct: Communist Party Conference endorses 'Socialism

	Meyerhold	Theatre	Art and culture	Politics and society
		May: Stravinsky, Cocteau, *Oedipus the King*, Paris. June: Gliere, *The Red Poppy*, Bolshoi, Moscow. Sept: Toller, *Hoppla! We're Alive*, dir. Piscator, Berlin. Oct: Blue Blouses tour Germany.	piano concerto with Persymfans Moscow. sept: death of I. Duncan. Oct: *The Jazz Singer*, USA, first sound film.	in One Country'. Trotsky expelled from Communist Party.
1928	March: Griboyedev, *Woe to Wit*, Meyerhold State Theatre.	Reorganization of Blue Blouses by trade unions. Jan: Hasek, *The Good Soldier Schweyk*, dir. Piscator, Berlin. June: Piscator theatre, Berlin, goes bankrupt. Aug: Mikhail Chekhov emigrates; Brecht/Weill, *The Threepenny Opera*, Berlin. Oct: Moscow Jewish Theatre in Berlin.	Sholokov, *And Quiet Flows the Don*, published. March: exhibition, 'Photography of the Last 10 Years', Moscow; film, *October*, dir. Eisenstein. April: Mayer becomes director of Bauhaus. May: RAPP founded; Gorky returns to USSR. Dec: *Novy Lef* ceases publication.	April: first Five-Year Plan inaugurated.
1929	Feb: Mayakovsky, *The Bedbug*, Meyerhold State Theatre. July: Selvinsky, *The Second Commander*, Meyerhold State Theatre.	International Union of Theatre Workers founded; Piscator, *The Political Theatre*, published; Group Theatre, NY, founded; last number of *The Mask*. Aug–Nov: Das Rote Sprachrohr in USSR. Sept: Mehring, *The Merchant of Berlin*, dir. Piscator. Berlin.	Remarque, *All Quiet on the Western Front*; Doblin, *Berlin Alexanderplatz*, published. Jan: film, *Man with a Movie Camera*, dir. Vertov. Feb: exhibition of Soviet art, New York. March: film, *The New Babylon*, dir. Kozintsev and Trauberg.	Collectivization of agriculture begins. May: Berlin police fire on May Day demonstrators. Oct: Wall Street crash. Dec: Stalin's fiftieth birthday publicly celebrated.

1930	March: Mayakovsky, *The Bathhouse*, Meyerhold State Theatre. April: Meyerhold State Theatre in Berlin and Paris. May: attacked in *Linkskurve*, German CP journal.	Jan: Shostakovich, *The Nose*, Leningrad. Feb: Mayakovsky, *Moscow's Burning*, dir. Radlov, State Circus, Moscow. March: Brecht/Weill, *The Rise and Fall of the City of Mahagonny*, Leipzig. April: Gruppe Junge Schauspieler in Meyerhold Theatre, Moscow. Oct: Piscator in Moscow. Dec: Brecht/Eisler, *The Measures Taken*, Berlin.	April: film, *Earth*, dir. Dovzhenko; suicide of Mayakovsky; death of Golovin. Aug: Mayer relieved of post at Bauhaus. Nov: International Congress of Revolutionary Writers, Kharkov.	April: first number of *Literaturnaya Gazeta* appears. Aug: death of Diaghilev. Sept: Lunacharsky resigns as Commissar for Education.	June: Allied troops leave Rhineland. Aug: Pilsudski takes measures against Polish communists. Nov: anti-communist laws, Finland.
1931	Oct: Zon Theatre closed for repairs. Winter: Meyerhold State Theatre tours Leningrad, Tashkent, etc.	Jan: Wolf, *Tai Yang Erwacht*, dir. Piscator, Berlin. Feb: Brecht, *Man Equals Man*, dir. Brecht, Berlin.	Jan: Tretyakov in Berlin. April: Piscator in Moscow. Summer: Eisler in Moscow; Vertov in Berlin. Nov: film, *Kameradschaft*, dir. Pabst. Dec: Heartfield exhibition, Moscow.		July: German bank crisis. Aug: British 'national' government. Sept: Japan invades Manchuria.
1932	Work on Erdman, *The Suicide*. Summer: Meyerhold State Theatre moves into Passage	First Manifesto of Theatre of Cruelty. Okhlopkov appointed director	Jan: Bauhaus dissolved. May: Brecht in Moscow; film, *Kühle Wampe*, dir. Dudov and		Jan: Japanese occupation of Shanghai. April: second Five-Year Plan

Year	Meyerhold	Theatre	Art and culture	Politics and society
	Theatre, Moscow.	of Realistic Theatre, Moscow. Sept: Gorky, *Yegor Bulychev*, Vakhtangov Theatre, Moscow.	Brecht.	inaugurated; Hindenburg beats Hitler for president of Germany. July: Nazis win 38% of seats in Reichstag. Nov: USSR–France non-aggression pact.
1933	Dec: Lermontov, *Masquerade* (second version), State Academic Drama Theatre, Leningrad.	Lorca, *Blood Wedding*. Brecht, Reinhardt, Piscator, Toller, etc., leave Germany.	Dec: death of Lunacharsky.	Jan: Hitler becomes chancellor of Germany; Roosevelt president of USA. Feb: Reichstag fire. March: Dachau concentration camp opened. Nov: USSR–USA diplomatic relations established.
1934	March: Dumas, *The Lady of the Camellias*, Meyerhold State Theatre.	Pitoëff director of Théâtre aux Mathurins, Paris.	Sept: All-Union Congress of Soviet Writers endorses 'socialist realism'.	Sept: USSR admitted to League of Nations. Dec: Kirov assassinated.
1935	Jan: Tchaikovsky, *The Queen of Spades*, Maly Theatre, Leningrad.	Federal Theatre Project, USA, inaugurated. Feb: Odets, *Waiting for Lefty*, New York. April: Mei Lan-fang appears in Moscow.	Aksenov sentenced to death. April: Brecht in Moscow.	Trials of former communist leaders begin. April: Moscow metro opened. Aug: Alexei Stakhanov cuts 102 tons of coal in one shift.
1936			First public television transmission. March: death of Glazunov. June: death of Gorky.	Feb: Popular Front government in Spain. March: Germany occupies Rhineland.

			May: Popular Front government in France. July: Spanish Civil War begins. Aug: trial of Zinoviev and Kamenev.
1937			Jan: trial of Pyatakov and Radek. April: Guernica bombed.
1938	Jan: Meyerhold State Theatre closed. March: invited by Stanislavsky to work at Opera Theatre. Oct: appointed director, Stanislavsky Opera Theatre. Dec: Lermontov, *Masquerade* (third version), Pushkin Theatre, Leningrad.	Artaud, *The Theatre and Its Double*, published. Aug: death of Stanislavsky.	March: Germany annexes Austria; trial of Bukharin and Rykov. April: fall of French Popular Front government.
1939	March: Verdi, *Rigoletto*, Stanislavsky Opera Theatre (production begun by Stanislavsky). 13 June: All-Union Conference of Theatre Directors. 20 June: arrested and imprisoned. 17 July: Zinaida Raikh murdered.	Aug: Tretyakov shot as a spy.	March: Germany annexes Czechoslovakia; Franco takes power in Spain. Summer: Britain and France fail to make alliance with USSR. Aug: USSR–Germany non-aggression pact. Sept: Germany invades Poland; Britain and France declare war on Germany.
1940	1 Feb: Meyerhold tried in prison. 2 Feb: Meyerhold shot in prison.	Oct: former Zon Theatre opens as Tchaikovsky Concert Hall.	

Appendix 2
Meyerhold's productions

Completed productions

The following productions were mounted by the Company of Russian Dramatic Artists under the direction of A.S. Kosheverov and V.E. Meyerhold, in Kherson. A.S. Kosheverov was Meyerhold's co-director for all of them, and all were designed by M.A. Mikhailov.

22 Sept 1902: A. Chekhov, *The Three Sisters*
24 Sept 1902: A. Ostrovsky, *Artists and Admirers*
26 Sept 1902: A. Chekhov, *Uncle Vanya*
29 Sept 1902: S. Naidenov, *Vanyusha's Children*
1 Oct 1902: A. Trofimov, *The Queen Bee and the Drones*, and I. Shcheglov, *A Woman's Trifle*.
3 Oct 1902: E. Paleron, *In the Kingdom of Boredom*, and adapted from Y. Delière, *The Last Guest*
4 Oct 1902: V. Trakhtenberg, *The Comet*
6 Oct 1902: G. Hauptmann, *Drayman Henschel*
8 Oct 1902: V. Nemirovich-Danchenko, *Gold*, and V. Kornileva, *Under a Fragrant Branch of Lilac*
10 Oct 1902: A. Chekhov, *The Seagull*
11 Oct 1902: L. Fulda, *School Friends*, and A. Myurzhe, *According to the Memorandum Book*
15 Oct 1902: L.L. Tolstoy, *Crazy Nights*
17 Oct 1902: H. Sudermann, *Long Live Life*
20 Oct 1902: A. Ostrovsky, *The Embalmer's Marriage*
21 Oct 1902: A. Ostrovsky and N. Soloviev, *The Marriage of Belugin*
24 Oct 1902: S. Przybyszewski, *The Golden Fleece*, and L. Yakovlev, *Woman's Curiosity*
25 Oct 1902: E. Zola, *Thérèse Raquin*
26 Oct 1902: V. Nemirovich-Danchenko, *The Last Will and Testament*
27 Oct 1902 (mat): M. Severnaya, *Little Olga from Podyachesky*
27 Oct 1902 (eve): V. Nemirovich-Danchenko, *The Price of Life*
31 Oct 1902: H. Heijermans, *The Death of 'Hope'*
1 Nov 1902: G. Hauptmann, *Lonely Lives*
3 Nov 1902: A. Ostrovsky, *It's a Family Affair — We'll Settle it Ourselves*
5 Nov 1902: A. Chekhov, *Ivanov*
7 Nov 1902: L.N. Tolstoy, *The Power of Darkness*
10 Nov 1902: G. Hauptmann, *The Sunken Bell*
12 Nov 1902: H. Sudermann, *Honour*
15 Nov 1902: J.K. Jerome, *Women's Logic (Miss Hobbs)*
17 Nov 1902: N. Timkovsky, *The Strong and the Weak*
19 Nov 1902: M. Gorky, *Philistines*
21 Nov 1902: A. Ostrovsky and N. Soloviev, *A Happy Day*
24 Nov 1902: H. Sudermann, *The Butterfly War*
28 Nov 1902: A. Schnitzler, *The Last Masks*
29 Nov 1902: H. Ibsen, *The Wild Duck*
30 Nov 1902: A. Ostrovsky, *Late Love*
4 Dec 1902: A.K. Tolstoy, *The Death of Ivan the Terrible*
7 Dec 1902: H. Ibsen, *Hedda Gabler*

10 Dec 1902: M. Tchaikovsky, *A Symphony*
12 Dec 1902: F. Filippi, *Benefactors of Mankind*
15 Dec 1902 (mat): D. Averkiev, *Funny Old Times*
15 Dec 1902 (eve): H. Sudermann, *The Vale of Content*, and I. Shcheglov, *The Mousetrap*
19 Dec 1902: V. Krylov, *A Spoiled Child*, and I. Shcheglov, *On Tour*
24 Dec 1902: Z. Rishpen, *Life and Death*
26 Dec 1902: A. Ostrovsky, *Sin and Misfortune Are Common to All*
27 Dec 1902: I. Platon, *People*
29 Dec 1902: A. Ostrovsky and S. Gedeonov, *Vasilisa Melentieva*
30 Dec 1902: P.P. Beinberg, *Without the Sun*
31 Dec 1902: J. Lemaître, *Backstage*
3 Jan 1903: I. Potapenko, *A Fairy Tale*
6 Jan 1903: A.K. Tolstoy, *Tsar Fyodor Ivanovich*
7 Jan 1903: K. Shengerr, *The Turners*, and V. Alexandrov, *The Spark That Started the Forest Fire*
9 Jan 1903: E. Chirikov, *In the Yard and In the Barn*
10 Jan 1903: V. Trakhtenberg, *Victory*
14 Jan 1903: M. Tchaikovsky, *The Wrestlers*
16 Jan 1903: H. Ibsen, *Doctor Stockmann (An Enemy of the People)*
17 Jan 1903: N. Rakshanin, *A Fit*
19 Jan 1903: D. Belsky, *Life Under the Tsars*
21 Jan 1903: I. Potapenko, *Someone Else's Things*
23 Jan 1903: M. Praga, *An Ideal Wife*
24 Jan 1903: G. Hauptmann, *Michael Kramer*
26 Jan 1903: F. von Shenton (version by N. Budkevich and V. Meyerhold), *The Acrobats*
31 Jan 1903: V. Protopopov, *Beyond Life*
4 Feb 1903: N. Nekrasov, *Autumnal Boredom*, and R. Bracco, *The Unfaithful*
6 Feb 1903: I. Potapenko, *Life*
7 Feb 1903: E. Labiche, *The Straw Hat*
9 Feb 1903 (mat): L. Urusov (after A.K. Tolstoy), *Prince Silver*
9 Feb 1903 (eve): P. Yartsev, *The Magician*
14 Feb 1903: N. Ermolov, *The Magic Flute*
15 Feb 1903: H. Faber, *Eternal Love*

The following productions were mounted by the same company in Sevastopol:
18 May 1903: M. Maeterlinck, *The Intruder*
21 May 1903: M. Gorky, *The Lower Depths*
26 May 1903: V. Tunoshensky, *A Provincial Cleopatra*
27 May 1903: H. Ibsen, *The Lady from the Sea*
5 June 1903: A. Bisson and F. Carré, *Monsieur Directeur*

The following productions were mounted by the Comrades of the New Drama under
    Meyerhold's direction, in Kherson. Some productions were directed by members of the
    company under Meyerhold's general supervision. All were designed by M.A. Mikhailov.
16 Sept 1903: A. Dumas *père, Kean*
19 Sept 1903: A. Schnitzler, *Fair Game* and *Literature*
20 Sept 1903: O. Mirbeau, *Business is Business*
21 Sept 1903 (mat): N. Gogol, *Marriage*
21 Sept 1903 (eve): A. Pleshcheyev, *Not the Last*
26 Sept 1903: R. Bracco, *The Triumph of Life*
28 Sept 1903: V. Meyer-Ferstner, *The Crown Prince*
1 Oct 1903: G. Hauptmann (trans. V. Meyerhold), *Before Sunrise*

2 Oct 1903: A. Ostrovsky, *The Forest*
4 Oct 1903: H. Bahr, *The Star*
7 Oct 1903: A. Chekhov, *Swansong*
8 Oct 1903: A. Ostrovsky, *Rabid Money*
11 Oct 1903: R. Bracco, *Lost in the Darkness*
14 Oct 1903: G. Hauptmann, *Colleague Crampton*
18 Oct 1903: F. Filippi, *The Great Stars*
21 Oct 1903: H. Sudermann, *Native Land*
24 Oct 1903: A. Schnitzler, *The Fairy Tale*
31 Oct 1903: H. Christiansen, *Dolly*, and N. Persyaninova, *The Lady Philanthropist*
2 Nov 1903 (mat): A. Ostrovsky, *Poverty No Crime*
2 Nov 1903 (eve): S. Naidenov, *No. 13*
7 Nov 1903: W. Shakespeare, *A Midsummer Night's Dream*
8 Nov 1903: S. Balutsky, *The Bachelors Club*
11 Nov 1903: N. Persyaninova, *A Barren Flower*
13 Nov 1903: I. Radzivillovich, *One's Past*
19 Nov 1903: I. Potapenko, *University*
21 Nov 1903: A. Chekhov, *The Wedding*
26 Nov 1903: A. Ostrovsky, *Wolves and Sheep*
27 Nov 1903: H. Ibsen, *Nora (A Doll's House)*
30 Nov 1903: A. Ostrovsky, *The Poor Bride*
3 Dec 1903: V. Krylov, *The Prank*, and A. Chekhov, *The Proposal*
4 Dec 1903: S. Naidenov, *A Wealthy Man*
9 Dec 1903: I. Potapenko, *Redemption*
12 Dec 1903: A. Federov, *Wind-fallen Trees*
14 Dec 1903: H. Sudermann, *Midsummer Eve's Fire*
17 Dec 1903: A. Kryukovsky, *Moneyed Toffs*, and A. Chekhov, *The Jubilee*
19 Dec 1903: S. Przybyszewski, *Snow*
26 Dec 1903: A. Griboyedev, *Woe from Wit*
29 Dec 1903: A. Schnitzler, *The Last Supper*
30 Dec 1903: L. Mey, *The Tsar's Bride*
31 Dec 1903: F. von Shentam, *Eve the Golden*
4 Jan 1904: N. Polovoy, *Siberian Close-stool*
8 Jan 1904: G. Hauptmann, *The Red Cock*
9 Jan 1904: G. Hauptmann, *The Feast of Reconciliation*
11 Jan 1904: A. Sukhovo-Kobylin, *The Case*
13 Jan 1904: H. Sudermann, *The Destruction of Sodom*
15 Jan 1904: H. Ibsen, *Little Eyolf*, and A. Bernikov, *Pilgrims of Romance*
17 Jan 1904: P. Yartsev, *Matrimony*
20 Jan 1904: H. Ibsen, *Ghosts*
22 Jan 1904: M. Maeterlinck, *Monna Vanna*
29 Jan 1904: M. Halbe, *Youth*
2 Feb 1904: W. Shakespeare, *The Merchant of Venice*
3 Feb 1904: A. Ostrovsky, *The Jokers*
4 Feb 1904: A. Chekhov, *The Cherry Orchard*

The following productions were mounted by the same company in Tiflis:
15 Oct 1904: M. Halbe, *The Stream*
25 Oct 1904: E. Brieux, *The Red Rose*
1 Nov 1904: A Schnitzler, *The Director of the Puppet Theatre*

30 Nov 1904: O. Efremova and S. Trefilov (after L.N. Tolstoy), *Katyusha Maslova*
14 Dec 1904: H. von Hofmannsthal, *The Woman in the Window*
16 Dec 1904: O. Mirbeau, *The Thief*
26 Dec 1904 (mat): G. Hauptmann, *Schluck und Jau*
26 Dec 1904 (eve): L.N. Tolstoy, *The Fruits of Enlightenment*
30 Dec 1904: A. Ostrovsky, *The Snow Maiden*
31 Dec 1904: V. Trakhtenberg, *The Fire Bird*
4 Jan 1905: A. Sumbatov, *Treachery*
8 Jan 1905: O. Ernst, *Flaxmann the Teacher*
14 Jan 1905: I. Potapenko, *The Wing Bound Down*
18 Jan 1905: A. Strindberg, *The Father*
22 Jan 1905: V. Nemirovich-Danchenko, *The Fir Tree*
28 Jan 1905: A. Kosorotov, *The Gush of Spring*
4 Feb 1905: G. Hauptmann, *Rosa Berndt*
13 Feb 1905: V. Trakhtenberg, *How They Gave up Smoking*
15 Feb 1905: M. Gorky, *Summer Folk*
20 Feb 1905: M. Federov (after H. Beecher Stowe), *Uncle Tom's Cabin*
25 Feb 1905 (mat): J. Verne, *Captain Grant's Children*
25 Feb 1905 (eve): F. Wedekind (trans V. Meyerhold), *The Tenor*

The following productions were mounted by the Comrades of the New Drama under
    Meyerhold's direction, in Nikolayev. All were designed by K.K. Kostin.
30 March 1905: S. Naidenov, *The Life of Avdotin*
4 April 1905: E. Chirikov, *Ivan Mironich*
7 April 1905: K. Balmont, *Liturgy of Beauty*
19 April 1905: S. Naidenov, *The Prodigal Son*
22 April 1905: A. Holz and O. Jerike, *The Dreamer*

The following productions were mounted by the same company in Tiflis:
20 Feb 1906: H. Ibsen, *Love's Comedy*, and S. Olgina (after A. Chekhov), *The Surgery*
21 Feb 1906: O. Dymov, *By Bureaucratic Means*
23 Feb 1906: V. Trakhtenberg, *Fimka*
24 Feb 1906: E. Chirikov, *The Jew*
27 Feb 1906: I. Potapenko, *The Secret Councillor's Dream*
1 March 1906: M. Gorky, *Children of the Sun*
2 March 1906: E. Brieux, *Damaged Goods*
12 March 1906 (mat): S. Razumovsky, *The Young Storm*
12 March 1906 (eve): A. Svirsky, *Prison*
15 March 1906: Sholom Ash, *In the Path of Zion*
16 March 1906: G. Hauptmann, *Hannele*
19 March 1906: M. Maeterlinck, *The Death of Tintagiles*, and A. Strindberg, *Miss Julie*
22 March 1906: I. Potapenko, *The New Life*

The following productions were mounted by the same company in Rostov-on-the-Don:
18 April 1906: A. Schnitzler, *The Green Cockatoo*
19 April 1906: A. Schnitzler (adapted by V.E. Meyerhold), *The Call of Life*

The following productions were mounted by the same company in Poltava:
7 June 1906: H. Ibsen, *Ghosts*, co-dir. O.P. Narbekova
10 June 1906: M. Maeterlinck, *The Miracle of Saint Anthony*

11 June 1906: O. Dymov, *Cain*

18 June 1906: D. Przybyszewska, *Sin*

15 July 1906: O. Hartleben, *Education for Marriage*

16 July 1906: M. Gorky, *Philistines*

10 Nov 1906: H. Ibsen, *Hedda Gabler*, des. N.N. Sapunov (settings) and V.D. Milioti (costumes), V.F. Komissarzhevskaya Theatre, Petersburg

13 Nov 1906: S. Yushkevich, *In the City*, co-dir. P.M. Yartsev, des. V.K. Kolenda, music by A.K. Lyadov, V.F. Komissarzhevskaya Theatre, Petersburg

22 Nov 1906: M. Maeterlinck, *Sister Beatrice*, des. S. Yu. Sudeikin, V.F. Komissarzhevskaya Theatre, Petersburg

4 Dec 1906: S. Przybyszewski, *The Eternal Fable*, co-dir. P.M. Yartsev, des. V.I. Denisov, V.F. Komissarzhevskaya Theatre, Petersburg

18 Dec 1906: H. Ibsen, *Nora (A Doll's House)* (reworked version of a production already in the theatre's repertoire), V.F. Komissarzhevskaya Theatre, Petersburg

30 Dec 1906: A. Blok, *The Fairground Booth*, co-dir. G.I. Chulkov, des. NN. Sapunov, music by M.A. Kuzmin; and M. Maeterlinck, *The Miracle of Saint Anthony* (revision of earlier production, with new design), des. V.K. Kolenda, V.F. Komissarzhevskaya Theatre, Petersburg

8 Jan 1907: G. Heiberg, *Love's Tragedy*, des. V. Ya. Surenyants, V.F. Komissarzhevskaya Theatre, Petersburg

22 Jan 1907: H. Ibsen, *Love's Comedy*, des. V.I. Denisov, V.F. Komissarzhevskaya Theatre, Petersburg

12 Feb 1907: H. von Hofmannsthal, *Zobeida's Wedding*, des. B.I. Anisfeld, V.F. Komissarzhevskaya Theatre, Petersburg

22 Feb 1907: L. Andreev, *The Life of Man*, des. V.E. Meyerhold (plan) and V.K. Kolenda, V.F. Komissarzhevskaya Theatre, Petersburg

27 May 1907: L. Andreev, *To the Stars*, V.R. Gardin Company, Casino Theatre, Terioki, Finland (now Zelenogorsk, USSR)

13 June 1907: 'An Evening of New Art': readings by poets (A. Blok, S. Gorodetsky, V. Pyast, and others), and two scenes from the musical romances of P.I. Tchaikovsky, des. N.N. Saven, Musical Studio, Ollila

20 June 1907: An evening of adaptations and dances from R. Strauss, *Salomé*, des. N.N. Saven, Musical Studio, Ollila

15 Sept 1907: F. Wedekind, *Spring Awakening*, des. V.I. Denisov, V.F. Komissarzhevskaya Theatre, Petersburg

10 Oct 1907: M. Maeterlinck (trans V. Bryussov), *Pelleas and Melisande*, des V.I. Denisov, music by V.A. Spiess von Eschenbruch, V.F. Komissarzhevskaya Theatre, Petersburg

6 Nov 1907: F.K. Sologub, *Death's Victory*, des. V.E. Meyerhold, V.F. Komissarzhevskaya Theatre, Petersburg

The following productions were mounted by an unnamed company under the direction of Meyerhold and R.A. Ungern, in Vitebsk (and later in Minsk, Kherson, Poltava, Kiev, Kharkov and other cities in the south and west). All were designed by K.K. Kostin.

17 Feb 1908: M. Maeterlinck, *Sister Beatrice*

19 Feb 1908: A. Blok, *The Fairground Booth*; and F. Wedekind (trans V.E. Meyerhold and S. Gorodetsky), *The Vampire (Earth Spirit)*

20 Feb 1908: H. von Hofmannsthal *Electra*

21 Feb 1908: H. Ibsen, *Hedda Gabler*

22 Feb 1908: F.K. Sologub, *Death's Victory*

23 Feb 1908: L. Andreyev, *The Life of Man*

24 Feb 1908: G. Hauptmann, *Charlemagne's Hostage*

12 March 1908: H. Ibsen, *Builder Solness* (*The Master Builder*)

13 March 1908: K. Hamsun, *At the Gates of the Kingdom*

30 Sept 1908: K. Hamsun, *At the Gates of the Kingdom*, des. A. Ya. Golovin, Alexandrinsky Theatre, Petersburg

6 Dec 1908: P. Potemkin, *Petrushka*, des. M.V. Dobuzhinsky, music by V.F. Nuvel; E.A. Poe (version by V. Trakhtenberg), *The Fall of the House of Usher*, des. M.V. Dobuzhinsky (settings) and V. Ya. Chambers (costumes), music by V.G. Karatygin; Count F.L. Sologub, *Please Be Seated!*, des. I. Ya. Bilibin, The Cove, Petersburg

19 March 1909: N. Gogol, *A Lawsuit*, des. Prince A.K. Shervashidze, Alexandrinsky Theatre, Petersburg

30 Oct 1909: R. Wagner, *Tristan and Isolde*, cond. E.F. Napravnik, des. Prince A.K. Shervashidze, Mariinsky Theatre, Petersburg

? Jan 1910: D. Merezhkovsky, *Paul I* (two scenes), private flat, Petersburg

9 March 1910: E. Hardt (trans P. Potemkin, M.A. Kuzmin and V. Ivanov), *Tantris the Fool*, des. Prince A.K. Shervashidze, music by M.A. Kuzmin, Alexandrinsky Theatre

19 April 1910: P. Calderón (trans K. Balmont), *The Adoration of the Cross*, des. S. Yu. Sudeikin, Tower Theatre (V. Ivanov's flat), Petersburg

12 Oct 1910: A. Schnitzler (transcription by Dr Dapertutto (V.E. Meyerhold)), *Columbine's Scarf*, des. N.N. Sapunov, music by P. Donani, House of Interludes, Petersburg

9 Nov 1910: J.-B. Molière, *Don Juan*, co-dir. Count S.I. Tolstoy, des. A. Ya. Golovin, music by J.P. Rameau, arr. by V.G. Karatygin, Alexandrinsky Theatre, Petersburg

3 Dec 1910: E.A. Znosko-Borovsky, *The Transfigured Prince*, des. S. Yu. Sudeikin, House of Interludes, Petersburg

6 Jan 1911: M. Mussorgsky, *Boris Godunov*, cond. A.K. Kouts, des. A. Ya. Golovin, Mariinsky Theatre, Petersburg

23 March 1911: Yu. Belyaev, *The Red Café*, des. A. Ya. Golovin, music by M.A. Kuzmin, Alexandrinsky Theatre, Petersburg

28 Sept 1911: L.N. Tolstoy, *The Living Corpse*, co-dir. A.L. Zagarov, des. K.A. Korovin, Alexandrinsky Theatre, Petersburg

8 Nov 1911: Volmar Lucinius (V.N. Soloviev), *Harlequin, the Marriage Broker*, des. K.I. Evseyev, music by V.A. Spiess von Eschenbruch, Assembly Rooms of the Nobility, Petersburg

21 Dec 1911: C.W. Gluck, *Orpheo*, cond. E.F. Napravnik, chor. M.M. Fokine, des. A. Ya. Golovin, Mariinsky Theatre, Petersburg

? Jan 1912: Dr Dapertutto (V.E. Meyerhold), *In Love*, des. V.I. Shukhayev and A.E. Yakovlev under direction of A. Ya. Golovin, music by C.A. Debussy, semi-circular platform in the home of O.K. and N.P. Karabchevsky, Petersburg

5 March 1912: K. Balmont, *Three Blossoms* (second scene), music by E. Grieg, Tenishevsky School Hall, Petersburg

9 June 1912: Dr Dapertutto (V.E. Meyerhold), *In Love*, des. N.I. Kulbin, music by C.A. Debussy; Volmar Lucinius (V.N. Soloviev), *Harlequin, the Marriage Broker*, des. N.I. Kulbin, music by Yu. L. de Bourg (after J. Haydn and F. Araya), Fellowship of Artists, Painters, Writers and Musicians, Terioki, Finland (now Zelenogorsk, USSR)

29 June 1912: P. Calderón (trans K. Balmont), *The Adoration of the Cross*, des. Yu. M. Bondi, Fellowship of Artists, Painters, Writers and Musicians, Terioki

14 July 1912: A. Strindberg, *Crimes and Crimes*, des. Yu. M. Bondi, Fellowship of Artists, Painters, Writers and Musicians, Terioki

15 July 1912: G.B. Shaw (adapted by V.E. Meyerhold), *You Never Can Tell*, Fellowship of Artists, Painters, Writers and Musicians, Terioki

6 Nov 1912: F.K. Sologub, *Hostages of Life*, des. A. Ya. Golovin, Alexandrinsky Theatre, Petersburg

18 Feb 1913: R. Strauss (libretto by H. von Hofmannsthal, trans M. Kuzmin), *Electra*, cond. A.K. Kouts, des. A. Ya. Golovin, Mariinsky Theatre, Petersburg

11 June 1913: G. D'Annunzio, *Pisanelle*, chor. M.M. Fokine, des. L. Bakst, music by Ildebrando Pizzetti, Châtelet Theatre, Paris

12 Dec 1913: F. Noziere and H. Muller, *Seville Café*, des. K.A. Veshilov, music by M.V. Vladimirov (from Spanish melodies), A.S. Suvorin Theatre, Petersburg

30 Jan 1914: A. Pinero, *Mid-Channel*, des. A. Ya. Golovin, Alexandrinsky Theatre, Petersburg

7 April 1914: A. Blok, *The Unknown Woman* and *The Fairground Booth*, co-dir. Yu. M. Bondi, des. Yu. M. Bondi, music by M.A. Kuzmin, production by the Vs. Meyerhold Studio at Tenishevsky School Hall, Petersburg

15 Aug 1914: G. de Maupassant (version by O. Metenya), *Mademoiselle Fifi*, des. S. Yu. Sudeikin, A.S. Suvorin Theatre, Petrograd

20 Sept 1914: E. Wolf-Ferrari, *Secret Susannah*, cond. M.A. Bikhter, des. S. Yu. Sudeikin, performance by L. Ya. Lipkovsky, Mariinsky Theatre *salon*, Petrograd

11 Oct 1914: A. Bobrishchev-Pushkin, *Victory Celebration*, des. S. Yu. Sudeikin, Mariinsky Theatre, Petrograd

10 Jan 1915: M. Lermontov, *Two Brothers*, des. A. Ya. Golovin, Alexandrinsky Theatre, Petrograd

12 Feb 1915: An evening at the Studio of Vs. Meyerhold, des, A.V. Rykov, Vs. Meyerhold Studio, Petrograd

18 Feb 1915: Z. Hippius, *The Green Ring*, des. A. Ya. Golovin, music by V.G. Karatygin, Alexandrinsky Theatre, Petrograd

23 April 1915: P. Calderón, *The Constant Prince*, des. A. Ya. Golovin, music by V.G. Karatygin, Alexandrinsky Theatre, Petrograd

26 April 1915: G.B. Shaw, *Pygmalion*, des. P.B. Lambin, Alexandrinsky Theatre, Petrograd

9 Jan 1916: A. Ostrovsky, *The Storm*, des. A. Ya. Golovin, Alexandrinsky Theatre, Petrograd

29 Jan 1916: M. Glinka (scenario by M. Fokine), *Argon's Desire*, chor. M.M. Fokine, cond. N.A. Malko, des. A. Ya. Golovin, Mariinsky Theatre, Petrograd

18 April 1916: A. Schnitzler (transcription by Dr Dapertutto (V.E. Meyerhold)), *Columbine's Scarf*, des. S. Yu. Sudeikin, The Comedians' Rest, Petrograd

21 October 1916: D. Merezhkovsky, *The Romantics*, co-dir. Yu. L. Rakitin, des. A. Ya. Golovin, Alexandrinsky Theatre, Petrograd

25 Jan 1917: A. Sukhovo-Kobylin, *Krechinsky's Wedding*, co-dir. A.N. Lavrentev, des. B.A. Almedingen, Alexandrinsky Theatre, Petrograd

27 Jan 1917: A Dargominsky, *The Stone Guest*, des. A. Ya Golovin, Mariinsky Theatre, Petrograd

24 Feb 1917: M.P. Mussorgsky, *A Marriage*, part of concert for the magazine *Contemporary Music*, cond. A. V. Gauk, Petrovsky School Hall, Petrograd

25 Feb 1917: M. Lermontov, *Masquerade*, des. A. Ya. Golovin, music by A.K. Glazunov, Alexandrinsky Theatre, Petrograd

24 April 1917: O. Wilde, *An Ideal Husband*, des. A. Ya. Golovin, School of Scenic Art, Mikhailovsky Theatre, Petrograd

30 Aug 1917: A. Sukhovo-Kobylin, *The Case*, co-dir. A.N. Lavrentev, des. B.A. Almedingen, Alexandrinsky Theatre, Petrograd

23 Oct 1917: A. Sukhovo-Kobylin, *The Death of Tarelkin*, des. B.A. Almedingen, Alexandrinsky Theatre, Petrograd

14 Dec 1917: N. Rimsky-Korsakov, *The Snow Maiden*, cond. A.K. Kouts, des. K.A. Korovin, Mariinsky Theatre, Petrograd

15 Dec 1917: H. Ibsen, *The Lady from the Sea*, co-dir. N.A. Stravinskaya, des. A. Ya. Golovin, Alexandrinsky Theatre, Petrograd

8 April 1918: L.N. Tolstoy, *Peter the Baker*, des. A. Ya Golovin, music by R.I. Mervolf, Alexandrinsky Theatre, Petrograd

30 May 1918: I. Stravinsky, *The Nightingale*, cond. A.K. Kouts, des. A. Ya. Golovin, Mariinsky Theatre, Petrograd

7 June 1918: H. Ibsen, *Nora (A Doll's House)*, des. V.E. Meyerhold (plan) and V.V. Dmitriev, Theatre at the House of Workers, Petrograd

7 Nov 1918: D. Ober, *Fenella (The Dumb Woman from Portichi)*, co-dir. S.D. Maslovskaya, cond. D.I. Pokhitonov, des. P.B. Lambin, Mariinsky Theatre, Petrograd

7 Nov 1918: V.V. Mayakovsky, *Mystery-Bouffe*, co-dir. V.V. Mayakovsky, des. K.S. Malevich, Theatre of Music Drama, Petrograd

6 Aug 1920: H. Ibsen, *Nora*, First Soviet Theatre in the name of Lenin, Novorossisk

7 Nov 1920: E. Verhaeren (adapted by V.E. Meyerhold and V.M. Bebutov), *The Dawns*, co-dir. V.M. Bebutov, des. V.V. Dmitriev, First Theatre of RSFSR, Moscow

1 May 1921: V.V. Mayakovsky, *Mystery-Bouffe*, co-dir. V.M. Bebutov, des. V.P. Kiselev, A.M. Lavinsky, V.L. Khrakovsky, First Theatre of RSFSR, Moscow

7 Aug 1921: H. Ibsen (adapted by V.E. Meyerhold, V.M. Bebutov and O.P. Zhdanova), *The League of Youth* (revived in 1922 at the Actors' Theatre under the title, *Stensgard's Escapade*), co-dir and des. V.M. Bebutov and O.P. Zhdanova, First Theatre of RSFSR, Moscow

20 April 1922: H. Ibsen (adapted by V.E. Meyerhold), *Nora (The Tragedy of Nora Helmer, or how a wife from a bourgeois family opted for independence and work)*, des. V.E. Meyerhold, Actors' Theatre, Moscow

25 April 1922: F. Crommelynck (trans I. Aksenov), *The Magnanimous Cuckold*, des. L.S. Popova and V.V. Lyutse, music by N.N. Popov and from contemporary jazz, Actors' Theatre and Meyerhold Free Workshop, GVYTM, Moscow

24 Nov 1922: A. Sukhovo-Kobylin, *The Death of Tarelkin*, des. V.F. Stepanova, Vs. Meyerhold Workshop, GITIS, Moscow

4 March 1923: M. Martinet (trans S. Gorodetsky, adapted by S.M. Tretyakov), *Earth Rampant* (*Night*), co-dir. S.M. Tretyakov, des. L.S. Popova, Vs. Meyerhold Theatre, Moscow

15 May 1923: A. Ostrovsky, *A Profitable Post*, co-dir. A.B. Velizhev, des. V.A. Shestakov, Theatre of the Revolution, Moscow

7 Nov 1923: A. Faiko, *Lake Lyul*, co-dir. A.M. Room, des. V.A. Shestakov, Theatre of the Revolution, Moscow

19 Jan 1924: A. Ostrovsky (adapted by V.E. Meyerhold), *The Forest*, des. V.E. Meyerhold (plan) and V.F. Fedorov, Theatre in the name of Vs. Meyerhold (TIM), Moscow

15 June 1924: M. Podgaetsky and others (after I. Ehrenburg and B. Kellerman), *D.E. (Give Us Europe)*, des. V.E. Meyerhold (plan) and I. Yu. Shlepyanov, TIM, Moscow (premiere in Leningrad)

29 Jan 1925: A. Faiko, *Teacher Bubus*, des. V.E. Meyerhold (plan) and I. Yu. Shlepyanov, music by F. Chopin and F. Liszt, TIM, Moscow

20 April 1925: N. Erdman, *The Mandate*, des. V.E. Meyerhold (plan) and I. Yu. Shlepyanov, TIM, Moscow

9 Dec 1926: N. Gogol (adapted by V.E. Meyerhold and M. Korenev), *The Government Inspector*, des. V.E. Meyerhold (plan) and V.P. Kiselev, music by M.F. Gnesin and romances of Russian composers, State Theatre in the name of Vs. Meyerhold (GosTIM), Moscow

26 Jan 1928: F. Crommelynck (trans I. Aksenov), *The Magnanimous Cuckold*, des. L.S. Popova and V.V. Lyutse, GosTIM, Moscow

12 March 1928: A. Griboyedov (adapted by V.E. Meyerhold and M. Korenev), *Woe to Wit* (*Woe from Wit*), des. V.A. Shestakov (settings) and N.P. Ulyanov (costumes and make-up), music from classical works selected and arranged by B.V. Asafiev, GosTIM, Moscow

13 Feb 1929: V.V. Mayakovsky, *The Bedbug*, co-dir. V.V. Mayakovsky, des. V.E. Meyerhold (plan) and Kukriniksy (scenes 1–4), A.M. Rodchenko (scenes 5–9), music by D.D. Shostakovich, GosTIM, Moscow

24 July 1929: I. Selvinsky, *The Second Commander*, des. V.E. Meyerhold (plan) and S.E. Vakhtangov, music by V. Ya. Shebalin, GosTIM, Moscow (premiere in Kharkov)

16 March 1930: V.V. Mayakovsky, *The Bathhouse*, co-dir. V.V. Mayakovsky, des. V.E. Meyerhold (plan), S.E. Vakhtangov and A.A. Deineka, music by V. Ya. Shebalin, GosTIM, Moscow

7 November 1930: M. Podgaetsky, N. Mologin and others (after I. Ehrenburg and B. Kellerman), *D.S.E.* (*Give Us a Soviet Europe*), des. V.E. Meyerhold (plan), I. Yu. Shlepyanov and others, GosTIM, Moscow

7 Feb 1931: Vs. Vishnevsky, *The Last Fight*, des. V.E. Meyerhold (plan) and S.E. Vakhtangov, music by V. Ya. Shebalin, GosTIM, Moscow

4 June 1931: Yu. Olesha, *A List of Blessings*, des. V.E. Meyerhold (plan), S.E. Vakhtangov, I.I. Leistikov, K.K. Savitsky, music by G.N. Popov, GosTIM, Moscow

26 Dec 1932: J.-B. Molière, *Don Juan*, des. A. Ya. Golovin, music by J.P. Rameau arr. V.G. Karatygin, State Academic Drama Theatre, Leningrad

28 Jan 1933: Yu. German, *Prelude* (*Professor Kelberg*), des. I.I. Leistikov, music by V. Ya. Shebalin, GosTIM, Moscow

14 April 1933: A. Sukhovo-Kobylin, *Krechinsky's Wedding*, des. V.A. Shestakov, music by M.L. Starokadomsky, GosTIM, Moscow (premiere in Leningrad)

25 Dec 1933: M. Lermontov, *Masquerade*, des. A. Ya. Golovin, music by A.K. Glazunov, State Academic Drama Theatre, Leningrad

19 March 1934: A. Dumas *fils*, *The Lady of the Camellias*, des. V.E. Meyerhold (plan) and I.I. Leistikov, music by V. Ya. Shebalin, GosTIM, Moscow

25 Jan 1935: P. Tchaikovsky (adapted from A. Pushkin by V.E. Meyerhold and V. Stenich), *The Queen of Spades*, cond. S.A. Samosud, des. L.T. Chupyatov, State Academic Maly Opera Theatre, Leningrad

25 March 1935: A. Chekhov, *33 Fainting Fits* (*The Jubilee, The Bear, The Proposal*), des. V.E. Meyerhold, V.A. Shestakov, GosTIM, Moscow

25 Sept 1935: A. Griboyedov, *Woe to Wit* (*Woe from Wit*), des. V.E. Meyerhold and V.A. Shestakov (decor), N.P. Ulyanov (costumes and make-up), music from classical works selected and arranged by B.V. Asafiev, GosTIM, Moscow (premiere in Leningrad)

10 Feb 1937: A. Pushkin, *The Stone Guest* (concert performance), music by V. Ya Shebalin, GosTIM, Moscow

29 Dec 1938: M. Lermontov, *Masquerade*, des. A. Ya. Golovin, music by A.K. Glazunov, State Academic Theatre in the name of Pushkin, Leningrad

Uncompleted productions

1902: L. Mey, *The Woman from Pskov*

1905: M. Maeterlinck, *The Death of Tintagiles*, des. S. Yu. Sudeikin (Acts 1, 2, 3), N.N. Sapunov (Acts 4 and 5), Music by I.A. Sats, Art Theatre Studio, Moscow

1905: G. Hauptmann, *Schluck und Jau*, co-dir. V.E. Repman, des. N.P. Ulyanov, music by R.M. Glier, Art Theatre Studio, Moscow

1905: S. Przybyszewski, *Snow*, des. V.I. Denisov, Art Theatre Studio, Moscow

1905: H. Ibsen, *Love's Comedy*, des. V.I. Denisov, Art Theatre Studio, Moscow

1908: O. Wilde, *Salomé*, chor., M.M. Fokine, des. L.C. Bakst, music by A.K. Glazunov, Mikhailovsky Theatre, Petersburg

1908–9: A.K. Tolstoy, *Tsar Fyodor Ivanovich*, des. D.S. Stelletsky, Alexandrinsky Theatre, Petersburg

1913: C.W. Gluck, *Queen of the May*, des. A. Ya. Golovin, Alexandrinsky Theatre, Petersburg

1921: I. Aksenov, *The Struggle and the Victory* (mass spectacle), des. A.A. Vesnin and L.S. Popova, public square, Moscow

1922: G.B. Shaw (trans I. Aksenov), *Heartbreak House*, des. S.M. Eisenstein, Actors' Theatre, Moscow

1922: 'AsGoTret' (N. Aseyev, S. Gorodetsky, S.M. Tretyakov), *Spinball* (*The Versailles Tourists Who Bumped into a Landmine*), des. V.N. Palmov and N. Rosenfeld, Theatre of the Revolution, Moscow

1923: P. Mérimée, *La Jacquerie*, Vs. Meyerhold Theatre, Moscow

1925: G. Bizet, *Carmen*, TIM, Moscow

1925–6: A. Pushkin, *Boris Godunov*, des. S.P. Issakov, Vakhtangov Studio Theatre, Moscow

1927–30: S.M. Tretyakov, *I Want a Child*, des. V.E. Meyerhold and L.M. Lissitsky, GosTIM, Moscow

1929–32: N. Erdman, *The Suicide*, des. V.E. Meyerhold, I.I. Leistikov, N.V. Grigorovich, S.V. Kozikov, music by M.L. Starokadomsky, GosTIM, Moscow

1931–32: P. Hindemith, *News of the Day*, Maly Opera Theatre, Leningrad

1936: V.V. Mayakovsky (adapted by V.E. Meyerhold and A. Fevralsky), *A Fairy Comedy* (*The Bedbug*), des. V.E. Meyerhold, music by D.D. Shostakovich, GosTIM, Moscow

1936: A. Pushkin, *Boris Godunov*, des. V.A. Shestakov, music by S.S. Prokofiev, GosTIM, Moscow

1937: L. Seifullina, *Natasha*, des. F.V. Antonov, music by V. Ya. Shebalin, GosTIM, Moscow

1937: E. Gabrilovich (after N. Ostrovsky), *One Life* (*How the Steel Was Tempered*), des. V.A. Stenberg, music by G.N. Popov, GosTIM, Moscow

1939: S. Prokofiev (libretto V. Katayev), *Semyon Kotko*, des. A.G. Tyshler, cond. M.N. Zhukov, Stanislavsky State Opera Theatre, Moscow

Other productions to which Meyerhold contributed

20 Feb 1918: P. Claudel, *Exchange*, dir. A. Ya. Tairov, des. G.B. Yakulov, Kamerny Theatre, Moscow

8 August 1921: R. Wagner (adapted by V.M. Bebutov and V. Shershenevich), *Rienzi*, dir. V.M. Bebutov, des. G.B. Yakulov, First Theatre of RSFSR, Moscow

18 March 1922: Students of GVYTM, *The Paris Commune*, dir. and des. students of GVYTM, Club of the Krasnopresensky Three Mines Factory, Moscow

3 Nov 1922: E. Toller, *The Machine Wreckers*, dir. P.P. Repnin, des. V.P. Komardenkov, Theatre of the Revolution, Moscow

26 Jan 1923: E. Toller, *Masses and Man*, dir. A.B. Velizhev, des. V.A. Shestakov, Theatre of the Revolution, Moscow

23 Jan 1926: S.M. Tretyakov, *Roar, China!*, dir. V.F. Fedorov, des. S.M. Efimenko, TIM, Moscow

8 Nov 1927: V.E. Meyerhold and R. Akulshin, *A Window on the Country*, des. V.A. Shestakov, music by R.I. Mervolf, GosTIM, Moscow

19 Dec 1929: A. Bezymensky, *The Shot*, dir. V.F. Zaichikov, S.V. Kozikov, A.E. Nesterov, F.P. Bondarenko, des. V.V. Kalinin, L.P. Pavlov, music by R.I. Mervolf, GosTIM, Moscow

10 March 1939: G. Verdi, *Rigoletto*, dir. K.S. Stanislavsky, des. M.P. Bobyshov, Stanislavsky State Opera Theatre, Moscow

July 1939: Public presentation and parade of Leningrad Institute of Physical Culture, created in conjunction with L.P. Orlov and N.P. Ser, with music by S.S. Prokofiev, Palace Square, Leningrad (6 July 1939) and Red Square Moscow (18 July 1939)

Films by Meyerhold

1915: O. Wilde (scenario by V.E. Meyerhold), *The Portrait of Dorian Gray*, 2124m, co-dir. M. Doronin, des. V.E. Egorov, camera A.A. Levitsky, Russian Golden Series film, premiere 1 Dec 1915

1916: S. Przybyszewski (scenario by V. Akhramovich), *The Strong Man*, 7 reels, co-dir. M. Doronin, V. Akhramovich, des. V.E. Egorov, camera S.G. Bendersky, Era films, premiere 9 Dec 1917

1917: F.K. Sologub, *Witchcraft*, des. V.E. Tatlin, film uncompleted

Radio productions by Meyerhold

17 April 1935: A. Pushkin, *The Stone Guest*, music by V. Ya. Shebalin
24 March 1937: A. Pushkin, *Russalka*, music by V. Ya. Shebalin

Notes

1 A life

1. Konstantin Stanislavsky, *My Life in Art* (Moscow: Foreign Languages Publishing House, n.d.), p. 493.
2. *Sovetskaya Muzika*, no. 3 (1974), p. 53.
3. Quoted in Leo Wiener, *The Contemporary Drama of Russia* (New York: AMS Press, 1924), p. 120.
4. N.D. Volkov, *Meierkhol'd*, 2 vols. (Moscow: Academia, 1929), vol. 1, p. 41.
5. See Erast Garin, *S Meierkhol'dom* (Moscow: Iskusstvo, 1974), pp. 40–1.
6. Diary, TsGALI, Moscow, f. 998, op. 1, ed. khr. 626, 1. 82.
7. V.E. Meierkhol'd, *Perepiska 1896–1939* (Moscow: Iskusstvo, 1976), p. 44.
8. Edward Braun (ed.), *Meyerhold on Theatre* (London: Eyre Methuen, 1969), p. 41.
9. Quoted in Konstantin Rudnitsky, *Meyerhold the Director* (Ann Arbor: Ardis, 1981), p. 56.
10. Meierkhol'd, *Perepiska*, p. 29.
11. See, for example, Theodore Komisarjevsky, *Myself and the Theatre* (London: Heinemann, 1929), p. 72.
12. A translation is published in *The Drama Review*, vol. 21, no. 4 (1977), pp. 87–99.
13. Leon Trotsky, *Literature and Revolution* (New York: Russell & Russell, 1955), p. 142.
14. F.D. Reeve, *Twentieth-Century Russian Plays* (New York: Norton, 1973), p. 175.
15. V.E. Meierkhol'd, *Stat'i, pis'ma, rechi, besedi*, 2 vols. (Moscow: Iskusstvo, 1968), vol. 1, p. 261.
16. Yuri Yurev, *Zapiski*, 2 vols. (Moscow–Leningrad: Iskusstvo, 1963), vol. 2, p. 170.
17. S. Volkov, *Sovetskaya Muzika*, no. 3 (1974) p. 53.
18. For a complete list of Dr Dapertutto's productions, see appendix 2.
19. Meierkhol'd, *Stat'i*, vol. 1, p. 182.
20. Braun, *Meyerhold on Theatre*, p. 63.
21. Quoted in George Gibian and H.W. Tjalsma, *Russian Modernism: Culture and the Avant Garde, 1900–1930* (Ithaca: Cornell University Press, 1976), p. 25.
22. Gibian and Tjalsma, p. 69.
23. Jay Leyda, *Kino* (London: George Allen & Unwin, 1983), pp. 86, 87.
24. N.A. Arzumanova and T.I. Kireeva, *Vstrechi s proshlym* (Moscow: Sovetskaya Rossiya, 1983), p. 284.
25. Volkov, *Meierkhol'd*, vol. 2, pp. 162–3.
26. Leyda, p. 82.
27. *Ibid.*, p. 87.
28. Quoted in Mikhail Guerman, *Art of the October Revolution* (London: Collet's, 1979), p. 43.
29. Ilya Ehrenburg, *First Years of Revolution* (New York: Macgibbon & Kee, 1962), p. 136.
30. A. Schouvaloff and V. Borovsky, *Stravinsky on Stage* (New York: Stainer & Bell, 1982), p. 17.
31. V. Kandinsky, *Programma Instituta Khudozhestvennoi Kultury* (Moscow: 1920).
32. Oliver M. Sayler, *The Russian Theatre* (New York: Brentano's, 1922), p. 293.
33. Huntly Carter, *The New Spirit in the Russian Theatre* (New York: Brentano's, 1929), p. 203.
34. Mikhail Zharov, *Zhizn', teatr, kino* (Moscow: Iskusstvo, 1967), pp. 113, 114.

35. See Lawrence Senelick, *Russian Dramatic Theory from Pushkin to the Symbolists* (Austin: University of Texas Press, 1981), p. 10.
36. Meierkhol'd, *Stat'i*, vol. 2, p. 26.
37. Yu. A. Dmitriev and K.L. Rudnitsky, *Istoria Russkogo Sovetskogo dramaticheskogo teatr* (Moscow: Prosveshchenie, 1984), p. 46.
38. Meierkhol'd, *Stat'i*, vol. 2, pp. 35–6.
39. See Paul Schmidt, *Meyerhold at Work* (Austin: University of Texas Press, 1980), pp. 74–5.
40. Quoted in R. Segal, *The Tragedy of Leon Trotsky* (Harmondsworth: Penguin, 1983), p. 286.
41. Quoted in E.H. Carr, *The Russian Revolution from Lenin to Stalin 1917–1929* (London: Macmillan, 1980), p. 117.
42. Edward Braun, *The Theatre of Meyerhold* (London: Eyre Methuen, 1979), p. 182.
43. Quoted in James H. Symons, *Meyerhold's Theatre of the Grotesque* (Cambridge: Rivers Press, 1973), pp. 96–7.
44. Trotsky, p. 238.
45. Luda Schnitzler *et al.* (eds.), *Cinema in Revolution*, trans. David Robinson (London: Secker & Warburg, 1973), pp. 21–2.
46. Unidentified press cutting, TsGALI, Moscow, f. 2392, op. 1, ed. khr. 327, l. 127.
47. Garin, p. 26.
48. A.E. Nesterov, 'God raboty klubno-metodologicheskogo i laboratorii pri gektemase im Meierkhol'da', typescript, TsGALI, Moscow, f. 963, op. 1, ed. khr. 1561, l. 5–9.
49. *Gogol i Meierkhol'd* (Moscow, 1927); '*Revizor*' *v teatr imeni Vs. Meierkhol'da* (Leningrad, 1927); D. Talnikov, *Novaia reviziia 'Revizora'* (Moscow, 1927).
50. See Rudnitsky, pp. 320–1; L. Lozowick, 'Theatre Chronicle', *Hound and Horn*, October–December 1930, p. 95; etc.
51. Mark Mestechkin, 'V iyune 1924 goda . . .', *Teatr*, no. 2 (February 1974), p. 49.
52. Quoted in Wiktor Woroszylski, *The Life of Mayakovsky* (London: Gollancz, 1972), p. 487.
53. Braun, *Meyerhold on Theatre*, pp. 258, 273.
54. Quoted in Susan P. Compton *et al.*, *Vladimir Mayakovsky: Three Views* (London: Scorpion Press, 1982), p. 12.
55. Schmidt, p. 202.
56. Boris Filippov, *Actors without Make-up* (Moscow: Progress, 1977), pp. 43–4.
57. M.A. Valenti *et al.* (eds.), *Vstrechi s Meierkhol'dom* (Moscow: Vserossiiskoe Teatral'noe Obshchestvo, 1967), pp. 440, 439.
58. Rudnitsky, p. 511.
59. Braun, *Meyerhold on Theatre*, p. 250.
60. Valenti *et al.*, p. 589.
61. Meierkhol'd, *Perepiska*, p. 350.
62. Schnitzler *et al.*, p. 177.
63. Ehrenburg, p. 138.

2 The fourth dimension

1. Constantin Stanislavsky, *An Actor Prepares* (London: Bles, 1937), pp. 75 and 258. Italics as in original.
2. Braun, *Meyerhold on Theatre*, p. 52.
3. Sayler, p. 208.
4. André van Gyseghem, *Theatre in Soviet Russia* (London: Faber & Faber 1943), p. 24.
5. Braun, *Meyerhold on Theatre*, pp. 253 and 256.
6. L.D. Vendrovskaya and A.V. Fevralsky (eds.), *Tvorcheskoe nasledie V.E. Meyerkhol'da* (Moscow: Vserossiiskoe Teatral'noe Obshchestvo, 1978), p. 46.
7. Quoted in Mordecai Gorelik, *New Theatres for Old* (London: Dennis Dobson, 1947), p.

215. Wagner's *Art and Revolution* was published in Russia in 1906.

8. Rudnitsky, p. 102.
9. *Ibid.*, p. 110.
10. Valenti *et al.*, p. 515.
11. A. Gladkov, 'Meyerhold Speaks', *The Drama Review*, vol. 18, no. 3 (September 1974), p. 108.
12. Yurev, pp. 188–9.
13. L. Arnshtam, 'Meierkhol'd i Muzika', *Sovetskaya Muzika*, no. 3 (1974), p. 58.
14. Braun, *Meyerhold on Theatre*, p. 120–1.
15. Schmidt, p. 160.
16. Braun, *Meyerhold on Theatre*, p. 120.
17. 'Meyerhold Address: Revolution, Art, War', *The Drama Review*, vol. 18, no. 3 (September 1974), p. 72.
18. From *Love of Three Oranges*, quoted in Braun, *Theatre of Meyerhold*, p. 146.
19. Braun, *Meyerhold on Theatre*, p. 170.
20. A. Karaganov, *Vsevolod Pudovkin* (Moscow: Iskusstvo, 1983), p. 13.
21. Ehrenburg, pp. 130–1.
22. Boris Alpers, *The Theatre of Social Mask* (New York: Group Theatre, 1934), p. 23.
23. van Gyseghem, pp. 14, 15.
24. Stanislavsky, *My Life in Art*, p. 430.
25. M. Zagorsky, 'Kak reagiruet zritel'?', *LEF*, no. 2 (6) (1924), p. 148.
26. Garin, p. 46.
27. Ehrenburg, p. 130.
28. Quoted in Rudnitsky, p. 268.
29. van Gyseghem, p. 20.
30. Zagorsky, p. 151.
31. S. Eisenstein, 'Montazh attraktsionov', *LEF*, no. 3 (1923), pp. 70ff.
32. N. Gorlov, 'O futurizmakh i futurizme', *LEF*, no. 4 (1924), p. 15.
33. Lozowick, p. 99.
34. Quoted in Rudnitsky, p. 269.
35. Braun, *Theatre of Meyerhold*, p. 155.
36. Valenti *et al.*, p. 183.
37. Igor Il'insky, *Sam o sebe* (Moscow: Iskusstvo, 1984), pp. 219, 223.
38. Schmidt, p. 143.
39. Vendrovskaya and Fevralsky, p. 46.
40. Alma H. Law, 'The Death of Tarelkin: A Constructivist Vision of Tsarist Russia', *Russian History*, vol. 8, part 3 (1981), p. 153.
41. Quoted in Rudnitsky, p. 209.
42. Alpers, p. 143.
43. A. Lacis, quoted in K. Eaton, 'Brecht's Contacts with the Theatre of Meyerhold', *Comparative Drama*, no. 1 (1977), p. 10.
44. Alpers, p. 4.
45. Quoted in Rudnitsky, p. 80.
46. Meierkhol'd, *Stat'i*, vol. 1, p. 104.
47. A. Golovin, quoted in Yurev, vol. 2, p. 186.
48. B. Alpers, quoted in Yu. Golovashenko, 'Etapy geroicheskoi temy', *Teatr*, no. 2 (February 1974), p. 17.
49. Alexander Bakshy, *The Path of the Modern Russian Stage and Other Essays* (London: Cecil Palmer & Hayward, 1916), p. 62.
50. Zagorsky, pp. 144, 145.
51. I. Uvarova, 'Teatr Budushchego', *Dekorativnoe Iskusstvo CCCP*, no. 4 (1977), p. 42.

52. For further details, see Valenti *et al.*
53. Gibian and Tjalsma, p. 25.
54. Norris Houghton, *Return Engagement* (New York: Putnam, 1962), p. 12.
55. Reeve, p. 173.
56. E. Zamyatin, 'The Modern Russian Theatre', in Ellandea and Carl R. Proffer (eds.), *Russian Futurism* (Ann Arbor; Ardis, 1980), p. 202.
57. L.H. Hedgbeth, 'Meyerhold's *D.E.*', *The Drama Review*, vol. 19, no. 2 (1975), p. 33.
58. Valenti *et al.*, p. 311.
59. Braun, *Meyerhold on Theatre*, p. 171.
60. Valenti *et al.*, p. 516.
61. Zagorsky, pp. 141–51.
62. TsGALI, Moscow f. 963, op. 1, ed. khr. 335.
63. For a fuller discussion of these issues (though one vitiated by a complete misunderstanding of Meyerhold's attitude) and other examples of early Soviet attempts to monitor audience reaction, see: L. Kleberg, 'The Audience as Myth and Reality: Soviet Theatrical Ideology and Audience Research in the 1920s', *Russian History*, vol. 9, parts 2–3 (1982), pp. 227–41.
64. Meierkhol'd, *Stat'i*, vol. 2, p. 51.
65. Zagorsky, p. 141.
66. Il'insky, p. 227.
67. Hedgbeth, p. 24.
68. Braun, *Meyerhold on Theatre*, p. 60.

3 The actor's business

1. Meierkhol'd, *Stat'i*, vol. 1, p. 141.
2. *Ibid.*, vol. 2, p. 37.
3. Garin, p. 34.
4. Valenti *et al.*, p. 432.
5. M. Zharov, 'V 1919 godu', *Teatr* (February 1974), p. 47.
6. Yurev, vol. 2, p. 172.
7. Volkov, *Meierkhol'd*, vol. 2, p. 52.
8. Norris Houghton, *Moscow Rehearsals* (New York: Harcourt Brace, 1936), p. 114.
9. D. Shostakovich, 'Iz vospominariy', *Sovetskaya Muzika*, no. 3 (1974), p. 54.
10. Golovashenko, p. 26.
11. Quoted in Rudnitsky, p. 56.
12. Quoted in Yu. M. Krasovskii, *Nekotorye problemy teatral'noi pedagogiki V.E. Meierkhol'da (1905–1907)* (Leningrad, 1981) p. 16.
13. See chapter 2 above, especially note 46.
14. Braun, *Meyerhold on Theatre*, p. 129.
15. *Ibid.*, p. 147.
16. M. Gordon, 'Biomechanics', *The Drama Review*, vol. 18, no. 3 (September 1974), p. 74.
17. *Petrograd Gazette*, 13 February 1915, quoted in Marjorie L. Hoover, *Meyerhold: The Art of Conscious Theatre* (Amherst: University of Massachusetts Press, 1974), p. 85.
18. Braun, *Meyerhold on Theatre*, p. 153.
19. *Ibid.*, p. 155.
20. See A.Z. Yufit *et al.* (eds.), *Russkii Sovetskii teatr, dokumenty i materialy, 1917–1921* (Leningrad: Iskusstvo, 1968), pp. 347–9.
21. Golovashenko, p. 16.
22. Garin, p. 27.

23. *Ibid.*, pp. 53–4.
24. Il'insky, p. 224.
25. Trotsky, p. 11.
26. *Ibid.*, p. 135.
27. *Ibid.*, p. 254.
28. Gorelik, p. 345.
29. V. Pluchek, 'V sentyabre 1929 goda', *Teatr*, no. 2 (February 1974), p. 50.
30. Lozowick, p. 98.
31. Braun, *Meyerhold on Theatre*, p. 198.
32. C. Coquelin, *The Art of the Actor* (London: George Allen & Unwin, 1932), p. 31.
33. Gordon, p. 76.
34. Braun, *Meyerhold on Theatre*, p. 198.
35. Il'insky, p. 228.
36. Braun, *Meyerhold on Theatre*, pp. 124–5.
37. See Braun, *Theatre of Meyerhold*, pp. 47–8; but see also Vendrovskaya and Fevralsky, p. 121.
38. Braun, *Meyerhold on Theatre*, p. 99.
39. *Ibid.*, p. 86.
40. *Ibid.*, p. 149.
41. Ronald Levaco, *Kuleshov on Film: Writings by Lev Kuleshov* (Berkeley: University of California Press, 1974), p. 7.
42. Braun, *Meyerhold on Theatre*, p. 270.
43. For terminology here, see Chris Pike, *The Futurists, the Formalists and the Marxist Critique* (London: Ink Links, 1979), *passim.*
44. Braun, *Meyerhold on Theatre*, pp. 199, 200.
45. Garin, p. 30.
46. *Ibid.*, pp. 52, 53.
47. A. Fevralsky, quoted in A. Law, 'Meyerhold's *The Magnanimous Cuckold*', *The Drama Review*, vol. 26, no. 1 (1982), p. 62.
48. P. Yartsev, quoted in Braun, *Meyerhold on Theatre*, p. 68.
49. See P.A. Markov, *The Soviet Theatre* (London: Gollancz, 1934), p. 67.
50. Braun, *Meyerhold on Theatre*, pp. 67–8.
51. Rudnitsky, p. 381.
52. Braun, *Meyerhold on Theatre*, p. 230.
53. A. Law, 'Meyerhold's *Woe to Wit* (1928)', *The Drama Review*, vol. 18, no. 3 (1974), p. 93.
54. See e.g. Arnshtam, p. 56.
55. Vendrovskaya and Fevralsky, p. 96.
56. Zharov, p. 113.
57. Sayler, pp. 216–17.
58. V.L. Yureneva, quoted in Rudnitsky, p. 381.
59. Gladkov, p. 111.
60. Yurev, vol. 2, p. 187.
61. A. Symons, 'The Ideas of Richard Wagner', in E. Bentley, *The Theory of the Modern Stage* (Harmondsworth: Penguin, 1968), p. 288.
62. Braun, *Meyerhold on Theatre*, p. 56.
63. van Gyseghem, p. 28.
64. V.L. Yureneva, quoted in Rudnitsky, p. 476.
65. Hedgbeth, p. 29.
66. Law, 'Meyerhold's *Woe to Wit* (1928)', p. 102.
67. Krasovskii, p. 17.
68. Braun, *Meyerhold on Theatre*, p. 321.

69. Il'insky, p. 226.

70. Valenti *et al.* pp. 213–14.

71. See D.H. du Prey, 'The Training Sessions of Michael Chekhov', *Theatre Papers*, 3rd series (Dartington College, 1979), p.5.

72. S. Serova, 'Meierkhold's Principles and the Theory of Chinese Theatrical Art', *Papers presented to XXth International Congress of Chinese Studies* (Moscow, 1968), p. 6.

73. Quoted in Yurev, vol. 2, p. 186.

74. Alpers, p. 37.

75. Il'insky, p. 231.

76. Thirteen biomechanical exercises are described in detail in Gordon, pp. 80–8. However, it should be noted that several photographs published with the descriptions are wrongly identified, and some of the exercises as described are impossible to do.

77. Houghton, *Moscow Rehearsals*, p. 39.

78. Meyerhold always began this exercise with the 'catcher' leaning against something like a table (see Garin, p. 34). In ten years of teaching this exercise, I have never had the catcher lean against anything, and wonder why Meyerhold did.

79. Braun, *Meyerhold on Theatre*, p. 141.

80. Quoted in Rudnitsky, p. 172.

81. Braun, *Meyerhold on Theatre*, p. 150.

82. *Ibid.*, p. 148.

83. Garin, p. 36.

84. Hoover, p. 85.

85. Sayler, p. 216.

86. Braun, *Meyerhold on Theatre*, p. 148.

87. Quoted in Braun, *Theatre of Meyerhold*, p. 70.

88. Quoted in Rudnitsky, p. 224.

89. Braun, *Meyerhold on Theatre*, p. 148.

90. Valenti *et al.*, pp. 436–7.

91. Lozowick, p. 101.

92. Coquelin, p. 77. Italics added.

93. *Ibid.*, p. 11.

94. *The Set Roles of the Actor's Art*, (Moscow: GVYRM, 1922), translated by Marjorie L. Hoover, reproduced in Hoover, pp. 297–310.

95. Braun, *Meyerhold on Theatre*, p. 131.

96. Quoted in Volkov, *Meierkhol'd*, vol. 1, p. 280.

97. Braun, *Meyerhold on Theatre*, p. 219.

98. Garin, p. 32.

99. Gladkov, p. 110.

100. Filippov, p. 42.

101. Braun, *Meyerhold on Theatre*, p. 227.

102. Garin, p. 28.

103. Meyerhold, quoted in Nikolai Gorchakov, *The Theater in Soviet Russia* (Oxford University Press, 1957), p. 58. See also Rudnitsky, p. 65.

104. S. Tretyakov, 'Tekst i rechemontazh', *Zrelishcha*, no. 27 (1923).

105. Braun, *Meyerhold on Theatre*, p. 222.

106. Yurev, vol. 2, p. 188.

107. Houghton, *Moscow Rehearsals*, p. 106.

108. Law, 'Meyerhold's *Woe to Wit* (1928)', p. 94.

109. Braun, *Meyerhold on Theatre*, p. 127.

110. Gorchakov, p. 204.

4 The *mise-en-scène*

1. Braun, *Meyerhold on Theatre*, p. 92.
2. Law, 'Meyerhold's *Woe to Wit*', p. 104.
3. J. Cooper, *Four Russian Plays* (Harmondsworth: Penguin, 1972), p. 189.
4. Carter, p. 220.
5. *Ibid.*, p. 331.
6. Markov, *The Soviet Theatre*, p. 83.
7. See F. Deak, 'Meyerhold's Staging of *Sister Beatrice*', *The Drama Review*, vol. 26, no. 1 (1982), p. 43.
8. See Law, 'Meyerhold's *Woe to Wit*', p. 104.
9. See Houghton, *Moscow Rehearsals*, p. 107; Rudnitsky, p. 508; etc.
10. Valenti *et al.*, p. 433.
11. van Gyseghem, p. 25.
12. Joseph Gregor and René Fulop-Miller, *The Russian Theatre* (London: Harrap, 1930), p. 49.
13. E.A. Znosko-Borovsky, *Russkii teatr nachala XX veka* (Prague: Plamya, 1925), p. 304.
14. *Ibid.*, p. 307.
15. Quoted in Rudnitsky, p. 146.
16. Braun, *Meyerhold on Theatre*, p. 100.
17. Znosko-Borovsky, p. 315.
18. Victor Erlich, *Russian Formalism*, 3rd edn (New Haven: Yale University Press, 1981), p. 76.
19. Garin, p. 42.
20. Sayler, pp. 212–13.
21. van Gyseghem, p. 20.
22. Braun, *Meyerhold on Theatre*, p. 31.
23. Garin, p. 46.
24. 'Programma uchebnoi podgruppy robochei gruppy Konstruktivistov INKhUKa', quoted in Christina Lodder, *Russian Constructivism* (New Haven: Yale University Press, 1983), p. 3.
25. Braun, *Meyerhold on Theatre*, p. 57.
26. Quoted in Lodder, p. 173. 'Movement' near the end of the passage might be better translated 'section'.
27. Quoted in Angelica Zander Rudenstine (ed.), *Russian Avant-garde Art* (London: Thames & Hudson, 1981) p. 399.
28. Lodder, p. 177.
29. Carter, p. 78.
30. Lodder, pp. 175–6. *Cinema Truth* was the name of Dziga Vertov's film newspaper. 'Godunov's system' probably refers to the stage rigging system.
31. Lodder, p. 177.
32. Eisenstein, p. 71.
33. Gorchakov, p. 205.
34. Quoted in Hedgbeth, p. 36.
35. Walter Benjamin, *Moscow Diary* (Cambridge, Mass.: Harvard University Press, 1986), pp. 33–4.
36. *Ibid.*, p. 40. Tairov's Kamerny Theatre appeared in Berlin in 1923.
37. Carter, p. 215.
38. Quoted in Rudnitsky, p. 113.
39. V. Verigina, quoted in Rudnitsky, p. 171.
40. Braun, *Meyerhold on Theatre*, p. 321.
41. Quoted in *ibid.*, p. 216.

42. Meyerhold, quoted in Rudnitsky, p. 113.
43. Braun, *Meyerhold on Theatre*, p. 105.
44. B. Brecht, 'The Literarization of the Theatre', *Brecht on Theatre* (London: Methuen, 1973), p. 43.
45. Vendrovskaya and Fevralsky, p. 349.
46. Quoted in Braun, *Meyerhold on Theatre*, p. 83.
47. Quoted in Serova, p. 8.

5 Rhythm

1. Meyerhold quoted in Schmidt, p. 155.
2. Braun, *Meyerhold on Theatre*, p. 32.
3. Quoted in Rudnitsky, p. 68.
4. S. Volkov, 'K 100-letiyu so dnya rozhdeniya Vs. E. Meierkhol'da', *Sovetskaya Muzika*, no. 3 (1974), p. 54.
5. Arnshtam, p. 56.
6. See Vendrovskaya and Fevralsky, pp. 46–54.
7. A. Gladkov, 'Meierkhol'd Govorit', *Novy Mir*, no. 8 (1961), pp. 216–17.
8. Arnshtam, p. 56.
9. Znosko-Borovsky, p. 311.
10. Valenti *et al.*, p. 320.
11. N.F. Chuzhak, 'Pod znakom zhiznestroennia', *LEF*, no. 1 (1923), p. 32.
12. Garin, p. 36.
13. See chapter 3 above.
14. Hsui Ta-chun, 'The Expression of Sound in Singing', *Collected Treatises on Chinese Classical Drama* (Peking, 1959), vol. 7, p. 175.
15. Deak, p. 50.
16. Znosko-Borovsky, p. 308.
17. Markov, *Soviet Theatre*, pp. 80–1.
18. van Gyseghem, p. 17.
19. Houghton, *Moscow Rehearsals*, p. 18.
20. Quoted in Rudnitsky, p. 377.
21. N. Gogol, *The Government Inspector* (London: Methuen, 1968), p. 107.
22. See Arnshtam, p. 57.
23. S. Auslender, quoted in Hoover, p. 38.
24. Meyerhold, quoted in Schmidt, p. 155.
25. Golovashenko, p. 17.
26. Braun, *Meyerhold on Theatre*, p. 322.
27. Meierkhol'd, *Perepiska*, p. 45.
28. Bakshy, p. 72.
29. Braun, *Meyerhold on Theatre*, p. 137.
30. V.E. Meyerhold, V.M. Bebutov, I.A. Aksenov, *Ampluya aktera* (Moscow, 1922); translated by M.L. Hoover, reproduced in Hoover, p. 309.
31. Golovashenko, p. 18.
32. See e.g. Braun, *Meyerhold on Theatre*, p. 294.
33. Erlich, p. 280.
34. van Gyseghem, p. 34.
35. Braun, *Meyerhold on Theatre*, p. 318.
36. Houghton, *Moscow Rehearsals*, p. 103–4.

6 Meanings

1. Valenti *et al.*, p. 280.
2. van Gyseghem, p. 35.
3. Braun, *Meyerhold on Theatre*, p. 48.
4. Gorchakov, p. 54.
5. Quoted in Schmidt, p. 71.
6. Quoted in Pike, p. 13.
7. Braun, *Meyerhold on Theatre*, p. 141.
8. A. Rodchenko, 'Puti sovremennoi fotografii', *Novy Lef*, no. 9 (1929), p. 39.
9. Vendrovskaya and Fevralsky, p. 47.
10. Braun, *Meyerhold on Theatre*, pp. 70–1.
11. See Arzumanova and Kireeva, p. 272.
12. Yurev, vol. 2, p. 186.
13. *Ibid.*, p. 171.
14. Sayler, p. 214.
15. van Gyseghem, p. 31.
16. Garin, pp. 48, 50.
17. A. Benois, 'Balet v Aleksandrinske', *Rech*, 19 November 1910, p. 3.
18. Braun, *Meyerhold on Theatre*, p. 127.
19. A. Gvozdev, quoted in Rudnitsky, p. 311.
20. P.A. Markov, quoted in Rudnitsky, pp. 351–2.
21. V.W. Turner, *The Ritual Process* (Harmondsworth: Penguin, 1974), p. 81.
22. E. Le Roy Ladurie, *Carnival* (London: Scolar Press, 1980), p. 316.
23. Quoted in Rudnitsky, p. 349.
24. Markov, *Soviet Theatre*, p. 79.
25. Gregor and Fulop-Miller, p. 123.
26. N. Bukharin, 'What is Art?' from *Historical Materialism* (1921); reproduced in M. Solomon, *Marxism and Art* (Hassocks: Harvester Press, 1979), p. 205.
27. See F. Deak, 'Russian Mass Spectacles', *The Drama Review*, vol. 19, no. 2 (June 1975), pp. 7–22.
28. Vahan Barooshian, *Brik and Mayakovsky* (Mouton: The Hague, 1978), p. 25.
29. Quoted in Lodder, p. 228.
30. Eisenstein, pp. 70–1.
31. Markov, *Soviet Theatre*, p. 70.
32. S. Eisenstein, *The Film Sense* (London: Faber, 1968), p. 17.
33. Braun, *Meyerhold on Theatre*, pp. 318–19.
34. Yu. Belyaev, quoted in Rudnitsky, p. 153.
35. P. Markov, quoted in Braun, *Meyerhold on Theatre*, p. 196.
36. See chapter 2 above.
37. Quoted in Pike, p. 14.

7 *Masquerade*

1. See, for example, Meierkhol'd, *Stat'i*, vol. 1, pp. 301–3.
2. Quoted in Rudnitsky, p. 211.
3. Unidentified press cutting, TsGALI, Moscow, f. 998, op. 1, ed. khr. 3370, 11. 31, 32.
4. Yu. B., *Vecher vremya*, 31–8–16.
5. Meierkhol'd, *Stat'i*, vol. 1, p. 302.
6. *Ibid.*, p. 303.
7. Yurev, vol. 2, p. 195.

8. *Ibid.*, p. 195.
9. *Ibid.*, p. 220.
10. Meierkhol'd, *Stat'i*, vol. 2, p. 440.
11. *Ibid.*, vol. 1, p. 247.
12. Znosko-Borovsky, p. 310.
13. Meierkhol'd, *Stat'i*, vol. 1, p. 300.
14. See A. Ya. Golovin, *'Maskarad' Lermontova v teatral'nyx eskizax A. Ya. Golovina* (Moscow–Leningrad: Izdanie Vserossiiskogo Teatral'nogo Obshchestva, 1941).
15. Vendrovskaya and Fevralsky, p. 48.
16. Meierkhol'd, *Stat'i*, vol. 2, p. 284.
17. Yurev, vol. 2, p. 210.
18. See Braun, *Meyerhold on Theatre*, p. 137.
19. English version of M.Y. Lermontov, *Masquerade*, by Valya Hine and Robert Leach (unpublished).
20. TsGALI, Moscow, f. 998, op. 1, ed. khr. 110.
21. J. Willett, (ed.), *Brecht on Theatre* (London: Eyre Methuen, 1973), p. 86.
22. Alpers, p. 157.
23. Arnshtam, p. 56.
24. M.A. Yakovlev, and Yu. Yurev, *Maskarad: drama M. Yu. Lermontova 'Maskarad' v postanovke V.E. Meierkhol'd (k gastrolyam Leningradskogo Gos. Akad. Th. dramy Alek.)* (Leningrad, n.d.).
25. Meierkhol'd, *Stat'i*, vol. 1, p. 299.
26. Rudnitsky, p. 235.

8 Meyerhold and Mayakovsky

1. A Fevral'skii, *Pervaya Sovetskaya p'esa – 'Misteria-Buff V.V. Mayakovskogo* (Moscow: Sovetskii Pisatel', 1971), p. 13.
2. A. Gladkov, 'Meierkhol'd govorit', *Novy Mir*, no. 8 1961, p. 223.
3. *Izvestia*, 26 February 1929.
4. 'Vstuplen'e na obsudenum p'ese V.V. Mayakovskogo 'Klop' v Klub im. Oktyabr'skoi Revolyutsii (pri Moskovsko–Kazanskoi)', 11 January 1929, TsGALI, Moscow, f. 998, op. 1, ed. khr. 550.
5. See, for instance, Woroszylski, pp. 437, 438.
6. Meierkhol'd, *Stat'i*, vol. 2, p. 360.
7. Woroszylski, p. 437.
8. 'Poet v teatr', *Literaturnoe Obozrenie*, no. 11 (1978), pp. 107, 108.
9. Woroszylski, p. 487.
10. Trotsky, p. 145.
11. V.V. Mayakovsky, programme note to production of *The Bedbug*, Theatre of Satire, Moscow, n.d.
12. G. Daniels, (trans.) *The Complete Plays of Vladimir Mayakovsky* (New York: Simon & Shuster, 1968), p. 46.
13. Mayakovsky, programme note.
14. Il'insky, p. 198.
15. M. Glenny (ed.), *Three Soviet Plays* (Harmondsworth: Penguin, 1966), p. 37.
16. Woroszylski, p. 438.
17. Trotsky, pp. 238–9. Trotsky's translator renders Griboyedov's play title 'Woes from Being Too Wise'. *Woe from Wit* is a more usual translation; when Meyerhold staged it, he renamed it *Woe to Wit*.
18. Gladkov, p. 224.

19. Quoted in Rudnitsky, pp. 448–9.
20. See *Literaturnoe Obozrenie*, no. 11 (1978), p. 111.
21. Elizabeth A. Warner, 'The Quack Doctor in the Russian Folk and Popular Theatre', *Folklore*, vol. 93 no. 2 (1982), pp. 171–2.
22. Woroszylski, p. 445.
23. *Ibid.*, p. 445.
24. *Ibid.*, p. 487.
25. *Ibid.*, p. 484.
26. 'Poet v teatr', p. 108.
27. Quoted in Rudnitsky, p. 274.
28. Woroszylski, p. 445.
29. Quoted in Hoover, p. 179.
30. 'Poet v teatr', p. 109.
31. *Klop*, Gosudarstvennyi Bolshoi Dramatich. Teatr. Filial, Leningrad, 1929, p. 10.
32. Woroszylski, p. 440.
33. *Pravda*, 24 February 1929.
34. Gorchakov, p. 218.
35. A. Uglov, 'Misteria Buff', *Kommunisticheskii Trud*, 7 May 1921.
36. I. Boelza, *Handbook of Soviet Musicians* (London: Pilot, 1943), p. 48.
37. D. Shostakovich, 'Reminiscences', *Soviet Literature*, no. 6 (1983), p. 101.
38. A. Gladkov, 'Meyerhold Speaks', in Proffer, p. 218.
39. K. Rudnitsky, 1981, p. 445.
40. *Klop*, p. 10.
41. *Pravda*, 24 February 1929.
42. Rudnitsky, p. 253–4.
43. *Ibid.*, p. 254.
44. V.V. Mayakovsky, *Teatr i kino*, vol. 1 (Moscow: Khudozhestvennaya Literatura, 1954), p. 322.
45. Fevral'skii, p. 73.
46. *Klop*, p. 7.
47. Proffer, p. 218.
48. Il'insky, p. 195.

9 The legacy

1. Quoted in S. Yutkevich, 'V.E. Meierkhol'd i teoriya kinorezhissury', *Iskusstvo Kino*, no. 8 (1975), p. 82.
2. B. Brecht, 'The Modern Theatre is the Epic Theatre', in Willett, p. 37.
3. B. Brecht, 'Interview with an Exile', in Willett, p. 65.
4. B. Brecht, *Poems*, (London: Eyre Methuen, 1976), p. 331.
5. Vendrovskaya and Fevralsky, pp. 95–7.
6. B. Brecht, 'Alienation Effects in Chinese Acting', in Willett, p. 93.
7. For all these, see Select Bibliography.
8. M. Davidow, *People's Theatre: From the Box Office to the Stage* (Moscow: Progress, 1977), p. 71.
9. See chapter 1, note 50 above.

Select bibliography

Alpers, Boris, *The Theatre of the Social Mask*, New York: Group Theatre, 1934
Arzumanova, N.A., and Kireeva, T.I., *Vstrechi s proshlym*, Moscow: Sovetskaya Rossiya, 1983
Bakshy, Alexander, *The Path of the Modern Russian Stage and Other Essays*, London: Cecil Palmer & Hayward, 1916
Barooshian, Vahan, *Brik and Mayakovsky*, The Hague: Mouton, 1978
Benjamin, Walter, *Moscow Diary*, Cambridge, Mass.: Harvard University Press, 1986
Bennett, Tony, *Formalism and Marxism*, London: Methuen, 1979
Bentley, Eric (ed.), *The Theory of the Modern Stage*, Harmondsworth: Penguin, 1968.
Bradby, David, James, Louis, and Sharratt, Bernard (eds.), *Performance and Politics in Popular Drama*, Cambridge University Press, 1980
Bradshaw, Martha (ed.), *Soviet Theatres, 1917–1941*, New York: Research Program on the USSR, 1954
Braun, Edward (ed.), *Meyerhold on Theatre*, London: Eyre Methuen, 1969
   The Theatre of Meyerhold, London: Eyre Methuen, 1979
Brukson, Y., *Teatr Meierkhol'da*, Moscow: Kniga, 1925
Carter, Huntly, *The New Spirit in the Russian Theatre, 1917–28*, New York: Brentano's, 1929
Cheremin, G.S., *V.V. Mayakovskii v literaturnoi kritike 1917–1925*, Leningrad: Izdatel'stvo, 1985
Compton, Susan P., Morgan, Edwin, Braun, Edward, Kalinovska, Milena, *Vladimir Mayakovsky: Three Views*, London: Scorpion Press, 1982
Coquelin, C., *The Art of the Actor*, London: George Allen & Unwin, 1932
Dana, H.W.L., *Handbook on Soviet Drama*, New York: The American Russian Institute, 1938
Dickinson, Thomas H. (ed.), *The Theatre in a Changing Europe*, New York: Putnam, n.d. [1937]
Dmitriev, Yu.A., and Rudnitsky, K.L., *Istoria Russkogo Sovetskogo dramaticheskogo teatra*, Moscow: Prosveshchenie, 1984
Eagleton, Terry, *Marxism and Literary Criticism*, London: Methuen, 1983
Ehrenburg, Ilya, *First Years of Revolution*, New York: Macgibbon & Kee, 1962
Eisenstein, Sergei, *The Film Sense*, London: Faber, 1970
Elam, Keir, *The Semiotics of Theatre and Drama*, London: Methuen, 1980
Elliott, David, *Alexander Rodchenko*, Oxford: Museum of Modern Art, 1979
   Mayakovsky: Twenty Years of Work, Oxford: Museum of Modern Art, 1982
Erlich, Victor, *Russian Formalism*, 3rd edn, New Haven: Yale University Press, 1981
Fevral'skii, A., *Pervaya Sovetskaya p'esa – 'Misteria-Buff' V.V. Mayakovskogo*, Moscow: Sovetskii Pisatel', 1971
Filippov, Boris, *Actors without Make-Up*, Moscow: Progress, 1977
Frankel, Tobia, *The Russian Artist*, London: Macmillan 1972
Garin, Erast, *S Meierkhol'dom*, Moscow: Iskusstvo, 1974
Gibian, George, and Tjalsma, H.W., *Russian Modernism: Culture and the Avant Garde, 1900–1930*, Ithaca: Cornell University Press, 1976
Golovin, A.Ya., *'Maskarad' Lermontova v teatral'nyx eskizax A.Ya. Golovina*, Moscow–Leningrad: Izdanie Vserossiiskogo Teatral'nogo Obshchestvo, 1941
Gorchakov, Nikolai A., *The Theater in Soviet Russia*, Oxford University Press, 1957
Gorelik, Mordecai, *New Theatres for Old*, London: Dennis Dobson, 1947

Gourfinkel, Nina, *Vsevolod Meyerhold – Le théâtre théâtral*, Paris: Gallimard, 1963
Gray, Camilla, *The Russian Experiment in Art 1863–1922*, London: Thames & Hudson, 1971
Gregor, Joseph, and Fulop-Miller, René, *The Russian Theatre*, London: Harrap, 1930
Guerman, Mikhail, *Art of the October Revolution*, London: Collet's, 1979
Hoover, Marjorie L., *Meyerhold: The Art of Conscious Theatre*, Amherst: University of Massachusetts Press, 1974
Houghton, Norris, *Moscow Rehearsals*, New York: Harcourt Brace, 1936
  Return Engagement, New York: Putnam, 1962
Il'insky, Igor, *Sam o sebe*, Moscow: Iskusstvo, 1984
Khaichenko, Grigory Arkad'evich, *Sovetskii dramaticheskii teatr za 50 let: 1917–1967*, Moscow, 1967
Komisarjevsky, Theodore, *Myself and the Theatre*, London: Heinemann, 1929
Krasovskii, Yu.,M., *Nekotorye problemy teatral'noi pedagogiki V.E. Meierkhol'da (1905–1907)*, Leningrad, 1981
Levaco, Ronald, *Kuleshov on Film: Writings by Lev Kuleshov*, Berkeley: University of California Press, 1974
Leyda, Jay, *Kino*, London: George Allen & Unwin, 1983
Lodder, Christina, *Russian Constructivism*, New Haven: Yale University Press, 1983
Luppol, I. (ed.), *Pushkin*, Moscow, 1939
Markov, P.A., *The Soviet Theatre*, London: Gollancz, 1934
Markov, Vladimir, *Russian Futurism: A History*, New York: Macgibbon & Kee, 1969
Meierkhol'd, V.E., *Perepiska 1896–1939*, Moscow: Iskusstvo, 1976
  Stat'i, pis'ma, rechi, besedi, 2 vols., Moscow: Iskusstvo, 1968
Miller, Alex (trans.), *Vladimir Mayakovsky: Innovator*, Moscow: Progress, 1976
Nilsson, Nils Ake (ed.), *Art, Society, Revolution*, Stockholm: Almqvist & Wiksell, 1979
Pike, Chris, *The Futurists, the Formalists and the Marxist Critique*, London: Ink Links, 1979
Proffer, Ellandea and Carl R. (eds.), *Russian Futurism*, Ann Arbor: Ardis, 1980
Red'ko, A.E., *Teatr i evolutsiya teatral'nyx form*, Leningrad: Izdanie M. i S. Sabashnikovykh, 1926
Rostotskii, B.E., *O rezhissorskom tvorchestve V.E. Meierkhol'da*, Moscow: Iskusstvo, 1960
Rudenstine, Angelica Zander (ed.), *Russian Avant-garde Art*, London: Thames & Hudson, 1981
Rudnitsky, Konstantin, *Meyerhold the Director*, Ann Arbor: Ardis 1981
Sayler, Oliver M., *The Russian Theatre*, New York: Brentano's, 1922
Schmidt, Paul (ed.), *Meyerhold at Work*, Austin: University of Texas Press, 1980
Schnitzler, Luda *et al.* (eds.), *Cinema in Revolution*, translated and with additional material by David Robinson, London: Secker & Warburg, 1973
Senelick, Lawrence (ed.), *Russian Dramatic Theory from Pushkin to the Symbolists*, Austin: University of Texas Press, 1981
Slonim, Marc, *Russian Theatre from the Empire to the Soviets*, New York: World Publishing Co., 1961
Smirnov, Yury Aleksandrovich, *V.V. Mayakovsky i sovetskii teatr*, Leningrad: Ministerstvo Kul'tury RSFSR, 1982
Stanislavsky, Konstantin, *My Life in Art*, Moscow: Foreign Languages Publishing House, n.d.
Symons, James H., *Meyerhold's Theatre of the Grotesque*, Cambridge: Rivers Press, 1973
Trabskii, A.Ya. *et al.* (eds.), *Russkii Sovetskii teatr, dokumenty i materialy, 1921–1926*, Leningrad: Iskusstvo, 1975
Trotsky, Leon, *Literature and Revolution*, New York: Russell & Russell, 1955 (first published 1924)
Valenti, M.A. *et al.* (eds.), *Vstrechi s Meierkhol'dom*, Moscow: Vserossiiskoe Teatral'noe Obshchestvo, 1967
van Gyseghem, André, *Theatre in Soviet Russia*, London: Faber & Faber, 1943

Vendrovskaya, L.D. and Fevralsky, A.V. (eds.), *Tvorcheskoe nasledie V.E. Meierkhol'da*, Moscow: Vserossiiskoe Teatral'noe Obshchestvo, 1978

Volkov, Nikolai, *Meierkhol'd*, Moscow: Zrelishcha, 1923

Volkov, N.D., *Meierkhol'd*, 2 vols, Moscow: Academia, 1929

Wiener, Leo, *The Contemporary Drama of Russia*, New York: AMS Press, 1924

Willett, John, *The New Sobriety*, London: Thames & Hudson, 1978

Williams, Robert C., *Artists in Revolution*, London: The Scolar Press, 1978

Woroszylski, Wiktor, *The Life of Mayakovsky*, London: Gollancz, 1972

Worrall, Nick, *Vladimir Mayakovsky*, Theatre Checklist No. 13, London: TQ Publications, 1977

Yufit, A.Z., *et al.* (eds.), *Russkii Sovetskii teatr, dokumenty i materialy, 1917–1921*, Leningrad: Iskusstvo, 1968

Yurev, Yuri, *Zapiski*, 2 vols; Moscow–Leningrad: Iskusstvo, 1963

Zharov, Mikhail, *Zhizn', teatr, kino*, Moscow: Iskusstvo, 1967

Znosko-Borovsky, E.A., *Russkii teatr nachala XX veka*, Prague: Plamya, 1925

INDEX